This book explores the role of focu
interface between focus structure ai
ture and the intonation associated w
level of f-structure (focus structure
which topic and focus constituents
(Phonological Form) and semantics and is sensitive to lexical ....
Dr. Shir argues that f-structure and not LF (Logical Form) is the input to a semantic rule of Predication. She provides an account of intonation, the interpretation of indefinites, coreference, donkey anaphora, negation, association with focus, quantifier scope, interpretations of *wh*-in-situ, anaphora, subject–object asymmetries, etc. One of the major results of Dr. Shir's analysis is that *wh*-movement turns out to be subject to the same constraint which accounts for anaphora and other subject–object asymmetries.

CAMBRIDGE STUDIES IN LINGUISTICS

General Editors: S. R. ANDERSON, J. BRESNAN,
B. COMRIE, W. DRESSLER, C. EWEN, R. HUDDLESTON,
R. LASS, D. LIGHTFOOT, J. LYONS, P. H. MATTHEWS,
R. POSNER, S. ROMAINE, N. V. SMITH, N. VINCENT

The dynamics of focus structure

In this series

Supplementary volumes

Earlier issues not listed are also available

THE DYNAMICS OF FOCUS STRUCTURE

NOMI ERTESCHIK-SHIR

Ben-Gurion University of the Negev

CAMBRIDGE
UNIVERSITY PRESS

CAMBRIDGE UNIVERSITY PRESS
Cambridge, New York, Melbourne, Madrid, Cape Town, Singapore, São Paulo

Cambridge University Press
The Edinburgh Building, Cambridge CB2 2RU, UK

Published in the United States of America by Cambridge University Press, New York

www.cambridge.org
Information on this title: www.cambridge.org/9780521592178

First published 1997
This digitally printed first paperback version 2006

A catalogue record for this publication is available from the British Library

Library of Congress Cataloguing in Publication data

Erteschik-Shir, Nomi.
The dynamics of focus structure / Nomi Erteschik-Shir.
   p.   cm. – (Cambridge studies in linguistics; 84)
Includes bibliographical references and indexes.
ISBN 0 521 59217 8 (hardback)
1. Grammar, Comparative and general – Topic and comment. 2. Focus
(Linguistics) I. Title. II. Series.
P298.E78 1998
415–dc21   96–52931 CIP

ISBN-13 978-0-521-59217-8 hardback
ISBN-10 0-521-59217-8 hardback

ISBN-13 978-0-521-02417-4 paperback
ISBN-10 0-521-02417-X paperback

לזכר אבי, מאיר ארטשיק

Contents

Acknowledgments

This book developed out of my ongoing enterprise to show that certain syntactic constraints do not belong in the realm of syntax and in particular that focus structure constrains *wh*-movement. During my sabbatical at Brandeis University in 1990–91 I presented a paper at a variety of colloquia entitled "What's what?" which addressed this issue. I originally envisioned a book based on the ideas in that paper. However, once I started developing a theory of focus structure it soon became clear that its repercussions are theoretically much more extensive and required a much broader investigation of a large variety of grammatical questions. I was therefore torn between a wish to concentrate on a limited number of questions and to investigate them in depth or to give a more superficial analysis of a larger chunk of topics. I chose the latter tack because of my wish to convince both syntacticians and semanticists of the need to view the full array of these topics from a focus-structure-theoretical perspective. I hope that the informal semantics of focus-structure theory outlined here will stimulate enough interest so that a more adequate formal version will be developed.

I am grateful to many colleagues and friends for their encouragement, support, comments, criticisms, and collaboration. For both professional and personal contributions to the making of this book over the years, I thank Dorit Ben-Shalom, Shoshana Benjamin, Edit Doron, Gerda Elata, Elisabet Engdahl, John Frampton, Jane Grimshaw, Eva Hajičová, Caroline Heycock, Katalin É. Kiss, Fred Landman, Shalom Lappin, Hagit Lurie, Anita Mittwoch, Tova Rapoport, Tanya Reinhart, Betsy Ritter, Roger Schwarzschild, Petr Sgall, Joe Taglicht, and Karina Wilkinson.

I have also benefited from the comments and questions of participants in workshops and conferences in which I presented parts of this book. These include meetings of the Israel Association of Theoretical Linguistics, the Conference in honor of Roman Jakobson in Prague, the ESSLLI workshop organized by Barbara Partee and Jaroslav Peregrin, the Workshop on Focus in Paris, the conference on Focus and Natural Language Processing at Schloss

Wolfsbrunnen in Germany, and also colloquia at the following universities: Tel-Aviv University, Ben-Gurion University, Rutgers University, CUNY, SOAS, Hebrew University, Brandeis University, UQAM and the University of Arizona, Tucson. The questions and comments of the students in my courses over the years have also been very useful.

I am indebted to reviewers of the complete manuscript and of sections which have been submitted to other volumes. These have to some extent been acknowledged in the text. I particularly thank Louise McNally and Peter Culicover, organizers of the Workshop on the Limits of Syntax and editors of the ensuing volume, for constructive and insightful comments.

Special acknowledgement goes to Suzie Ganot for her friendship and much needed assistance. My other colleagues in the department of Foreign Literatures and Linguistics at Ben-Gurion University have been very supportive as well.

I am grateful to the staff of Cambridge University Press which has not only been extremely competent but also very kind.

I want to thank my mother and my daughters, Tamar and Dafna. From them I have received constant encouragement and help of a variety of kinds. I also want to express my appreciation to Avigdor Link for his unfailing friendship during the various stages of work on the book.

Support for this research was provided in part by grant No. 90-00267 from the United States–Israel Binational Science Foundation (BSF), Jerusalem, Israel.

Introduction

Observe the following sentence pair:

(1) a. Who did everyone talk to?
     b. Who talked to everyone?

(1a) is ambiguous, allowing either an individual answer as in (2a) or a pair-list answer as in (2b). (1b), however, is unambiguous and allows only an answer such as (2a).

(2) a. Sam.
     b. Sam talked to Mary, Peter talked to Susan, . . .

This subject–object asymmetry has received much attention (May 1985, Engdahl 1986, Kim and Larson 1989, Chierchia 1991 among others). The fact that context may determine which interpretation to assign to (1a) has, however, been ignored.

If (1a) is uttered in the following context

(3) Tell me about everyone. Who did everyone talk to?

only the pair-list reading is available. Alternatively, if the quantifier is emphatically stressed only the individual answer is allowed:

(4) Who did EVERYONE talk to?

I intend to use these phenomena to illustrate how a focus-structure account must be applied to capture the discourse facts, the ambiguity in (1a), and the lack of ambiguity in (1b). The precise details of the argument can be left vague for the moment, but it will involve at least the following two assumptions:

1. Topics have wide scope.

2. The pair-list reading, but not the individual reading, involves a particular dependency type which I call an "I-dependency." I-dependencies are restricted by the Subject Constraint which constrains I-dependencies to structures in which the subject is interpreted as the sentence topic.

First, I introduce the basic concepts related to focus structure: Topic and Focus. For the purposes of this introduction a basic diagnostic test for each will suffice. In the following Topic-test (Reinhart 1981), X must be the topic of Speaker B's assertion.

> Topic-test: Speaker A: Tell me about X.
>   Speaker B: . . . X . . .

The focus is identified as the stressed constituent.

Let us first examine what happens if *everyone* functions as the topic:

(5)   Speaker A: Tell me about everyone.
        Speaker B:
        a.   Sam went to the beach, Peter went to school, . . .
        b.   *Everyone went to the beach.

The fact that the response in (b) is not possible shows that *everyone* is not a possible topic. What happens when *everyone* is specified as a topic is that each of the individual members of the set defined by the quantifier become topics, rather than the set as a whole. This is what we find in the "list"-response in (5a). Let us now return to (1a). It follows from what has just been said about the topic properties of *everyone* that if it is interpreted as the topic of the question, the list interpretation necessarily ensues, explaining why the individual reading is blocked in the context (3). If, however, *everyone* is not interpreted as the topic of the question only the individual answer should be possible. One way of blocking the topic-reading of the quantifier is to assign stress to it, as in (4), and make it a focus. (4) is no longer ambiguous and allows only the individual answer (2a). The ambiguity of (1a) therefore follows from the two different focus structures, i.e., two different assignments of topic and focus. When the quantifier is interpreted as the topic of the sentence, the pair-list reading ensues, and when the quantifier is focused only the individual answer reading occurs.

The puzzle presented by the lack of ambiguity in (1b) remains to be solved. In the spirit of what has been said up to now, we can rephrase the puzzle as follows: what prevents *everyone* from being a possible topic in this question? The answer to this question (to be discussed in detail in chapter 6) is the Subject Constraint which constrains dependencies such as the one found between the quantifier and the *wh*-phrase in the list reading to a "canonical" f-structure, one in which the syntactic subject and the topic are identified.

My principal concern in this book is to explore the role of focus structure in Grammar. I examine the interface between focus structure and syntax, the semantics of focus structure and the intonation associated with it. I define a grammatical level of f-structure (focus structure), an annotated structural description (SD) in which topic and focus constituents are marked. F-structure feeds both PF (Phonological Form), and semantics and is sensitive to lexical information. It feeds PF since this level provides the explicit phonetic spell-out including intonation. I argue that f-structure and not LF (Logical Form) is the input to a semantic rule of Predication. Under this view, the model of grammar takes the following shape:

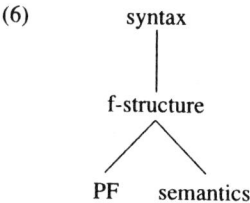

(6)   syntax
              |
              |
          f-structure
            /\
           / \
         PF   semantics

The f-structural framework provides a natural account of quantifier scope, interpretations of *wh*-in-situ, anaphora, subject–object asymmetries, etc. One major result of my analysis is that *wh*-movement turns out to be constrained by the same constraint which accounts for subject–object asymmetries.

The f-structure-theoretical approach to interpretation is dynamic in that it assumes a theory of discourse which defines the state of the common ground both before and after the utterance of a sentence. I adopt and modify Reinhart's (1981) file metaphor for the organization of the common ground. The common ground is viewed as having the following structure: it consists of a set of file cards which represent existing discourse referents. The common ground propositions form entries on these file cards. Only propositions which are interpretable as properties of a particular discourse referent are entered on the file card for that discourse referent. Common ground information is thus ordered according to the "topics" defined by each discourse referent. The set of file cards is also ordered as follows: a well-defined subset of the cards are located on *top of the file*. The cards in this location are licensed as potential topics of an utterance. Thus, the state of the file before the utterance of the sentence determines the potential f-structures licensed for it. Focusing an NP in the sentence results in positioning either a new card (if the NP is indefinite) or an existing card from the file (if the NP is definite) on top of the file. Focusing thus triggers a new state of the file.

F-structure theory is a pragmatic theory which is concerned with felicity conditions on the relation between sentences and context. Thus Topic can be assigned only to constituents for which file cards are available on top of the file, i.e., cards which have been positioned there by the application of the f-structure rules to previous utterances.

F-structure affects truth conditions. Rooth (1985) among others has shown that Focus assignment may determine truth conditions. Chierchia (1992a) shows that Topic is what forms the restrictor on adverbs of quantification. Partee (1992) discusses the idea that the restriction of tripartite discourse representations is akin to Topic and that nuclear scope is the Focus. Following Reinhart (1981), I adopt the Strawsonian view that the topic is the pivot for assessment and show that f-structures involving both main and subordinate assignments of topic and focus are required for interpretation. In particular, I show in chapter 5 that quantifier scope is determined by f-structure. F-structure theory thus forms part and parcel of semantics. It is a property of dynamic semantic theories that the borderline between pragmatics (involving circumstance of use) and semantics is blurred. F-structure theory blurs this line further. I discuss this issue in chapter 1, section 1.4.1 and in chapter 3, section 3.6. The discourse model assumes the following discourse rules:

F-structure rules

I   TOPIC instructs the hearer to locate on the top of his file an existing card (or an existing set of cards) with the relevant heading and index.

II   FOCUS instructs the hearer to either
        (i) open a new card and put it on the top of the file. Assign it a *heading* and a new index (in the case of an indefinite) or
        (ii) locate an existing card and put it on the top of the file (in the case of a definite)

III   PREDICATION instructs the hearer to evaluate the predicate with respect to the topic where the predicate is taken to be the complement of the topic.

If the result of the evaluation is TRUE the UPDATE rule applies:

IV   UPDATE instructs the hearer to enter the predicate on the topic card and then to copy all entries to all cards activated by the focus rule.

The following interaction illustrates the application of these rules: A is speaking, B is listening. Since cards for the speakers are available on top of the file, the first person is licensed as the topic of (7):

   A says:

(7)   I [have a dog].   [It] is brown.
             FOC   TOP

B's update:

1. Select the card for A (first person) from the top of the file. (TOPIC rule)
2. Evaluate "A has a dog" with respect to A. (PREDICATION)
3. If 2 yields TRUE, enter "e has a dog" on A's card. (UPDATE)
4. Open a new card, label it dog_2. Put it on top of the file. (FOCUS rule (i))
5. Enter "A_1 has e" on this card. (UPDATE)

The following cards are now on top of the hearer's file and are available as future topics:

A_1	= heading	dog_2
e has dog_2	= entry	A_1 has e

Chapter 1 concerns the interpretation of f-structure and defines the basic notions Topic and Focus in terms of the discourse theory associated with f-structure. I show following Strawson (1964) and Reinhart (1981) that sentences are evaluated with respect to their topics: if T is the topic of a sentence S then we check our knowledge of T to verify S. This chapter continues to examine indefinite subjects of intransitive individual-level predicates. I argue that such subjects must be topics. I introduce subordinate f-structures to account for such indefinite topics.

In chapter 2 I show, following Reinhart (1983, 1986), that coreference is determined by f-structure. I then offer an analysis of the interpretation of donkey sentences in terms of f-structure.

Chapter 3 offers an f-structure-theoretical analysis of questions, negation, and contrast as well as *only* and *even*.

Chapter 4 shows how intonation is assigned to f-structure in PF.

Chapter 5 discusses scope phenomena as a type of R-dependency (relevant to the speaker's file). I argue that Topics, by definition, have wide scope. Scope thus follows from f-structure without special stipulation.

Chapter 6 proposes a constraint on I-dependencies. A distinction is made between R-dependencies and I-dependencies (relevant to the hearer's file). I show that all phenomena which are classified as I-dependent (anaphora, multiple *wh*-questions, *wh-* and its trace, negative polarity among others) are constrained by the Subject Constraint, a syntactic constraint on f-structure.

The conclusion to be drawn from this chapter is that a model of grammar which incorporates f-structure in the manner proposed in this book allows for a wide range of linguistic phenomena to be unified under one *single* syntactic constraint.

I restrict the discussion to English and similar languages. Discussion of the relevance of focus structure to syntax in previous work has generally concentrated on languages in which either the focus or the topic has a fixed syntactic position. The former can be exemplified by a focus-preposing language such as Hungarian. (See for example É. Kiss 1991, 1996; Szabolcsi and Zwarts 1993.) An example of the latter is a topic-prominent language such as Chinese. (See for example Huang 1984.) Languages such as Japanese which mark topic and focus morphologically have also been studied with a view to examine the relevance of topic and focus to the syntax. (See Kuno 1976, 1982, 1987.) There are two main reasons why the choice of English makes a stronger argument for my theory than a topic-prominent language, a focus-preposing language or one that marks both:

1. Whereas it is to be expected that topic and focus play a role in the syntax of topic-prominent languages or in focus-preposing languages, this is a much more surprising finding for a language such as English in which syntactic constraints have generally been assumed to be determined entirely by syntactic properties. My proposal is thus more significant because it claims that f-structure is responsible for syntactic constraints even in a language such as English, which lacks morphological or (overt) syntactic devices for marking focus or topic (in most cases).

2. My concern is to provide an in-depth study of one language to demonstrate the viability and explanatory power of my account in considerable detail. This approach is standard in contemporary linguistic (particularly syntactic) theory. Since I challenge the most common accounts of phenomena such as binding and extraction, it is imperative to offer an alternative account in terms of f-structure precisely for a language such as English for which syntactic accounts have been developed in most detail.

In the concluding chapter I suggest how f-structure theory, a fundamental part of Universal Grammar, can be extended to languages which mark topics and/or foci overtly.

I   *The interpretation of f-structure*

Watt's instructions were to give what Mr Knott left of this dish, on the days that he did not eat it all, to the dog. . . .

But was a dog the same thing as the dog? For in Watt's instructions there was no mention of a dog, but only of the dog, which could only mean that what was required was not any dog, but one particular dog, that is to say, not one dog one day, and the next another, and perhaps the next a third, no, but every day the same, every day the same poor old dog, as long as the dog lived. But a fortiori were several dogs the same thing as the dog?

Samuel Beckett, *Watt* (New York: Grove Press, 1959[1953]), pp. 91, 96

1.1   Focus structure

I use the term focus structure (f-structure) to characterize structural descriptions (SDs) annotated for topic and focus constituents. F-structure feeds both PF (Phonological Form) and Semantics.[1] It feeds PF since this level provides the explicit phonetic spell-out including intonation. (Intonation is discussed in chapter 4.) I argue that f-structure and not LF (Logical Form) is the input to a semantic rule of Predication.

This chapter introduces the discourse theory to which f-structure provides the input. Interpreting f-structure is a dynamic venture, in the sense that the f-structure of a sentence determines its information-change potential. A sentence is thus viewed as a means of changing the information state of the interpreter or hearer. The part of the information state which the hearer has in common with the speaker is the common ground. The f-structure theory of discourse defines the state of the common ground both before and after the utterance of a sentence. The common ground is viewed as having the following structure: it consists of a set of file cards which represent existing discourse referents. The common-ground propositions form entries on these file cards. Only propositions which are interpretable as properties of a particular discourse referent are entered on the file card for that discourse referent. Common-ground information is thus ordered according to the "topics" defined by each discourse referent.[2] The set of file cards is also ordered as follows: a well-defined subset of the cards is located on *top of the file*. The cards on top of the file are licensed as potential topics of an utterance. Thus, the state of the file before the utterance of the sentence determines the potential f-structures licensed for it. Focusing an NP results in positioning on top of the file either a new card (if the NP is indefinite) or an existing card from the file (if the NP is definite). Focusing thus triggers a new state of the file.[3]

F-structure theory is a pragmatic theory which is concerned with felicity conditions on the relation between sentences and context. Thus Topic can be assigned only to constituents for which file cards are available on top of the file, i.e., cards which have been positioned there by the application of the f-structure rules to previous utterances.

F-structure affects truth conditions. Chierchia (1992a) shows that Topic is what forms the restrictor on adverbs of quantification. Partee (1992) discusses the idea that the restriction of tripartite discourse representations is akin to Topic and that nuclear scope is the Focus. Following Reinhart (1981), I adopt the Strawsonian view that the topic is the pivot for assessment and show that f-structures involving both main and subordinate assignments of topic and focus are required for interpretation. In particular, I define a rule of Predication which allows for a dynamic assignment of truth values. This rule is viewed as a relation between the "topic" of a sentence and its predicate. Formally, Predication is a one-place function that maps topics to propositions, assigning them truth values. It operates on articulated f-structures in which Topic and Focus have been assigned. One of the main innovations provided by the theory of f-structure is therefore the introduction of the pragmatic notions Topic and Focus into the semantics. I provide arguments for the topic-centered rule of predication in section 1.4.1.

In this chapter I commence with a characterization of the terms Topic and Focus (sections 1.1.1–1.1.4). In section 1.2, I propose that truth values are assigned by a topic-centered rule of predication. I then define the level of f-structure and the ground rules for its interpretation: update rules are triggered by the topic and focus constituents in the sentence and define the changes in the discourse file (sections 1.3–5). In section 1.4, following Kratzer (1989a), I show that the subject of predication can be a Davidsonian spatio-temporal argument. This argument, when unactualized, necessarily functions as the topic of the sentence. I call a topic which defines spatial and/or temporal parameters a Stage Topic.

I then examine the individual/stage-level distinction in terms of f-structure in order to probe the nature of topics (section 1.6). I argue that sentences with stage-level predicates can be assigned an f-structure with a stage topic but that sentences with individual-level predicates cannot. It follows that the subject of intransitive individual-level predicates is necessarily the topic of the sentence. Therefore an NP which can be inserted in this position must be of the kind that qualifies as a topic. An analysis of these NPs thus sheds light on the nature of topics in general. One of the conclusions I draw from this investigation is that subordinate f-structures are required, i.e., f-structure marks both main and subordinate topics and foci.

In section 1.7, I discuss subordinate f-structure in more detail and propose a revised version of the update rules that takes into account subordinate f-structures.

In the last section I compare f-structure-theoretical discourse theory to Information Packaging (Vallduví 1992), Information structure (Lambrecht 1994), and Discourse Representation Theory (DRT) (Heim 1982 and Kamp 1981).

1.1.1 Topic

Both Topic and Focus are often characterized as the salient part of the sentence. This has caused much confusion in the past. For this reason and also because of the vast amount of material written on both notions, I will refrain from offering a proper review of the literature.[4] Instead, I will introduce the analysis of these notions assumed in this work.

The definition of Topic is derived from Reinhart (1981) who in turn draws on Strawson (1964: 97). According to Strawson the topic has three central properties:

a. The topic is what a statement is about.
b. The topic is used to invoke "knowledge in the possession of an audience."
c. "The statement is assessed *as* putative information *about its topic.*"

Strawson connects these three properties to explain why truth value gaps come about. He argues that if the topic is what a statement is about and therefore the statement is assessed with respect to the topic, the topic must have reference. If, however, the topic has no reference, the sentence cannot be evaluated as either true or false, since in such a case "a statement which, by hypothesis, is *about* something is really about nothing" (p. 98).

Reinhart adopts this view of topics and offers a formalization in terms of the context set à la Stalnaker (1978): "The *context set* of a given discourse at a given point is the set of propositions which we accept to be true at this point" (Reinhart 1981: 78). Each new assertion, if not rejected as false, adds a new proposition to the presuppositions in the context set. Reinhart suggests that the context set has internal organization, in particular, propositions in the context set are classified by their topics. Sentence topics thus determine under which entry a particular proposition is assessed. Take for example:

(1)   A: Tell me about John.
        A': Tell me about Mary.
        B: John invited Mary to dance.

This sentence can be understood to be "about" John or "about" Mary since it can naturally follow the requests made both by speaker A and by speaker A'. According to Reinhart, B's sentence, in the context of A, will be assessed as putative information about *John*. If the new information is not rejected, it is entered under the referential entry for *John*. Similarly, for B in the context of A'. Although the truth value of B's sentence will be the same in both contexts in this case, the way the sentence is evaluated is different.

In view of the fact that a sentence may have more than one potential topic (allowing it to occur naturally in several contexts), it is, in Reinhart's framework, associated with a set of possible pragmatic assertions (PPA) the content of each of which can be introduced into the context set, depending on the topic selected. Reinhart (1981: 80, her (44)) defines the set of PPAs of S (PPA$_{(S)}$) as follows:

(2) ϕ denotes the proposition expressed by a given sentence S
        PPA$_{(S)}$ = ϕ together with [<a, ϕ>: a is the interpretation of an NP expression in S][5]

The following definition of Topic results:

> To say that a sentence S uttered in a context C is about a_i, i.e., that the pair <a_i, ϕ> of PPA$_{(S)}$ is selected in C, is to say, first, that, if possible, the proposition θ expressed in S will be assessed by the hearer in C with respect to the subset of propositions already listed in the context set under a_i, and, second, that if is not rejected it will be added to the context set under the entry a_i. (p. 81)

The framework I will be developing differs from Reinhart's in two respects. First, I argue in section 1.4 that every sentence must have a topic since if topics are the pivots for assessment it is crucial that every sentence have one. Non-overt topics, I claim, are provided by the spatio-temporal parameters of the utterance. (Reinhart, in fact, speculates in a footnote that this may indeed be the case.) Second, I show that all topics are old or presupposed. In particular I claim that indefinite topics do not contradict this claim. In section 1.6.2.2, I introduce the notion "subordinate" f-structure to achieve this result. Another problem with the idea that topics are old, according to Reinhart, is that this requires that topichood be defined directly on referents, "or that the topic role of an expression can be identified by checking properties of its referents" (p.72). This, she shows, cannot be the case in view of the fact that the *same* referent may function both as the topic and as the focus in one sentence (Reinhart's (37)):

(3)   A: Who did Felix praise?
        B: Felix praised HIMSELF.

Reinhart argues that if *Felix* is the topic in B's response, then so is the anaphoric reflexive since the referent of these two NPs is the same. But the reflexive answers the *wh*-question and therefore must be interpreted as a focus. It follows that the reflexive is both a topic and a focus, a plain contradiction, according to Reinhart. In chapter 6, I argue that anaphors belong to the class of I-dependent NPs. As an I-dependent NP, the reflexive is interpreted via its dependency on its antecedent and this interpretation is constrained by the subject constraint which requires that the dependent is contained in the focus. The details of this account must await chapter 6.

Reinhart uses the term topic structure to indicate the topic assignment of a particular sentence. Focus structure, in turn, has been used to indicate focus assignment. In view of the fact that the framework I develop here essentially involves both topic *and* focus, I have elected to use the name focus structure as an abbreviation for "topic–focus" structure.

1.1.2   Focus

I adopt the definition of Focus in Erteschik-Shir (1973, 1986a):[6]

(4)   The Focus of a sentence S = the (intension of a) constituent c of S which
        the speaker intends to direct the attention of his/her hearer(s) to, by uttering
        S. (See Erteschik-Shir and Lappin 1979.)[7]

The definition of focus in terms of speakers' intentions entails that it is a discourse property which is assigned to a constituent in a context of conversation. For any sentence several focus assignments will generally be possible, one of which is realized in discourse. A sentence, in discourse, has only one main focus which is assigned to a syntactic constituent. This constituent may be an NP, a VP or even the whole S (as in an out-of-the-blue sentence). The topic of a sentence is excluded as a focus because it is by definition already in the hearer's attention. Hence, the focus constituent is selected freely among the nontopic constituents of the sentence. The fact that the focus is defined as the constituent to which the hearer's attention is drawn enables the constituents contained in it to provide the topics of the following sentences since these constituents have become part of the domain of what the hearer is now attending to.

The distinction between plain focus as defined here and contrastive focus has often been blurred. Contrast is contextually constrained to occur only if a contrast set is available:

(5)   A: Who wants to marry John, Janet or Ann?
      B: JANET wants to marry John.

B's answer is contrastive because it selects *Janet* from the contrast set provided in the context. If, however, no such context set were provided by A, *Janet* in B's answer would be a noncontrastive focus. Outside of context contrastive and noncontrastive foci may coincide. Contrastive foci are also distinct from plain foci in that they are not constrained to syntactic constituents:

(6)   He didn't tie his shoelaces, he UNtied them.

Contrastive and noncontrastive foci therefore do not necessarily overlap. Sentence stress, as clarified in chapter 4, is governed by the focus. If a sentence contains both a contrastive and a noncontrastive focus, the former will receive the main sentential stress. This may be why contrastive foci have often been mistaken for noncontrastive ones.

A further focus type with distinct properties is what I refer to as a Restrictive Focus. Restrictive foci, like contrastive ones require a context-specified set:

(7)   A: Which one of his friends wants to marry John?
      B: JANET wants to marry John.

Here the focus, *Janet*, is selected from the contextually specified or restrictive set of *John's friends*. *Janet* is, however, not contrasted with any other particular individual. Note that in B's answer, the set of *John's friends* qualifies as a topic. I show below that this set in fact provides the topic of a (subordinate) focus structure in which *Janet* is the focus. A similar f-structure is assigned to contrastive foci.

B's answer could, of course, also be a response to:

(8)   Who wants to marry John?

in which no contextually specified set is assumed. *Janet* in this case would
be a nonrestrictive, noncontrastive focus. B's answer therefore can occur in
three different context types and accordingly can be assigned three different
focus structures. I show below that restrictive foci have a different distribution than nonrestrictive ones. In particular, in sentences which have been
claimed to have multiple foci, I show that only *one* of these is a nonrestrictive
one. My claim that a sentence has only one focus therefore pertains to
nonrestrictive, noncontrastive foci. Such foci I refer to below as "main" foci.

1.1.3   Presupposition

In the discussion of topics in section 1.1.1, I claimed that topics are presupposed. The context-specified sets which provide the topics of restrictive and
contrastive foci are similarly presupposed. Presuppositions which are not
identified with topics also occur:

(9)   A: Who did you give the book to?
        B: I gave the book to Mary.
           TOP ——————— FOC

In the context of A's question, the topic in B's answer is "I," the focus is
"Mary" and the remainder of the sentence ("(I) gave the book to X") is
presupposed. In view of the fact that the topic is also presupposed, it is not
surprising that the claim has been made that the complement of the focus is
presupposed. It is, however, not always the case that an analysis in terms
of topic, focus, and presupposition "covers" the whole sentence. A natural
interpretation of the following sentence is one in which only the subordinate
clause has a focus structure. Here the matrix is used merely to qualify the
assertion:

(10)   I think that John FELL ASLEEP.
                      TOP   FOC

The matrix in this case is not presupposed. It is therefore possible to have a
sentence in which constituents are "left out": they function neither as topics
nor as foci. And they are not presupposed.

The bipartite sectioning of sentences can be observed in the current framework in the division between topic and "predicate." The term predicate is
used here to define the sentence part which complements the topic. (This use
of the term is clarified in section 1.2.)

1.1.4 Topics and foci: tests

Reinhart (1981) offers several Topic-tests. One of these, noted in the introduction, follows:

(11)   Speaker A: Tell me about X.
         Speaker B: ... X. ... X = TOPIC

X is the topic of speaker B's sentence because according to A's request B's sentence will necessarily be about X. (Should B not cooperate with A, we get a clear nonsequitur.)

Traditionally, focus has been identified as the constituent which answers a *wh*-question. The topic in the answer must already be introduced in the question, since it would make little sense for the question to be about one thing and the answer to be about another. Question–answer pairs therefore are useful to determine the topic and focus assignments in the answers. This works nicely in the following exchanges:

(12)   a. What did the children do? The children ATE THE CANDY.
                                            TOP   FOC
         b. What did the children eat? The children ate THE CANDY.
                                            TOP   FOC
         c. Who ate the candy? THE CHILDREN ate the candy.
                                  FOC   TOP

In (12a), the focus and the predicate coincide and complement the topic. In (12b), however, the focus constituent, *the candy*, is included in the predicate (*ate the candy)* since the predicate is the complement of the topic. Similarly, in (12c) (in which *the candy* is the topic), the focus *the children* is part of the predicate (*the children ate*).

Another way to test for potential "focus-hood" is the lie-test (Erteschik-Shir 1973):

(13)   Lie-test:
         Speaker A: John said that he knows Peter.
         Speaker B: a. That's a lie, he didn't.
                    b. That's a lie, he doesn't.

Each response indicates a different f-structure. (a), for example, takes the subject as a Topic and the whole VP as the Focus. The fact that (b) is a possible response indicates that the lower sentence can be the one that the speaker directs the hearer's attention to and hence the focus can fall on or within it. (Here the topic and focus both fall within the subordinate clause.) In this manner the lie-test distinguishes the main assertion of the sentence from the rest of the sentence. This test is not a test for focus per se, but rather a test for the main assertion or the main f-structure.

Finally, I should point out here that these tests are useful diagnostics which capture some of the properties of topics and foci. The f-structure-theoretical framework outlined here, however, stands on its own. The assignment of f-structure to a sentence is free (restricted only in that overt topics and (noncontrastive) foci must be syntactic constituents). F-structures are then interpreted by the proposed discourse theory. Intonation is assigned to f-structure according to the rules proposed in chapter 4. The prediction is that the intonation assigned renders the derived interpretation. In languages in which other markers of f-structure are used (syntactic structure or morphological marking, for example) it is again predicted that the interpretation be consistent with the overt marking of f-structure.

In this system, there will be clauses (and other sentence "parts") which belong neither to the topic nor to the focus constituents (e.g., the matrix in the case in which only the subordinate clause is focused.)

It is important to emphasize two points in which my approach differs from other approaches. (For discussion, see Erteschik-Shir and Lappin 1983.) a) Whereas Topic and Predicate "cover" the whole sentence this is only the case for Topic and Focus assignments when the Focus and Predicate are coextensive. b) The main focus is contained in the predicate, but again does not necessarily "cover" the whole predicate.

1.2   Predication[8]

Predication is viewed here as a relation between the "topic" of a sentence and its predicate. Formally, predication is a one-place function that maps topics to propositions, assigning them truth values. It operates on articulated f-structures in which Topic and Focus have been assigned.

I adopt a traditional definition of predication. According to Quine (1960): "The basic combination in which general and singular terms find their contrasting roles is that of *predication*: 'Mama is a woman', or schematically '*a* is an *F*' where '*a*' represents a singular term and '*F*' a general term. Predication joins a general term and a singular term to form a sentence that is true or false according as the general term is true or false of the object, if any, to which the singular term refers." I follow Strawson (1964) in saying that predication is an assessment for truth value of the predicate with respect to the Topic, i.e., "the statement is assessed *as* putative information *about its topic*."[9] Strawson's innovation is that for him the topic is not necessarily associated with the grammatical subject of the sentence (or with any other structural position). Rather, it is chosen in accordance with the context as illustrated in (14) and (15):

(14)   The King of France is bald.
     a. What is the King of France like?
     b. What bald notables are there?

(15)   The exhibition was visited by the King of France.

According to Strawson, in the context of the question in (14a), (14) has no truth value since the sentence cannot be verified. It cannot be *about* a nonexisting king. (15), however, has a possible f-structure in which "the exhibition" is chosen as the topic. This sentence will be assessed as false if the King of France is not among the visitors at the exhibition. Similarly, (14), in the context of (14b), is simply false. The context-dependent choice of topic thus determines the assignment of truth values. This view of topichood has been formalized in Reinhart (1981) as shown above.

I introduce a rule of Predication which assigns truth values by examining the truth of the predicate with respect to the topic. (The topic here functions as the "subject" of predication.) The rule of Predication thus applies to f-structures. This is the traditional use of the notion predication and should not be confused with syntactic predication as in Williams (1980), for example. Here Predication is a semantic rule which takes f-structures as its input and produces truth values as its output.[10]

1.3   The filing system

In this section I introduce the rules that interpret f-structures. F-structures are structural descriptions (SDs) with both topic and focus assigned. Topic and focus assignment is free, conditioned only by syntactic structure: foci and overt topics must form constituents.[11] It is possible to imagine a theory of f-structure which does not restrict topics and foci to syntactic constituents. Such a theory would, however, be totally unconstrained and would not enable the intonational, syntactic and semantic predictions to be made here. The free assignment of f-structure means that not all f-structure assignments will be interpretable. Others will be contextually constrained. The interpretive rules can be viewed as a filter which rules out incorrect f-structures.

I adopt and modify Reinhart's (1981) file metaphor for the organization of the context set. I assume a file consisting of a set of "cards" and a set of rules which determine the changes in the file induced by an utterance. The rules are based on the definitions of Topic and Focus given above. Topic and Focus are thus viewed as the basic elements of f-structures which in turn trigger the application of the discourse rules. In particular, incorporating Reinhart's (1981) basic insight into their nature, topics represent existing cards which must both be old and "prominent" in the discourse and these cards provide the locus for truth value assignment. The system also incorporates a basic idea from Heim (1982) namely that indefinites trigger the construction of new "cards" and definites presuppose the existence of old ones. Finally, the focus is, according to its definition here, the constituent to which the hearer's attention is drawn. Translated into the file system, this means that focused cards are placed prominently in the file.

Utterances are conceived of as a set of instructions by a speaker to a hearer to update and organize a file so that the file will contain all the information the speaker intends to convey. The file consists of indexed cards which represent existing discourse referents. Information is entered on these cards according to well-defined principles. Each card has an indexed "heading" and information pertaining to this heading can be entered on the card. Common ground information is thus ordered according to the "topics" defined by each discourse referent.[12]

An identifying "index" is assigned to the card heading by a function which maps the set of cards onto the set of discourse referents. The heading of a card is an attribute of the card (such as "dog"). When a card is first introduced, the constituent which introduces it determines the form of this heading. Once entries are added to the card, any other attribute can take the place of the index which uniquely identifies the card thus distinguishing between various "dog" cards.

The file itself can be viewed as a stack of such cards which is partitioned into two parts: the *top of the file* where "prominent" cards are to be found and the rest of the stack where nonprominent cards are to be found. The cards on top of the file are licensed as potential topics of an utterance. Thus, the state of the file before the utterance of the sentence determines the potential f-structures licensed for it.

F-structure theory is a pragmatic theory which is concerned with felicity conditions on the relation between sentences and context. Thus Topic can be assigned only to constituents for which file cards are available on top of the file, i.e., cards which have been positioned there by the application of the f-structure rules to previous utterances.

The following rules show how new cards are made out and how cards get to be on top of the file. Note that the instruction for a topic requires the topic card to be on top of the file. The instruction for focus puts a card on top of the file providing a potential future topic.

F-structure rules

I   TOPIC instructs the hearer to locate on the top of his file an existing card (or an existing set of cards) with the relevant heading and index.

II   FOCUS instructs the hearer to either
        (i) open a new card and put it on the top of the file. Assign it a *heading* and a new index (in the case of an indefinite) or
        (ii) locate an existing card and put it on the top of the file (in the case of a definite)

III   PREDICATION instructs the hearer to evaluate the predicate with respect to the topic where the predicate is taken to be the complement of the topic.

If the result of the evaluation is TRUE the UPDATE rule applies:

IV   UPDATE instructs the hearer to enter the focus on the topic card and then to copy all entries to all cards activated by the focus rule.

Topics are presupposed or old. They are distinguished in the file system as existing file cards (positioned on top of the file). Presuppositions that do not occur as topics are assumed to be existing entries on cards, i.e., if a predicate consists of both a presupposition and a focus, the presupposed part of the predicate is represented as an already existing entry on the topic card, whereas the focus is added to this presupposition by the Update rule.

It is important to note that the top of the file consists of more than one card. At the beginning of a discourse the following permanent cards are on top: the card for the speaker (first person), the card for the hearer (second person) and a card which signifies the here-and-now of the discourse situation. The focus rule then adds cards to the top of the file which join the cards already in that position.

Being on the top of the file is a well-defined notion which restricts the available topics. According to the Topic rule, being on top of the file means being available as the topic of the utterance which follows it.[13] I do not take a stand concerning how long a card remains on top of the file in a discourse. It is clearly *not* the case that the positioning of a new card on top of the file "covers" a card already there. The question might be clarified by a careful analysis of extended discourses within the framework outlined here. A few points relating to this issue are discussed in the section on discourse in chapter 2, section 2.2.

The focus rule applies to *all* constituents included in the focus constituent (each such consituent should therefore receive a separate focus marking), i.e., the number of new cards constructed by the focus rule equals the number of subconstituents of the focus constituent. I assume that cards are taken out not only for the focus constituent itself, but for all NP constituents contained in it. For each constituent, to which the hearer's attention is directed, a card is either opened or located. In the current framework "opening (or locating) a card" is the term I use to mean that the hearer's attention is directed to a constituent. Once a new card is opened and positioned on top of the file, it is available as a potential topic for the following sentence.

In view of the fact that any constituent can be a focus constituent, possible cards not only represent NPs but also cards for propositions, VPs, and APs. I assume that the headings of such cards take the form of nominalizations so that an account for pronominal reference to such constituents can be offered. In the following I do not discuss cards with nominalized heads.

The focus constituent may define a *set* of cards. "The students in my class," for example, forms such a set. The card which is positioned on top of the file by the focus rule in this case has the heading "the students in my class$_i$." This is a single card. There is a distribution mechanism for plurals that distributes the discourse referent to members of the set and constructs a card for each member of the discourse referent. The output of the distribution mechanism is a set of cards. Cards which contain a set of cards are called *restrictive* cards, the set they define is a *restrictive* set and the focus which introduces them is a *restrictive* focus.

In summary, the hearer's file, at any given point in a discourse, consists of two types of cards: those that are on top of the file (and provide potential topics) and those that are not. The latter consist of definite cards which can be accessed by focus rule (ii). Existential presupposition is associated with all the cards in the file. Presuppositions also take the form of existing entries on cards. Such entries may occur on cards whether they are on top of the file or not.

Let us examine the file system through a simple illustration. Assume the following interaction: A is speaking, B is listening. Remember that the cards for the speakers are available on top of the file, hence the first person is licensed as the topic of (16):

A says:

(16)   I [have a dog]. [It] is brown.
         FOC   TOP

B's update:

I.   Select the card for A (first person) from the top of the file. (TOPIC rule)

2.   Evaluate "A has a dog" with respect to A. (PREDICATION)

3.   If 2 yields TRUE,[14] enter "e has a dog" on A's card. (UPDATE)

4.   Open a new card, label it dog_2. Put it on top of the file. (FOCUS rule (i))[15]

5.   Enter "A_1 has e" on this card. (UPDATE)

The following cards are now on top of the hearer's file and are available as future topics:

A_1	= heading	dog_2
e has dog_2	= entry	A_1 has e

The heading of the card (indicated as the top line of the card) has a special status as "identifying" an individual to the hearer. In the new card for dog_2, the heading allows future definite references to this dog such as "the dog." Once further entries are added to a card in the continued discourse one or more of these entries may provide better ways of identifying the individual and may be added to it or even replace it, in this fashion commuting to the heading of the card. Our dog may be referred to as "the dog you have" (= "your dog") or "the brown dog." Entries can in this way be viewed as restrictions on the heading.

Entries and headings may "commute" up to a point. Assume that said dog is given a name in the discourse, "Chita," for example. This entry can also commute to the heading, yielding "the dog whose name is Chita," abbreviated as "Chita." It follows that once a name becomes the heading of a card it cannot be further restricted, thus ruling out "the Chita that is brown" as a way of referring to A's dog. (Chances are that future references to the dog (in this or future discourses) will employ this name rather than a modified definite description.) In this connection I show in section 1.3.1 below that the fact that, once it is available, a name must provide the heading of a card, follows from the nature of names: names are directly referential; knowing the intension of a name is the same as knowing its reference. Therefore, the name itself provides an identifying index for the card heading and no further index is required.

The entry for the second sentence in (16) can now be made by B. The pronoun, which is the only possible topic in this sentence, is interpretable only if entered on an available card from the top of the file. The features of the heading in card 2 match this pronoun, licensing the entry on this card.

The following steps are taken by B:

1. Select card 2 from the top of the file. (TOPIC rule)
2. Evaluate "e is brown" with respect to dog_2. (PREDICATION)
3. If 2 yields TRUE, enter "e is brown" on card 2. (UPDATE)

The updated card 2 is still on top of the file:

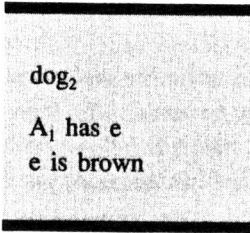

dog_2

A_1 has e
e is brown

Two further points have to be made here: in the f-structure model as just illustrated, pronouns must always be interpreted with respect to an available topic card, i.e., a pronoun is necessarily a topic. If no card is available on top of the file for this purpose, the pronoun cannot get interpreted. The pronoun *it* thus refers to the heading of the card just opened and is placed on top of the file, i.e., it refers to dog_2 which can, in view of the commutativity of entries, be described as the dog that A has.[16]

The second point has to do with uniqueness. When A says his first sentence, he is not saying that he has only one dog. He might have another dog or two. The utterance he makes does not make reference to those other dogs, and no cards are placed on top of the file for them. That is why the pronoun in the second sentence uniquely refers to the dog just introduced into the discourse.[17]

1.3.1   Generic cards

The file system applies to generics in the same way, with different results.[18] Generics are assumed to be name-like (see Carlson 1977). Whereas NPs which are not names must be indexed in order to identify the individual to which they refer, names, which are rigid designators, provide an inherent index as mentioned in the previous section. I use the following notation to make this intuition overt:

(17)   John thinks that he$_{\text{JOHN}}$ is going to succeed.

The purpose of noninherent indexes is to uniquely identify individual discourse referents and in particular to distinguish two different cards that happen to have the same heading. So, for example, two different books can be identified as book$_1$ and book$_2$. I may also know two different people by the name John and in that case one will be identified as John$_1$ and the other as John$_2$, but here, *John* is not a rigid designator, hence it functions like any other nonname definite. Generics are names of kinds and it is never the case that one generic name refers to two different kinds. Accordingly, there is no need to assign (noninherent) identifying indexes to generics. I conclude that the heading of a generic card consists of the (translation) of the noun with no other index.

Generics and names, like definites, are present in the file independent of immediate mention in the discourse.[19] Generics, however, differ from names in that they are also indefinite. (See Wilkinson 1991.) It follows from the discourse theory introduced here, that a new card can be made out for every focused generic in view of the fact that it is indefinite. Generics are therefore interesting in that they have properties of names, which means that the cards representing them are available in the file as are all definites. (This feature of generics allows them to be topics once they are elevated to the top of the file by the focus rule.) In addition they may be taken as indefinite, triggering the introduction of a *new* card by the focus rule. The fact that the file update can treat generics either as names or as indefinites explains the ambiguity of the pronoun in (18):

(18)   John smokes cigars. They stink.

The generic (unindexed) card with the heading "cigars" is elevated to the top of the file by the focus rule. The second sentence in (18) can therefore be entered on this generic card, rendering the interpretation in which the pronoun *they* refers to cigars in general. This follows from focus rule (ii) if the generic card is taken to be a name, i.e., definite. The following card results:

```
cigars

John smokes e
e stink
```

This interpretation is indexed as follows:

(19)   John smokes cigars. They$_{\text{CIGARS}}$ stink.

Since generics are also indefinite, focus rule (i) also applies, rendering a *new* card as follows:

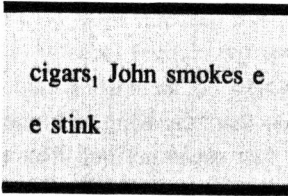

```
cigars₁ John smokes e

e stink
```

Note that a new genus is defined by this card, namely the kind of cigars John smokes. Here the entry "John smokes e" commutes to the top and functions as a restriction on the indefinite, as shown with respect to (16) above. The second sentence in (18) is entered on this card as well, rendering the interpretation in which the pronoun *they* indicates the kind described in the card heading, i.e., the kind of cigars smoked by John. This interpretation is indexed as follows:

(20)   John smokes cigars$_i$. They$_i$ stink.

The ambiguity in (18) is thus explained. The only case in which entries cannot commute to the heading, and therefore cannot function as restrictions, is in the case of names, which cannot be further restricted as noted above.

   Note that coreference in this system is not triggered by coindexing, but by entering the sentence containing the pronoun on the relevant topic card. Viewing generics as both definite (names) and indefinite enables the filing system to account for this type of ambiguity in a natural way.[20]

1.3.2   Truth values: Strawson's examples

Let us now return to Strawson's examples in (14) (repeated here for convenience) and reformulate his observations in the filing system framework.

(14)   The King of France is bald.
         a. What is the King of France like?
         b. What bald notables are there?

First let us examine the sentence in the context of (14a), posed by A: (14a), according to Strawson, is a question which does not arise and has no correct answer. The only correct *reply* to such questions would be: "There is no King of France." Let us imagine that B does answer (14a) and that the interchange is observed by C: in the context of (14a) "the King of France" is the unstressed topic of (14). C must therefore locate a card with this heading. But in a world such as ours in which there is no King of France, C will not be able to perform this task, since among C's existing cards no such card is to be found. It follows that C will not be able to evaluate (14) at all. This is how we get a truth-value gap. (14b), however, is a question about *bald notables*. (In this context "the King of France" is the (restrictive) focus of (14) and is therefore stressed). B is thus instructed to take out an existing card with this heading. In assessing (14), B will discover that "the King of France" is not among his list of bald notables (and, in fact could not be). Hence, in this context, (14) will be assessed as false.[21]

1.3.3   Restrictive focus

In this section I show how restrictive sets are manipulated by the topic and focus rules.

Assume that (14) is given as an answer to

(21)   Which of your friends is bald?

How does A go about answering this question? He locates the card for the restrictive set "my friends" on top of his file (B's question positions this card on top of A's file). Assume that such a "restrictive set" card looks as follows:

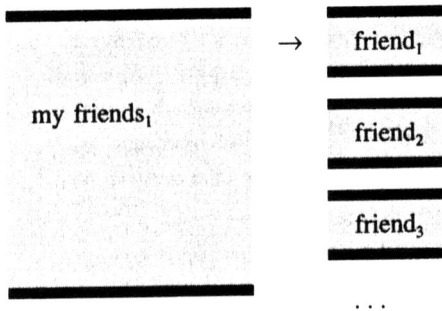

The individual cards for each friend contained in the discourse referent (which are constructed by the distribution mechanism for plurals) are *attached* to the card for the restrictive set of friends. In view of the fact that neither speaker nor hearer necessarily knows the exact number of friends, or has too many details about each friend or, for that matter, information concerning the set of friends in general, the availability of cards for the individuals in the restrictive set is not required. This is an important point in view of the occurrence of infinite restrictive sets. For example the set of integers. Depending on context the attached cards for the individuals contained in this set may in turn define restrictive sets: the set of even or odd numbers, for example. Clearly, an infinite set of attached cards is ruled out.

The only strict requirement on restrictive sets is that the set of friends be discoursally restricted. I assume that there is partial overlap of the entries on the individual attached cards and the restrictive set card. For example, if the restrictive card has the entry *are interesting*, the individual cards must have this entry too. On the other hand, if the entry *dispersed* is entered on the restrictive card, this entry cannot occur on the individual cards. Similarly, characteristics of one of my friends may not be true of them all.

A now proceeds as follows. He examines each individual friend-card and assesses whether the sentence is true of it. If this assessment comes out TRUE, he puts the card in pile K (= the set of bald friends), and if it does not, he puts it in the pile N (= the set of not-bald friends). In order to answer (21), A must partition the set F into the parts K and N, according to the definition *bald*. Assume that the set K includes Peter as its only member and Peter is known by his friends as "the King of France." In A's answer this constituent is stressed, hence focused as in (22):

(22)   THE KING OF FRANCE is bald. (Capitals = stressed constituent)

What A's answer does is cause B to select this card, which has the entry "e is bald" on it, from the set of friend-cards already on top of his file, and position it as a separate card on top of his file. Note that if the set of bald friends had more than one member, the card positioned on top via the answer would be a new restrictive card, namely the card for the set of A's bald friends. This card would have attached to it the cards for the individuals contained in this new restrictive set which in turn is attached to the original restrictive card:

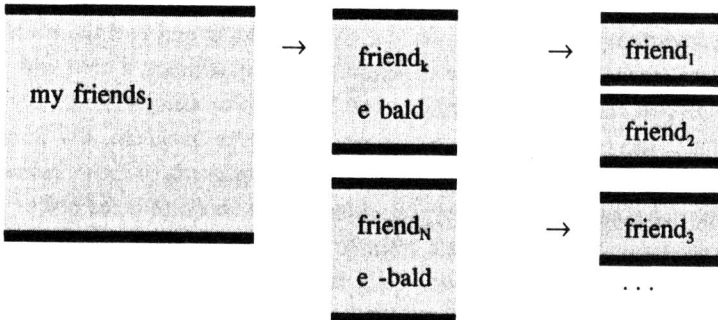

A restrictive focus thus differs from a regular focus in that it presupposes the partitioning of a discourse or utterance-specified set (F in this case). The new subset defined by the partitioning of the existing restrictive set is also a restrictive set. This reflects the operations on B's file and allows him to evaluate (22) as follows. B, in asking (21), constructs a set of cards for himself with the heading "A's friends." In order for B to assess (22) as a response to (21), the card for "the King of France" must be located in the set "A's friends". If it isn't (22) cannot be evaluated. If the card is located in the relevant set it is evaluated as usual.

Notice that the restrictive focus has the properties of both a focus and a topic. On the one hand it is stressed and triggers a search for a card as a proper focus should, on the other it functions as a topic with respect to predication. For one constituent to have properties of both topic and focus is possible only in a restrictive context, for which a restrictive set is available on the top of the file. A detailed analysis of such restrictive sets follows below (section 1.6.2.3) and in chapter 3 where I show that the partitioning of restrictive sets follows from general principles of (subordinate) update.

1.4   "Stage" topics

In this section I show that spatio-temporal arguments (à la Kratzer) may play the role of a topic.[22] In such a case the truth value of the sentence is determined by examining a card with a spatio-temporal heading. Let us look at the examples in (23):

(23)   a. The King of France is sitting in the chair.[23]
        b. A man arrived.
        c. It is raining.

As mentioned in above, a card which signifies the "here-and-now" of the discourse situation is always located on top of the file. It follows that spatio-temporal arguments may play the role of a topic and that the truth value of sentences with such topics is determined by examining a card with a spatio-temporal heading. Such topics I call Stage topics using stage in the theatrical sense, the place where events appear before an audience. My term "stage" corresponds to Kratzer's spatio-temporal argument, which "refers" to the slice or zone of time and space within which an event takes place. Thus, the term "stage" here does not refer to stages of individuals (as in Carlson's (1977) use of the term stage-level), but rather to the Time/Place at which the event expressed by the sentence takes place. Only stage-level predicates can have stage topics. My use of the term retains the connection between stage-level predicates and stage topics. Other terms which might be appropriate are "scene" or "situation." I have chosen the term "stage topic" because only stage-level predicates have such topics and because the event can be viewed as taking place on the stage defined by this topic. The model therefore includes a card which has the heading Time/Place and the index t where the index reflects the reference time and the presupposed location of the stage. I use the notation sTOP$_t$ for the heading of stage topics. This card is always available on top of the file.

As mentioned above, other cards which are permanently available on the top of the file are the cards for the speaker and the hearer: the "I" and "you" of the discourse. Together with the "stage," these cards form the "center" of the utterance (see Fillmore 1971).[24]

It makes little sense to talk about presupposition with respect to stage topics. Stage topics are rather discourse specified (if not overt), i.e., the indices of the existing "stage" card are fixed as the "here" and "now" of the current discourse (modulo the tense of the sentence).

Let us examine (23c) first. (23c) can be assessed only by examining the implicit stage topic made up of the here-and-now of the utterance. (23c) is assessed by examining this stage to see if *it is raining* there. In this case the whole sentence is taken as a focused event predicated of a stage topic. This f-structure is assigned to all out-of-the-blue sentences. (23c), which must be interpreted with a stage topic, results in the following entry in the hearer's file:

$_s$TOP$_t$

is raining (at) e

In this case the hearer selects the permanently available stage card from the top of the file. The focus "it is raining" is entered on the card if the sentence is evaluated as true.

Sentences (23a and b) can be assessed in two ways, depending on context. If "the King of France" is taken to be the topic, we proceed as in (14). We could, however, also choose "in the chair" as the topic for (23a). This would give us a stage topic made up of the location "in the chair" and the index t giving the time of the utterance. The sentence is assessed by examining this stage to see if the King of France is there. This assessment will again come out false, as in (15).

In (23b) it is possible to assess the sentence with respect to the stage topic (although this stage topic is implicit). In this case the whole sentence is taken as a focused event predicated of a stage topic which results in the following card in the hearer's file:[25]

$_s$TOP$_t$

a man arrived (at) e

In this case the hearer selects the permanently available stage card from the top of the file. The focus (predicate) "a man arrived" is entered on the card if the sentence is evaluated as true. A new card is made out for "a man":

---

man$_1$

e arrived (at)s$_t$

Note that only *one* man is asserted to have arrived. Although the sentence would not be false if two men had arrived, the hearer would be justified in considering the speaker a bad informant if s/he were to assert (23b) in such a case. I therefore conclude that indefinites predicated of stage topics are unique to that stage.[26]

The following illustrates the changes in the file in (23a) with the stage topic "in the chair":

[in the chair]$_t$

the King of France is sitting e

In order for the sentence to be interpreted as predicated of the topic "in the chair," this "location" must first be introduced into the discourse creating a card on top of the file. This card is derived by incorporating the specific location "in the chair" into the heading of the stage card available on top of the file. In this fashion the heading of the card will consist of the relevant time and place, thus situating the chair on the current stage of the discourse. The process of incorporating overt locations into current stage cards also applies to overt time descriptions. It follows that overt Time/Place arguments can (but do not necessarily) function as topics.[27]

1.4.1   Truth values revisited

Strawson's view that truth conditions are Topic-determined has been questioned (among others) by Donnellan (1981). In particular Donnellan demonstrates that his intuitions concerning whether or not a proposition has a truth value are not those predicted by Strawson. The first problematic example follows:

(24)   a. The King of France exists./There is a king . . .
         b. The King of France doesn't exist./There is no king . . .

According to Strawson, if the subject fails to refer no truth value can be assigned, but our intuition here is clear: the sentences in (24a) are false and the ones in (24b) are true. Note that the problem only arises if the King of France is taken as the topic of these sentences and this is what Donnellan assumes. But existential sentences take stage topics, hence the rule of predication applies correctly after all.

The next type of case Donellan uses to argue against Strawson involves a comparison between the existent and the nonexistent as illustrated in (25):

(25)   The readers of this paper will know more about presuppositions than the King of France.

Intuitively, this feels as much like a truth value gap as (14). Yet Donnellan argues that for Strawson (25) would come out false. Donnellan's "problem" with Strawson results from a confusion between sentence topic (as employed here) and discourse topic. Donnellan assumes that the topic of conversation is "the readers of this paper." This is indeed a possible discourse topic, but the sentence topic of the second phrase of the comparison must be "the King of France" which leads to the truth-value gap as expected.

Reinhart (1981) uses the following example to illustrate how the meaning of a sentence depends on the topic selected:

(26)   It's no wonder that *Carter* is considering withdrawing the *American athletes* from the *Olympic games.*

Here the topic can be either of the italicized phrases or else it can be a stage topic. According to Reinhart, what is considered to be a wonder in each case is that a given proposition holds of a given topic. The following two interpretations are derived with *Carter* and *American athletes*, as topics:

(27)   As for Carter, it's no wonder that he's considering withdrawing the American athletes from the Olympic games (because he's such a hard liner).

(28)   As for the American athletes, it's no wonder that Carter is considering withdrawing them from the Olympic games (because they are so bad they may lose).

Chierchia (1992a) recognizes that asymmetric readings of donkey sentences follow from topic selection and that quantification is over topics. Compare the interpretations of the italicized sentence in (29a and b) (Chierchia's (19), (20)):

(29)   a. Dolphins are truly remarkable. When a trainer trains a dolphin, *she usually makes it do incredible things.*
         b. Trainers from here are absolutely remarkable with all sort of animals. For example, if a trainer from here trains a dolphin, *she usually makes it do incredible things.*

In (29a) "dolphins" are introduced as the topic, in (29b) the topic is "trainers." According to Chierchia (29a) "is true iff most dolphins that are properly trained do incredible things. The presence of a dumb dolphin that was trained by scores of trainers and fails to perform, doesn't make [(29a)] false." (29b), however, "would be true iff most trainers from here that train a dolphin make it do wonderful things. The presence of a trainer who is unsuccessful with scores of dolphins wouldn't affect the truth of [(29b)]." Chierchia's Dynamic Type Theory (DTT) operates on structures which are T-marked (for topics). Chierchia's system therefore has some form of f-structure built into it. My purpose is to argue that an account of the phenomena dealt with here falls out of a well-developed theory of f-structure, which is independently necessary. Distinguishing f-structure properties from pure semantic properties allows both components to remain maximally simple.[28]

It has been argued by Rooth (1985, 1992) that Focus assignment determines pragmatic aspects of interpretation in cases of association with focus. This type of case will be examined in chapter 3 as cases involving subordinate f-structures in which the focus constituent with which the operator associates is selected from within a restrictive topic-set.

In Erteschik-Shir (1973: 105) I showed that interpretation depends on whether the focus occurs on a particular subordinate clause:

(30)   Oddly enough, here is the man who likes Peter.
        ≠ Here is the man who, oddly enough, likes Peter.

(31)   Oddly enough, there are people who like Peter.
        = There are people who, oddly enough, like Peter.

In (30) *oddly enough* cannot qualify the statement made by the relative clause since the relative clause is not a possible focus constituent (the clause is presupposed and as such constitutes an entry on the card for *the man$_i$*). In (31), on the other hand, the relative clause can be focused and therefore *oddly enough* can qualify it.[29] (32a) exemplifies a sentence in which the availability of two different f-structures accounts for the ambiguity:

(32)   a. Oddly enough, JOHN believes that Peter is a fool.
        b. Oddly enough, John believes that PETER is a fool.

In (32a) *oddly enough* qualifies the focus in the matrix (i.e., it is odd for John to hold the belief). In (32b), however, what is odd is that Peter is held to be a fool.

In chapter 5 I argue that it is a property of topics that they take wide scope. A topic provides a link to the preceding discourse in which it is introduced by a focus constituent which may or may not be restrictive. In the former case, its quantificational nature follows from the application of the rule of predication which requires assessment for every single member of this restricted set. A simple definite topic such as *the man* can be viewed as quantificational in that predication ranges over the "single" member of the topic-set. The link of the topic to the discourse also makes the contextual restriction of quantifiers fall out automatically. So, for example, the topic *everyone* must be interpreted as "everyone we are talking about," it is a context-specified set represented by a card with the heading *everyone$_i$*.[30]

Partee (1994) addresses the question of whether focus affects pragmatic or semantic aspects of interpretation. In particular she examines the Prague school view that "theme-rheme structure is always considered an aspect of linguistic meaning, whether it has any truth-conditional effects or not." In particular, Partee examines the relation between the restrictor and the notion "theme" (=topic) and the relation between the Nuclear Scope and the "rheme" (=focus).[31] Since the f-structure theoretical approach presented here concurs with this view, Partee's discussion is particularly pertinent.[32]

Partee offers two examples of D-quantifiers, one in which the tripartite structure is syntactically determined ((33)) and one which, according to Partee, is pragmatically or contextually determined ((34)).

(33)   A: Most logicians like linguistics.
        B: Most NICE logicians like linguistics.

(34)   Most ships pass through the lock at NIGHT.
        a. MOST (ships)(pass through the lock at night)
        b. MOST (ships that pass through the lock)(pass through the lock at night)

In section 1.6 I show that individual-level predicates such as *like* are restricted to take nonstage topics. The topic of (33) is therefore most likely to be the syntactic subject, in this case the generics: "logicians" and "nice logicians" which provide the domain of quantification. In (34), however, a stage topic is available rendering the (b) reading as follows: the stage topic is defined by the nonfocused spatio-temporal parameters of the sentence. In this case "passing through the lock" provides the spatial parameter and the present tense gives a generic reading. The stage topic thus provides the correct restrictor here as well.[33]

In this section I gave evidence that truth value is determined by complete f-structures. Both topic marking and focus marking are required for interpretation. Although the topic is derived contextually and is therefore pragmatically determined, its function in the sentence is clearly semantic as well. F-structure theory can therefore be seen as the distinction between semantics and pragmatics rather blurred. It is not clear to me that F-structure theory is any different from DRT in this respect, however.

1.5   F-structure: form

I have outlined a model in which the semantic rule of predication applies to f-structures upon which Topic and Focus have been annotated on the relevant syntactic constituents. According to this rule of predication the predicate is assessed as putative information about its topic and receives a truth value accordingly. In the following chapters, I develop a theory of topic and focus assignment.

The f-structures for the example in (12), from section 1.1.4, are assigned in (35a, c, and d) (35b and e) provide further f-structures for this sentence:

(35)   a. What did the children do?
                [the children]$_{TOP}$ [ate the candy]$_{FOC}$
        b. What happened to the candy?
                TOP$_i$ [the children ate [the candy]$_i$]$_{FOC}$

c. What did the children eat?

       [the children]$_{TOP}$ ate [the candy]$_{FOC}$

d. Who ate the candy?

       TOP$_i$ [[the children]$_{FOC}$ ate [the candy]$_i$]

e. What happened?

       sTOP$_t$ [the children ate the candy]$_{FOC}$

Let me go through (35a–e) one by one to explain the meaning of the annotation, to indicate the state of the file necessary for verifying each case and to show how the rule of predication applies. In (35a), the subject – *the children* – is taken as the topic and the whole VP is the focus. In order for *the children* to be the topic, there must be a card with that heading on the top of the file. According to the rule of predication the truth value of the sentence is determined as follows: evaluate the predicate with respect to the topic *the children*. If the sentence is assessed as true, the asserted information will be added as an entry on the card. This card will now have at least the following information on it:

the children$_1$

e ate the candy

Similarly for (35b): here the topic is the object *the candy*. Again, a card with the heading *the candy* must be on the top of the file. And if the sentence is assessed as true with respect to the topic *the candy*, the new entry will be added:

the candy$_1$

the children ate e

(35e) is more interesting, as none of the overt constituents of the sentence is identified as the topic. In such cases, as we saw in section 1.4, the topic is a stage topic:

> $_s$TOP$_t$
>
> the children ate the candy (at) e

(35c and d) illustrate cases in which the focus and predicate are not coextensive. Here it is because *ate* is presupposed, as indicated by the context provided by the question. (35c) has the same topic as (35a). Presuppositions signify existing entries on cards. As chapter 3 shows, a variable is entered on the topic card in a *wh*-question. The following topic card is on top of the file after applying the topic and focus rules to the question in (35c):

> **the children$_i$**
>
> **e ate X**

The answer in (35c) simply replaces the variable with the entry *the candy*, resulting in a card identical to the one we get after processing (35a). As noted, presuppositions are assumed to be existing entries on cards. Topics are also presupposed, but are distinguished in the file system as existing cards (positioned on top of the file).

The f-structures in (35) all have an initial TOP followed by a focus constituent. The f-structures associated with syntactic topicalization structures are isomorphic to the parallel f-structures without topicalization. The f-structure in (35b) exhibits a notational reflection of syntactic topicalization or can alternatively be viewed as an f-structure-theoretical variant of LF topic movement rendering the following structure:

(36)   [the candy$_i$]$_{TOP}$ [the children ate t$_i$]$_{FOC}$

The following f-structure is ruled out by the premise that a focus must constitute a syntactic constituent:

(37)   [the children ate]$_{FOC}$ [the candy]$_{TOP}$

From the perspective of discourse theory (37) is, however, merely a notational variant of (35b) or (36).

1.6   F-structure and the individual/stage-level distinction

According to Diesing (1989, 1992) and Kratzer (1989a) the different interpretations of individual and stage-level predicates follow from syntactic differences as follows.[34] Examine (38) from Kratzer:

(38)   a. Firemen are available.
            i. There are available firemen.
            ii. Firemen have the property that they are available.
       b. Firemen are altruistic.
            i. *There are altruistic firemen.
            ii. Firemen have the property that they are altruistic.

be available is a stage-level predicate and therefore (38a) receives both the existential reading (i) and the "property" reading (ii). *be altruistic*, however, is an individual-level predicate and therefore (38b) only gets the "property" reading. According to Diesing/Kratzer stage-level predicates differ from individual-level predicates structurally in two ways:

(a)   stage-level predicates have an extra argument position for spatio-temporal location.

(b)   the subjects of stage-level predicates are generated in spec, VP and are raised to spec, IP. Subjects of individual-level predicates are generated in the latter position with PRO filling spec, VP.

The structures are then interpreted as follows: the VP-external subject is mapped into the restrictive clause (to get reading (ii)) and the VP-internal subject is mapped into the nuclear scope, the domain of existential closure which renders existential readings as in (i). Stage-level predicates allow the interpretation of their subjects both in the s-structure position and in the position of the trace of movement, hence the ambiguity. (See Heim (1982), Diesing (1989, 1992), Kratzer (1989a) for the relevant semantic framework.)

I now intend to show that an analysis of the individual/stage-level difference in terms of f-structure allows for an account of the phenomena discussed by Diesing/Kratzer without the need for any added machinery such as LF reconstruction rules. The main advantage of an f-structure analysis is that the f-structure machinery is needed independently of the issue at hand, and that the relevant intonations will follow automatically. Another important consequence, I believe, is that under the view offered here, stage-level predicates do not differ from individual-level predicates in argument structure as Kratzer proposes.

Diesing suggests that the INFL associated with individual-level predicates assigns a special θ-role to their subjects which has the meaning " 'has the property x', where x is the property expressed by the predicate" (Diesing 1992: 26), i.e., in her framework, what I would call the Topic is a lexical role assigned by these predicates. Kratzer, on the other hand, argues that stage-level predicates differ from individual-level predicates in that they have an extra spatio-temporal argument.

I have already claimed that Kratzer's spatio-temporal argument can altern-atively be viewed as the topic of the sentences in which it occurs and that the whole sentence is predicated of this topic, i.e., that the whole sentence is focused. In my framework, this topic is *not* an argument, but is rather a generally available card in the file. If an f-structure with a stage topic is assigned to a sentence with an individual-level predicate, the interpretation will be ruled out pragmatically. (See below.)

A much discussed question is whether sentences with individual-level predicates have event arguments (see, for example, Chierchia 1992b). This question can be rephrased in the current framework as whether sentences with individual-level predicates have stage topics. Clearly, if we assume an indexed stage topic for such a sentence, we derive the wrong interpretation. (38b), for example, predicated of a stage time would mean: it is true of a certain time and place that *Firemen are altruistic*. What we would want to see is that the sentence is true *always*, i.e., of *all* times and places.[35] This result can be derived if we assume a generic reference time and a generic location for all such sentences, i.e., the temporal and locative parameters of the stage topic are generic. Under this view a stage topic is assumed for individual-level predicates, but the question of how to constrain it to a generic or unindexed one is left open.

One approach to blocking the possibility of a contextual stage topic in the interpretation of such sentences is to assume that one of the NPs in sentences with individual-level predicates (in this case the subject) occupies the posi-tion of the locative argument in lexical structure. The interpretation which follows from such an assumption is that it is true of (the location) *Firemen*, at any reference time, that *they are altruistic*. If the stage topic is "filled" with an individual, and individuals do not get their locative and temporal para-meters from context, it follows naturally that the sentence is true of all times and places in which this individual occurs.

For the purposes of the current discussion I assume that nongeneric stage topics are excluded for individual-level predicates and that an individual must play the role of main topic in such cases. I distinguish the meanings of stage- and individual-level properties, not their argument structures, nor the thematic roles which they assign. In chapter 2, I utilize the idea that individual-level predicates must be interpreted with generic stage topics to explain the different interpretations of donkey sentences.

Both individual-level and stage-level readings are available in principle for stage-level predicates. Very often, however, one reading will be pragmatically blocked. (39) from von Fintel (1989) presents a clear illustration that world knowledge is at stake:

(39) a. Your EYES are red. (stage level only)
      b. Your EYES are BLUE. (individual level only)

In special contexts the interpretations and intonations of (a) and (b) can be reversed. Both (a) and (b) can be assigned two different f-structures and the rule of predication will apply to derive two readings for each. The "bad" readings will be filtered out by the pragmatic component which brings world knowledge and contextual knowledge to bear on the output of the rule of predication.

1.6.1 Properties of topics: an examination of the subjects of individual-level predicates

If an individual-level predicate cannot occur in a sentence with a (nongeneric) stage topic, it follows that the only available topic for an *intransitive* predicate of this sort is the subject. This view depends on the assumption that every sentence must have a topic. It follows from the definition of topics as the pivot for assessment for truth value that this is so. An individual-level, intransitive predicate therefore necessitates that the VP is interpreted as a property of its subject, cum topic.[36]

If the subjects of individual-level predicates are necessarily interpreted as topics, as proposed here, then we can learn about the nature of topics by examining individual-level subjects. It is necessary to pay attention to the following point: as will become clear in chapter 4, foci are assigned stress. However, this is not only the case for the main focus of the sentence, but also for restrictive and contrastive foci. It is therefore possible to compose contexts for sentences with intransitive individual-level predicates in which the subject receives stress. This does *not* indicate that the subject is not the main topic of the sentence.

1.6.2 Definiteness

Milsark (1974, 1977) distinguishes two basic types of NPs: weak NPs which are permissible in existentials, and strong NPs which are not. Weak NPs include *a*, the cardinals, *sm* (=unstressed some), φ (plural and mass). Strong

NPs include the definites, i.e., *the*, demonstratives, pronouns, possessive DETs and the universals, i.e., *all, each, every*, etc., and generics. Since topics involve existing cards, it is predicted that strong, but not weak NPs can be topics, since the former, as we shall see, necessarily involve existing cards.[37]

1.6.2.1 Generic indefinites

First, let us examine indefinites in subject position:

(40)   A Frenchman is intelligent.

(41)   Dogs are intelligent.

The indefinite subjects in (40) and (41) can only get a generic reading if unstressed. If the subjects are stressed, a contrastive or restrictive reading is available.[38] A restrictive reading for (41) is brought about by a context such as:

(42)   What animals are intelligent?

Here the restrictive set is the generic set of "animal kinds" and the kind "dogs" is selected from this set. We will ignore contrastive and restrictive cases below.

   Two important questions are immediately raised: (a) Why don't we get an existential reading? and (b) What allows for the generic reading? According to Diesing/Kratzer the answer to (a) follows in Heim's framework from the requirement that indefinites must be bound by existential closure and must appear within the nuclear scope. Subjects of individual-level predicates are VP-external, therefore not within the nuclear scope. Indefinites on their existential interpretation are therefore ruled out in this position. (a) follows easily in the current framework: indefinites included in the focus domain are necessarily interpreted existentially. Their interpretation follows the first Focus rule: Focus instructs the hearer to open a new card and put it on the top of the file. Assign it a heading and a new index (in the case of an indefinite). Indefinites cannot, however, receive an existential interpretation as topics. In order for an NP to function as a topic it must be represented by an existing card on top of the file. An indefinite with a *new* index (i.e., an indefinite interpreted existentially) is derived by making out a new card, i.e., such a card is not available in the file at all, and therefore cannot occur on top of the file.

   The solution to (b) in Diesing, following Wilkinson (1986), is that NPs in the restrictive clause are bound by a default operator Gen (=generic) if there is no overt operator. The effect of this default operator can be made to follow as a property of the discourse theory proposed here, making the generic operator superfluous. Remember that TOPIC instructs the hearer to locate on the top of the file an existing card (or an existing set of cards) with the relevant heading and index. As discussed in section 1.3.1, our files include generic cards, e.g., cards with the headings *dogs* and *Frenchmen*. How does this work? If someone says (41), s/he assumes an existing card with the heading *dogs* on top of the hearer's file. Note that what is peculiar about this card-type is that it is a "name" card, which means that the heading functions as an identifying index. Such a card therefore does not pick out a particular instance of the kind in question.

Carlson (1977: 285) distinguishes indefinite singular generics from plural ones: the former speaks about the species by selecting an arbitrary representative of the kind. The procedure by which the arbitrary representative is selected can be made to follow from the procedure involved in the file-change operations triggered by f-structure, i.e., the generic card functions as a topic and the individual instance of the kind, as a focus.[39] In view of the fact that this manipulation of cards is subordinate to the update of the main assertion of the sentence, I call this type of file manipulation "subordinate update." Subordinate update is triggered by a subordinate f-structure with a subordinate topic and focus. For the case of indefinite singular generics, subordinate update applies to select an arbitrary representative *dog* from the "generic" card by taking the latter as the topic and the former as its focus. The sentence is then assessed with respect to this particular instance of *dog*. (I return to another example of subordinate update in the next section and review its properties in section 1.7.)[40]

For the plural generic, the sentence is assessed with respect to the entries listed on the "generic" card. Since the information listed for an arbitrary generic dog and the information listed on the generic card for *dog* is identical, the assessment will in effect come out the same.

1.6.2.2 Subordinate f-structure and specific indefinites
It is inaccurate to claim that indefinites do not occur as subjects of individual-level predicates:

(43) a. A friend of mine is intelligent.
      b. A certain student likes linguistics.
      c. A man who was wearing a brown hat knew enough French to help us.
      d. A student who I know likes linguistics.

The subjects in (43) are all specific. (Cf. de Hoop (1992), Diesing (1992), Enç (1990), Fodor and Sag (1982), Kennedy (1990), Lumsden (1988), Milsark (1974, 1977).) Since topics must be either generic or specific (i.e., a card with the relevant heading must exist), it is not surprising that specific indefinites are allowed as topics. It is, however, rather mysterious what it is that makes these indefinites specific. In each case the indefinite is modified in some way. Unmodified indefinites in topic position, as we saw above, are not allowed (except for generics and contrast).[41]

Another important issue concerns the notion of referentiality as it pertains to specific indefinites. It is often recognized that specific indefinites are specific only to the speaker and that the hearer is not assumed to have an available referent in these cases. These two issues are connected. First, let us examine the function of the relative clause in (43d). The complex subject must be assigned an f-structure to get interpreted. This f-structure does not involve predication, i.e., assessment, since only full sentences are assessed. The subordinate f-structure assigned is, however, interpreted by *subordinate update*, the process that associates subordinate topics with their foci. Subordinate update involves the application of the Topic, Focus and Update rules to a subordinate f-structure and differs from main f-structures only in that the rule of predication does not apply. Its role is to rearrange the cards according to the discourse rules and to make the relevant entries.

The file manipulation for (43d), for example, is equivalent to that of the following sequence of sentences:

(44)   I know a student. He likes linguistics.

In the first sentence of this sequence, "a student" is contained in the focus and hence a new card is introduced (by focus rule (i)) allowing for the introduction on top of the file of a new indexed card for "a student":

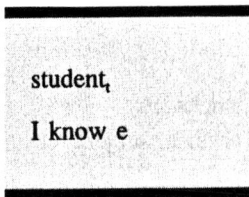

$$student_1$$

$$I\ know\ e$$

Once this card is opened, the indefinite is (speaker) referential and qualifies for topic status. The fact that the relative clause introduces a "subordinate" application of the rules is also what explains the speaker-perspective of the reference. When a speaker introduces a new referent by means of a relative clause s/he instructs the hearer to open a new card, position it on the top of the file, and then go on to the sentence (without the relative clause). Only the speaker, not the hearer, is assumed to already have a card for man_i. Note that subordinate update must occur prior to the file manipulation triggered by the main f-structure. Otherwise the card for the main topic would not be available, making the sentence uninterpretable. Subordinate f-structure and its associated update thus feed the main application of the rules. The head of the relative clause is thus the subordinate focus rendering the f-structure in (45):

(45)   [[a student]$_{FOC-SUB}$ [who I know e]]$_{TOP}$ [likes linguistics]$_{FOC}$

As the f-structures become more complex it will be necessary to distinguish subordinate f-structures from the main f-structure. I use the subscript *sub* on the subordinate f-structures to make this distinction clear. For simplicity, I ignore here the internal f-structure of the relative clause which contains the subordinate topic. Note that relative clauses are necessarily presupposed in this system because they represent existing entries on cards.

(43a) and (43b) work the same way. In the former, *a friend of mine* receives the following (subordinate) f-structure:

(46)   Top$_i$ [a friend of mine$_i$]$_{FOC}$

The subordinate topic is the available card for the speaker (first person). Again, *a friend* is in the subordinate focus domain which triggers the opening of a new card in the hearer's file. This card is placed on top of the file ready for the relevant entry. After the rules have been applied to (43a), the hearer's card looks as follows (A$_i$ = the speaker):

friend$_1$

e is a friend of A$_1$
e is intelligent

Finally, adjectives such as *certain* and *specific* provide the same service, i.e., they trigger a subordinate f-structure and a new card is opened by subordinate update as before. These adjectives simply mean that the speaker "has a reference" for the following NP.[42] (43b) renders the following card:

---

student₁

A₁ has reference for e

e likes linguistics

A further point should be made concerning the function of relative clause constructions as subordinate f-structures. In the preceding discussion we saw how relative clauses function to introduce new cards and to place them on the top of the file via an application of the focus rule. This occurs with definite heads as well. The analysis is parallel to the analysis of relatives with indefinite heads except that the definite represents an existing card in the file which is elevated to the top by the focus rule.

Subordinate f-structures do not involve assessment for truth value, but only a rearrangement of the cards. A subordinate f-structure is assigned whenever a card is located on top of the file for the subordinate topic which represents a phrase which is not analyzed as the *main* topic of the sentence. The subordinate focus functions to place cards on the top of the file. This is how the main topic, with respect to which the assessment of the sentence is performed, was derived in the case just examined. Subordinate f-structures are constrained primarily by the availability of subordinate topic cards on top of the file at the point at which the sentence is uttered.[43]

1.6.2.3 Partitives: restrictive subordinate f-structures

Partitives can be subjects of individual-level predicates, i.e., they qualify as topics. Yet, it is counterintuitive to propose that cards with partitive headings, such as the italicized ones in (47), must be available to the hearer:

(47)   a. *Two of the students* are intelligent.
        b. *Some of the students* like linguistics.

A card must, however, be available for the definite NP *the students* in both sentences in (47). Here again *the students* functions as a subordinate topic, i.e., the card with the heading *students*ᵢ must be on top of the file. Remember that a distribution mechanism applies to plural cards which constructs a card for each member of the discourse referent. What the partitive does is instruct the hearer to select *two* or *some* members from this set of student cards and to assess the sentence with respect to these members of this set only, i.e., the partitive triggers a partitioning of the set of students according to the focus rule. Note the intonation of the partitive topics (capitals indicate stress, for details see chapter 4):

(48)   a. TWO of the students are inTELLigent.
           b. SOME of the students are inTELLigent.

The stress on *two* and *some* indicates that these constituents are to be interpreted as foci within the larger topic constituent. The topic part of this constituent defines a set. The hearer has on top of his file a set card with the group heading *students*$_i$. Although the hearer does not necessarily have a set of (attached) cards representing the individual students, but only one individual card which defines the group, partitioning is still possible: he selects a subset from this set. This subset is defined by the focus constituent. When the subset is defined cardinally, the hearer must open a particular number of cards, in the case of (48a), it will include exactly two cards. These cards each have the heading:

(49)   student$_j$ ∈ {students$_i$}

This relation is represented by attaching the subset cards to the group card as above. The new cards do not represent specific students, i.e., two students are selected at random from the set of students defined by the subordinate topic. We have derived an analysis of partitive topics in which they trigger subordinate update by the f-structure rules.

     If the following f-structure is assigned to (48a), for example, the rules will apply to the subordinate f-structure to derive the relevant subset:

(50)   [[Two]$_{\text{FOC-sub}}$ of [the students]$_{\text{TOP-sub}}$]$_{\text{TOP}}$ [are intelligent]$_{\text{FOC}}$

The topic rule applied to the subordinate topic locates a (restrictive) set of cards or a group card on the top of the file. The focus rule then defines a new (subset) card as indicated by the subordinate focus constituent. This new card is positioned on top of the file and is given a new heading.

     For *some* (as well as *few, many*) there is no enumeration of individual cards, hence the partitioned subset consists of only one unindividuated card. In (48b) the subset will consist of any number of cards that counts as *some*. The card for such a subset is made available on top of the file by the focus rule making it accessible as a topic for the main f-structure.

     According to Enç (1990) specific indefinite NPs are either partitives or discourse linked in some other way. Here specific NPs are formed by subordinate f-structures including partitive subordinate f-structure.

I have examined subjects of intransitive individual-level predicates in order to gain insight into the properties of topics. I conclude that an unmodified indefinite (singular and plural) topic must be interpreted generically. Modified indefinites and partitives may receive a speaker-specific reading via subordinate update triggered by a subordinate f-structure.

1.6.3   Transitive f-structures

1.6.3.1   The Topic Constraint

So far I have limited the discussion to intransitive individual-level predicates. Two possible interpretations are available for transitive individual-level predicates: either the subject is interpreted as the topic as in (51) or else the object is the topic as in (52).

(51)   John knows a lawyer.

(52)   A lawyer knows Mary.

The appropriate f-structures follow:

(53)   a. [John]$_{TOP}$ [knows a lawyer]$_{FOC}$
        b. TOP$_i$ [a lawyer knows Mary$_i$]$_{FOC}$

Since (nongeneric) indefinites are not possible topics, each of these examples receives only one f-structure.[44]

If both subject and object were definite, each sentence would have two f-structures assigned to it:

(54)   John loves Mary.
        a. [John]$_{TOP}$ [loves Mary]$_{FOC}$
        b. TOP$_i$ [John loves Mary$_i$]$_{FOC}$

The f-structure we get depends on whether *Mary* or *John* are under discussion, i.e., whether a card with the heading *Mary*$_i$ or *John*$_j$ is on top of the file. The interesting case is when cards for both *John*$_j$ and *Mary*$_i$ are available, i.e., in the context of a question such as

(55)   a. What is the relationship of John to Mary?
        b. How does John feel about Mary?

These questions ensure that both cards are on top of the file since the relevant NPs are either topics or foci in the questions. (The former means that a card is already on top of the file, the latter means that a card is placed on top of the file.) I have made the assumption that only the f-structure (54a) would be available in such cases, i.e., that verification necessarily takes place as required by this f-structure. This point must now be argued for. The issue is whether (54) can be assessed under *Mary*$_i$ as opposed to *John*$_j$. This turns out not to be possible. If this were a possible assessment in the context of (55), the following answer should be possible and it is not:

(56)   Mary is loved by John.

The subject of the passive must be assigned to the Topic in f-structure. The fact that (56) is not a possible answer shows that the card for *Mary* cannot be the locus for assessment in this case.[45] (30) is, however, also about *Mary* in the sense that once the rules are applied the information that *John loves her*$_i$ should also be accessible on the card for *Mary* in the following discourse. This can be represented in f-structure as follows:

(57)   TOP$_{i\text{-sub}}$[John$_{\text{TOP}}$ [loves Mary$_i$]$_{\text{FOC}}$]$_{\text{FOC-sub}}$

The subscript *sub* indicates that this is a subordinate f-structure. What exactly are the implications of such a subordinate f-structure? Let us examine the state of the cards following the question (55b), for example. *John* is topic in the question; therefore the card for *John*$_j$ is on top of the file and the question is entered on this card (another reason assessment of the answer must occur on this card as well). The question introduces *Mary* in its focus; therefore the card for *Mary*$_i$ must be located and positioned on top of the file. Both cards are therefore available as potential topics on top of the file. The fact that the card for *Mary* is accessible means this card is updated as well. After the rules have been applied to (54), the two cards look as follows:

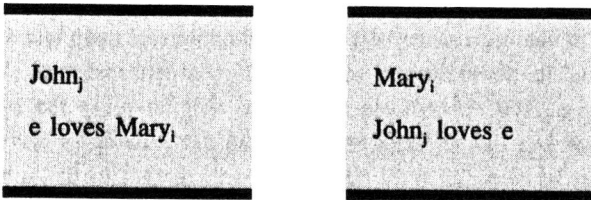

This analysis renders a symmetric reading of the sentence in which both subject and object are available topics. The intonation that goes with this f-structure is one in which the verb is stressed and both subject and object are destressed:[46]

(58)   He LOVES her.

I use pronouns in this illustration since this would be the natural response to the questions in (55). Since pronouns must be interpreted as topics, they are entered on the available topic cards. The question arises as to how it is ensured, when there are several pronouns, that these pronouns get the correct index:

John$_j$

he$_j$ loves her$_i$

Mary$_i$

he$_i$ loves her$_i$

The index j on the subject pronoun on the card for *John*$_j$ follows from the principle that pronouns receive their interpretation according to the heading of the card upon which they are entered. Since entries occur on cards for topics, it follows that pronouns require the existence of the relevant topic card on top of the file. Similarly the index i on the object pronoun on the card for *Mary*$_i$ is accounted for. The problem is to ensure the correct indexing on the other two pronouns, *her* on the card for *John*, and *he* on the card for *Mary*. I propose that the update rule is augmented as follows:

IV   UPDATE instructs the hearer to enter the focus on the topic card and then to copy all entries to all cards activated by the focus rule. Any index included in an entry on one card must by copied to all other cards with the same entry.

This update rule ensures that the indices on the two identical entries are the same.

A distinction has been made between the functions of main and subordinate f-structure. The determination of truth values depends exclusively on the main f-structure. The subordinate f-structure only involves the manipulation of the file, i.e., the selection of cards and the copying of entries. This means that predication can only take place with respect to the subordinate topic (i.e., on the card for *Mary*$_i$) by means of accommodation. Accommodation, in this view, is a process which triggers assessment for truth value on a subordinate topic. Subordinate update does not determine truth values under normal circumstances. Accommodation used in this sense makes subordinate f-structures identical to that of main f-structures in that the entry on the card for a subordinate topic is assessed for its truth value. When accommodation applies, a subordinate topic therefore functions as a main topic.

. Edit Doron (pers. com.) points out that the following interaction is possible:

(59)   A: How does John treat Mary?
          B: Well, I don't know, but she's TERRIFIED of him.

B's answer indicates that the question is about *Mary*. But note that without the hedging expressions, "well" and/or "I don't know," B's answer is impossible:

(60)   A: How does John treat Mary?
          B′: She's TERRIFIED of him.

What this indicates is that, as I predict, taking *Mary* as the topic is not possible without further ado. The hedging expressions are required exactly because this is the case. I suggest that these expressions prompt accommodation, i.e., the licensing of *Mary* as the card upon which the sentence is verified.

It follows that, in symmetric cases, when both the subject and object are candidates for topichood, the *subject* is taken as the main topic. The following f-structure, in which the object is the main topic and the subject is a subordinate one, must therefore be ruled out:

(61) $\text{TOP}_i[\text{John}_{\text{TOP-sub}} \ [\text{loves Mary}_i]_{\text{FOC-sub}}]_{\text{FOC}}$

There are several ways of formalizing this constraint. One possibility would be to say that the main topic cannot be c-commanded by a subordinate topic. Another would be to require that the subject be selected as the main topic whenever a card is available for it. Nonsubjects could then only be selected as main topics in those cases in which the subject does not qualify as a potential topic. The second version of the constraint can be viewed as an extension of the idea that the subject is the unmarked topic. I will refer to this constraint on main topic assignment as the Topic Constraint (on f-structure) and will formalize the constraint as follows:

> **Topic Constraint** (first version):[47]
> $*\text{TOP}_i[\text{SUBJECT}_{\text{TOP-sub}} \ [\ldots \text{NP}_i \ldots]_{\text{FOC}}]_{\text{FOC}}$

The "star" here is intended to mean that this f-structure is highly marked, i.e., only heavy contextual clues will render it possible. It is important to note that this constraint will have a different effect on sentences in which both the subject and object are nondeictic pronouns and those in which they are R-expressions. As we shall see in detail in chapter 2, pronouns are licensed only as topics (i.e., the relevant card must be available on top of the file).

R-expressions have "independent" reference and therefore are not restricted to topics. The Topic Constraint therefore almost always applies to pronouns. The constraint applies to R-expressions only if they represent available topic cards. The following two examples show how context makes the (italicized) objects main topics in spite of the fact that the subjects are available as well:

(62) A: So tell me about the earth. What do you know about the earth?
      B: It's round, it's a planet, the moon goes around *it*.

(63) A: Tell me about John.
      B: I personally can't stand *him*.

According to the topic test, (63) must be taken to be about the object. In this case we have two pronouns competing for the status as main topic. Although a card for the speaker is always available on top of the file, i.e., the first person is a potential topic at all points in the discourse, it is possible that a contextually introduced topic takes precedence, thus overruling the topic constraint.

According to the Topic Constraint, if both subject and object are candidates for topichood, the subject will be selected as the pivot for predication. The object will be selected if the subject is not a possible candidate (i.e., if it is indefinite), or if the context forces such an interpretation. The topic constraint thus reflects the intuition that when both subject and object are definite, only heavy contextual clues allow for the object to be interpreted as the topic.

The view that an unmarked f-structure is one in which the syntactic structure and the f-structure are isomorphic, i.e., subject is the topic and the VP is the focus, has been recognized for other languages as well. Schwartz (1976) argues that what he refers to as the Ilocano focus, which is actually the topic as defined here, is necessarily the subject. Anderson (1991) argues for Dinka, a major Western Nilotic language, that the preverbal noun phrase is a topic. Li and Thompson (1976: 484) argue that Subjects are essentially grammaticalized topics. This "is why many of the topic properties are shared by subjects in a number of languages." Reinhart (1981: 87) also claims that the syntactic subject is the preferred topic for the following reason: ". . . it is easier to interpret the sentence as being about its subject, than, say, about its object, since in the logical form, something is predicated directly of the subject's interpretation." More recently Lambrecht (1994) argues that the unmarked information-structure sequence is topic followed by focus and that the subject is the unmarked topic.

In this section the Topic Constraint was introduced. The Topic Constraint is a pragmatic constraint which constrains f-structures and it is part and parcel of f-structure theory. An f-structure in which the object is the topic renders a marked f-structure. Canonical or unmarked f-structures are those in which the topic precedes the focus.

1.6.3.2 Objects: why they misbehave

We have seen that individual-level predicates do not allow stage topics. The following reading will therefore be excluded:

(64)   sTOP$_t$ [John loves a girl]$_{FOC}$

Evidence is the ungrammaticality of individual-level sentences with nongeneric indefinites in both subject and object position:

(65)   *A boy loves a girl.

In transitive individual-level predicates either the subject or the object must be definite or strong, otherwise the rule of predication cannot apply, since no f-structure can be assigned. Introducing (65) with "once upon a time" makes it acceptable:

(66)   Once upon a time, a boy loved a girl.

Such an introduction in effect provides a stage topic. This is why neither of the NPs need be interpreted as a topic, licensing the two indefinites. What this means is that in special contexts, individual-level predicates can be interpreted with indexed stage topics. A reasonable approach to take is therefore to generate f-structures freely and to filter out those readings which are pragmatically implausible as suggested in section 1.6. Another illustration follows:

(67)   Look out! A boy has a gun.

Here again the sentence must be interpreted with stage topic, in this case with the current here-and-now.

My analysis of individual-level predicates differs from that of Diesing/Kratzer in that they predict that only the subjects of these predicates have the particular properties I have associated with topichood. Both Diesing and Kratzer are aware of this problem. Kratzer (1989a: 35) gives the following examples:

(68)   a. When Sue likes a movie, she recommends it to everyone.
         b. When Mary knows a foreign language, she knows it well.

We will return to a more detailed analysis of sentences such as these in chapter 2. For now, it suffices to say that the construction demands that the topic of the *when*-clause be indefinite. Compare (68) with (69):

(69)   a. When a lot is close to Lawrence Swamp, it is subject to many restric-
            tions.
        b. *When this lot is close to a swamp, construction must be kept 200 feet
            away from it.

(69a) illustrates the case predicted by Diesing/Kratzer. The subject of the
individual-level predicate goes into the restriction and when it is indefinite it
introduces a variable that can be bound by the implicit quantifier introduced
by the *when*-clause. When the indefinite is in object position as in (69b), it
goes into the nuclear scope and gets existential closure. The implicit quantifier cannot bind the indefinite and a case of vacuous quantification arises. The
sentences in (68) are structurally parallel to (69b) and should therefore be
ruled out. Such sentences do however exist and Kratzer proposes that these
ill-behaved objects are scrambled out of the VP at LF (adjoining to IP), and
can thus be mapped into the restriction. A positive aspect of this account is
that the ill-behaved objects are moved by the same scrambling rule which
operates in scrambling languages such as Japanese and German. A more
problematic aspect of the analysis is that it is totally unpredicted which
individual-level predicates allow this scrambling rule to apply at LF and
which do not.

My story is simpler: individual-level predicates do not have available an
interpretation with a stage topic. Hence, either the subject or the object of a
transitive individual-level sentence is in principle interpreted as the topic.
This theory predicts that topics can be found in object position. Under this
view (69b) is exceptional since here the object must be prevented from being
interpreted as a topic. First note the following parallel:

(70)   a. The proof contains a mistake.
        b. *A proof contains this mistake.

(71)   a. This house is close to a lake.
        b. *A house is close to the lake.

(72)   a. A girl likes this movie.
        b. Someone knows this language.

Other predicates like *contain* and *be close to* which block topic assignment
to their objects are (see Kratzer): *own*, *have*, and *require*. Predicates which
allow both subjects and objects as topics in addition to *like* and *know* are
appreciate, *love*, and other psychological predicates as well as *be responsible*
and *fit*. Let me name the first class, those for which only the subject can be
the topic, perspective predicates. Examine

(73)   a. ??A house is close to the lake.
         b. ?A lake is close to the house.

The reason (73b) is somewhat better than (73a) is that the relationship between the lake and the house is better seen from the perspective of *the house*. Assessment is most naturally done from a topic which provides the perspective from which the relationship presented by the sentence is "seen." The perspective, thus, enhances the topic reading of the object.[48]

Individual-level perspective predicates, in general, have as their only f-structure one in which the subject is the topic and the VP is the focus. They therefore present an instance of the isomorphism between syntax and f-structure which I assume is the unmarked case.

1.6.4   Stage-level interpretations

Stage-level predicates allow individual topics (subject, object, etc.) as well as stage topics. A stage topic, I argue, is available at all points in discourse as a card on top of the file with an index filled in by the spatio-temporal location of the context. Faber (1987: 348) offers the following test which can be used as a test for stage topics:

(74)   All of a sudden, Fred staggered in.

Any sentence following *all of a sudden* must be interpreted as predicated of the current stage topic available on top of the file.

I adopt Kratzer's basic ideas about spatio-temporal arguments. According to Kratzer (1989a), the spatio-temporal argument is represented in logical structure as a variable "l" which is supplied with a value by the context of use.[49] Kratzer has no explanation for why it is that the context of use can restrict the value of this variable. If, however, the spatio-temporal argument is viewed as the topic of the sentence (and the topic must be represented by a card on the top of the file) then topics (not only stage topics) will always be determined by the context of use. Kratzer supplies the following illustrations:

(75)   Manon is dancing on the lawn.

(76)   Manon is dancing this morning.

According to Kratzer, in (75) the context of use specifies the spatial extension of "l" and in (76) its temporal extension. This result follows from the f-structures assigned as well. The overt spatial or temporal expressions can be interpreted either as part of the focus constituent or as part of the topic. Assume that (75) is assigned the f-structure

(77)   sTOP$_{ti}$ [Manon is dancing [on the lawn]$_i$]

Here the sentence is evaluated with respect to the *lawn*, i.e., whether it is true of the lawn that Manon is dancing on it. The "now" defined by the time of the utterance and the tense of the sentence provides the temporal extension of the stage topic. Now examine a different f-structure:

(78)   sTOP$_t$ [Manon is dancing on the lawn]

In this case the stage topic is completely context defined. It is the here-and-now of the context. *The lawn*, which is contained in the focus constituent, is also contained in the more general location defined by the "here" since the sentence is assessed by evaluating whether it is true of the here-and-now that Manon is dancing on the lawn. It is possible to have both overt stage topics and overt locational constituents contained in the focus:

(79)   In America, linguistics is taught in many places.

This sentence can be evaluated with respect to the general location *America*. Evaluation with respect to *many places* would make no sense. The stage topic must therefore always have a relation of inclusion with any overt time and place argument contained in the focus.

1.7   Subordinate and main f-structure: take 2

Three different cases of subordinate f-structures have been examined above. In this section I show how the same process is involved in these three cases, namely applications of the topic rule, the focus rule and update. The predication rule is not applied to subordinate f-structures. I then give the revised set of rules for the interpretation of f-structure.

The first case is that of NP modifiers discussed in section 1.6.2.2. There I argued that modifiers of various kinds form subordinate f-structures, allowing for new cards to be introduced on top of the file and thus making the main topic of the sentence available.

The second case involves Restrictive f-structures discussed in 1.6.2.3. In these cases the subordinate f-structure is formed around a card on top of the file representing a discoursally available set which provides the subordinate topic. A subset of this topic set is focused triggering the partitioning of the set. This makes available a card for the new subset which is positioned on top of the file enabling it to play the role of main topic. The discussion of singular indefinite generics in section 1.6.2.1 also assumed that the card for the singular generic is made available through the application of the rules to such a subordinate f-structure. In this case the plural generic card is assumed to be available on top of the file and the singular card is derived by subordinately focusing on a single instance of this card, again triggering the construction of the card for a single instance of the genus. Clearly the generic set is not restrictive. The reason subordinate update works here is because the set need not be partitioned in order to derive an instance of the kind. This is because all such instances are identical.

The third case has to do with sentences with multiple topics discussed in section 1.6.3.1. I claim that the predication rule must apply only once and that the entries made on the remaining topic cards are updates triggered by subordinate f-structures. In this case the application of the rules to the subordinate f-structure must precede their application to the main f-structure. This is necessary so that the indices of the subordinate topics are copied onto the main entry, enabling correct evaluation of the sentence. Stage topics may also form subordinate f-structures if the sentence is evaluated with respect to another topic.

Although there are many different cases in which subordinate f-structure will be shown to play a role, I will give only one more illustration here.

(80)   As for John, he likes rock music.

The context in which "as for" phrases are used is one in which a set, in this case a set of people, is under discussion. *John* is selected from this set. The following f-structure is therefore appropriate:

(81)   As for $\left[\begin{array}{c} [John]_{FOC\text{-}sub} \\ \left\{ \begin{array}{c} person_1 \\ person_2 \end{array} \right\} \end{array} \right]_{TOP\text{-}sub}$, he$_{TOP}$ [likes rock music]$_{FOC}$

In the "as for" phrase *John* is focused. The card for *John* is therefore positioned on top of the file forcing *John* to be the topic of the immediately following sentence. It is correct that "as for" phrases can be used as a diagnostic of topic in the *following* phrase. It is not the case that the NP within the "as for" phrase is itself a topic. This also explains the following discrepancy noted in Reinhart (1981: 88):

(82)   a. She said about sharks that they won't attack unless they are very hungry.
        b. She said about a shark that he won't attack unless he is very hungry.
        c. A shark won't attack unless he is very hungry.

Whereas the plural generic occurs in the *about*-test for topics, the singular generic does not and in (82b) "a shark" receives only an existential reading.

If the NP following *about* is focused, as it is in the *as for*-test, and if, as I claim, an indefinite singular can get a generic interpretation only as a result of subordinate update on a generic topic set, then the generic reading is excluded in (82b) as required.

Subordinate f-structure and the resulting subordinate update also gives a fresh perspective on the problematic issue of whether topics should be associated with "old" information.[50] In the current framework topics represent old discourse referents. This follows from their status as representing available cards on top of the file. If main topics can be introduced by subordinate f-structure, i.e., via the availability of a subordinate topic, then the new derived main topic may indeed be new to the discourse. Topics are, however, never new at the point at which the Topic rule applies to them.

The following rules have now been obtained to interpret f-structure. They must be applied first to subordinate f-structures, then to the main f-structure.

I   TOPIC instructs the hearer to locate on the top of his file an existing card (or an existing set of cards) with the relevant heading and index.

II   FOCUS instructs the hearer to either
        (i) open a new card and put it on the top of the file. Assign it a heading and a new index (in the case of an indefinite) or
        (ii) locate an existing card and put it on the top of the file (in the case of a definite).

III   PREDICATION instructs the hearer to evaluate the main predicate with respect to the topic where the predicate is taken to be the complement of the topic.

If the result of the evaluation is TRUE the UPDATE rule applies:

IV   UPDATE instructs the hearer to enter the focus on the topic card and then to copy all entries to all cards activated by the focus rule. Any index included in an entry on one card must be copied to all other cards with the same entry.

These rules apply to f-structures which are syntactic structures (SDs) annotated for Topic and Focus. Topics, in particular stage topics, may be implicit but are marked in initial position in the f-structure as are all main topics. Main topics are, therefore, coindexed with the topic position when it is not itself in initial position, i.e., a subject.

According to C. Heycock (pers. com.), languages that mark topics morphologically, such as Japanese, do not allow for topic-marked phrases within embedded clauses (*when*- or *if*-clauses, for example). Neither does English allow topicalization in embedded clauses which do not provide the main assertion. Note that I do not assign a "topicalized" f-structure to subordinate topics. Only main topics are marked in this way in f-structure reflecting the special status of main topics with respect to predication and the fact that only main topics are overtly topic-marked in a variety of languages.

1.8   Information packaging, update semantics, information structure, and Discourse Representation Theory

Vallduví (1992, 1994)[51] presents a model of update semantics, Information Packaging, which is in many ways similar to the one defined here in that it takes as its aim to account for syntactic phenomena and intonation in terms of discourse structure. For Vallduví, the focus is the argument of an Update predicate, i.e., it determines the new entry on a file card. A "Link," in Vallduví's model, is similar to the topic in f-structure theory in that it designates the locus of update. A Link differs from a topic in that sentences that retain their topic from the previous utterance are without Links. In many of Vallduví's examples Links are subordinate f-structures which function to introduce new topics. Vallduví's system also includes the primitive "Tail" which represents the instruction to UPDATE-REPLACE. In chapter 3, I discuss the representation of presuppositions in the current framework as existing entries on file cards. Such entries may be manipulated by f-structure rules without the need for further primitives.

There are two major differences between Vallduví's framework and mine. The first one is that Vallduví claims no connection between the assignment of truth values and update semantics. I show in the following chapters that this is an integral aspect of f-structure theory with consequences for, among other issues, the account of quantifier scope, the interpretation of negative sentences and the interpretation of questions. The second difference is that Vallduví does not distinguish the top of the file as I do. One of the consequences of distinguishing those cards that are available as future topics is that it predicts possible sequences of sentences in discourse as I show in chapter 2. Moreover, in view of the fact that topics are not represented in Vallduví's framework unless they are overt new topics (Links), stage topics, which are often covert, cannot in any obvious way be incorporated in his system.

Lambrecht (1994)[52] defines a component of grammar which he calls Information Structure: "That component of sentence grammar in which propositions as conceptual representation of states of affairs are paired with

lexicogrammatical structures in accordance with the mental states of inter-
locutors who use and interpret these structures as units of information in
given discourse contexts." The basic categories of information structure are

(i)   Presupposition and Assertion
(ii)   Identifiability and Activation
(iii)   Topic and Focus

Only the notions in (ii) are unfamiliar. Identifiability is similar to the notion
"old." An identifiable entity is one which is assumed to be represented in the
hearer's mind. Existing cards in the current framework would be identifiable
in this sense. An activated element is one that is in prominence, possibly what
here is located on top of the file. Information structure thus has essentially the
same basic concepts as f-structure. Lambrecht also allows for the equivalent
of Stage topics. He also argues that sentences in which both the subject and
the object are pronouns have two topics. However, he does not distinguish
between main and subordinate topics. Neither does he relate topics to truth
value assignment. In order to explain stress assignment Lambrecht says
that nonasserted phrases may have informational structure just like asserted
phrases do. Here I achieve this effect by allowing for subordinate f-structures.
Lambrecht's framework is in many ways similar to what I propose here in
that he makes many of the same basic distinctions. He also provides a number
of valuable insights into how information structure determines intonation and
structure which I cannot go into here. What is lacking in Lambrecht's framework, however, is a tight framework that ties all the various notions together.
Moreover, as I show in the following chapters, the idea that truth value
assignment is read off f-structure together with the particular update semantics proposed here, allows for an explanation of a variety of syntactic and
semantic phenomena which Lambrecht's framework cannot provide.

   I now compare f-structure-theoretical discourse theory to Discourse Representation Theory (Heim 1982 and Kamp 1981). The framework developed
here differs essentially from the Kamp/Heim framework in that it makes use
of the notions Topic and Focus and "top of the file." This difference shows
up, for example, in cases in which indefinites are not included in the focus.
In a context in which John is a well-known car thief, I say to you:

(83)   Guess what happened! *John BOUGHT a car.* #It is red.[53]

The verb in the italicized sentence is focused, *a car* is not. For Heim it
is sufficient that an NP be indefinite for it to enable the reference in the
following sentence to be felicitous. According to the theory of discourse

developed here, the indefinite must be focused or included in the focus as well. Further differences are that DRT employs only one card per sentence or clause, whereas f-structure theory employs several, at least one for each referent. The use of the card heading is totally different here, resulting in much richer headings than in DRT which uses only indexes. Whereas in DRT all sentences are entered on cards, here only "true" information is entered.

This is not to say that there is no way of integrating the main tenets of the f-structure theoretical discourse theory with a version of DRT. In the Kamp/Heim framework logical representations consist of three parts:

1.   an unselective quantifier
2.   the Restrictive clause (the Restrictor)
3.   the Nuclear Scope.

As discussed in Partee (1992, 1994), there is a clear connection between the notion of "restrictive clause" in DRT and the notion of Topic on the one hand and the notions of nuclear scope and focus on the other. One of the main differences between the notion of topic introduced here and the restriction is that here a distinction is made between discourse-specified sets which can function as restrictive topics and infinite sets which cannot. This distinction is applied in chapter 3 to account for the difference between restrictive and nonrestrictive questions. It turns out that these two question types have different syntactic constraints. The fact that topic is a discourse defined notion is what allows this important distinction to be made. Another innovation of the f-structure-theoretical discourse theory is the use of subordinate f-structures. Finally, I see no natural way to define stage topics as restrictions in DRT.

However, only a semantics which takes into account the structure of discourse such as DRT has the potential to incorporate f-structure theory which is, by definition, a theory of discourse. This is why a promising line of investigation is to develop a theory which integrates f-structure and DRT. In Kamp's version of DRT the tripartite division of the sentence is represented by *duplex conditions* (See Kamp and Reyle 1993) illustrated in (84b) for (84a):

(84)   a. Every child is interesting.

         b.   x
            children(x) $\langle$every$\rangle$ x is interesting

The left side of the condition represents the restrictor, the right side the nuclear scope and the middle part is the quantifier. An initial proposal for combining DRT and F-structure is therefore to assign duplex conditions to *all*

Discourse Representation Structures (DRSs) and not just to quantified ones. The DRS of a simple sentence such as (85a) will therefore include the duplex condition (85b):

(85)   a. John is interesting.
        b.   x
                    ⟨⟩ x is interesting
            John(x)

On this view the left side of the condition represents the topic and the right side the focused predicate. The meaning of this condition is that it is true of *John* that he *is interesting*. If the topic is quantified as in (84), the condition renders the following interpretation: it is true of *every child* in the discourse-specified set of children (the topic set) that s/he *is interesting*.[54] Only referents which can be selected from the top of the file are licensed to occur on the left side of a duplex condition. This is how the f-structure-theoretical organization of the file may be built into DRT.

This view of how f-structure theory and DRT are to be combined provides a solution to the "separation" problem defined in Kamp and Reyle (1993), a problem they characterize as "one of the most urgent problems for natural language semantics" (p. 641). It is noted there that in temporally quantified sentences there is no available strategy for defining what goes on the left side and what on the right of the duplex condition. This strategy is now provided by f-structure theory. (Kamp and Reyle recognize that topic and focus are connected to this issue, but do not provide a solution.) One of the DRSs available for the sentence in (86a) is partially represented in (86b) which could be an answer to (87):

(86)   a. In 1975 Fred always had kippers for breakfast.
        b.   e
            [1975, for breakfast] (e)   ⟨always⟩ x had kippers
                    x
                Fred(x)

(87)   What did Fred have for breakfast in 1975?

(86b) is a simplified version of the duplex condition involved. There are, in fact, two such conditions, one subordinate to the other. *Fred* is the topic of the main predication, and the stage topic (with the parameters: *in 1975, for breakfast*) forms a subordinate f-structure. Subordinate duplex conditions must take over the role of subordinate f-structures if the two frameworks are to be merged.

In DRT each DRS displays a set of discourse referents, called the *universe* of the DRS. The theory of f-structure also assumes such a set of discourse referents which is represented as a set of "cards." In f-structure theory, however, the set of cards is structured: a subset of the cards constitutes the "top of the file." Cards which represent focused elements in sentences are placed on the top of the file and are thus licensed as future topics. Certain cards are permanently available on top of the file. These are the cards for the speaker, the hearer, and the here-and-now of the discourse (the "stage"). These three cards also provide potential topics. The organization of the universe of the DRSs into potential topic referents and "other" referents and, in particular, the idea of the stage topic also render the potential for interesting solutions to problems having to do with tense and aspect. For example, since anaphora in f-structure theory is licensed by the existence of a card on the top of the file, the view that tense can be anaphoric to an explicit temporal specification receives a natural account in this framework if tense is analyzed as anaphoric to a stage topic.

It is not my intention in this work to offer a full-fledged semantics for the discourse theory I propose. My intention is merely to indicate what role f-structure plays in semantic theory. This I do by offering a set of discourse rules and a rule of predication both driven by f-structure.

In this chapter I have defined f-structure and given the ground rules for its interpretation. I offered a discourse theory defined on f-structure and have shown how truth values are determined by applying the predication rule to articulated f-structures. Topics have been characterized by examining subjects of intransitive individual-level predicates and stage topics in stage-level predicates.

2   *Reference and coreference*

This chapter has four parts. In the first part I expand the notions of uniqueness introduced in chapter 1. There, the nature of topics was determined and it was concluded that they must be specific, i.e., that a card must be defined upon which the entry defined by the predication can be made. In this chapter I will investigate in more detail how new cards are opened and defined and what makes them specific or unique. I will show that this depends on whether the sentence is interpreted as predicated of a stage topic or whether it is interpreted as predicated of an individual topic. I treat the ambiguity which occurs in intensional contexts as the outcome of the two different f-structures; one in which there is a subordinate f-structure involving an individual giving rise to the specific reading, the other in which the subordinate f-structure involves an "intensional" stage giving rise to the nonspecific or transparent readings.

In the second part I discuss the function of focus structure in extended discourse. I distinguish three types of discourse chains; those in which the topic remains constant, those in which the topic changes according to the focus of the previous sentence and those in which a topic set is introduced allowing for any member of this set to be a topic in the following unit of discourse.

In the third part I offer an account of pragmatic anaphora along the lines proposed in Reinhart (1983, 1986). An f-structure-theoretical account for the distribution of coreferent pronouns is provided by the assumption that pronouns must be topics, i.e., they must access cards from the top of the file. The heading of the card on which the pronoun is entered determines its antecedent. I predict cases of backward anaphora showing that observations made by Reinhart follow from the f-structure framework introduced here.

The fourth part of the chapter shows that pronouns in donkey sentences are interpreted in the same way. The interpretation of donkey sentences is then shown to follow from f-structures in which the conditional is seen either as an individual or as a stage topic. The former f-structure derives the universal reading and the latter the existential reading.[1] It follows that the existential reading of donkey sentences is limited to stage-level predicates. I conclude this section by showing that a similar explanation can be given for opacity inducing predicates.

2.1 Uniqueness[2]

In this section I make a distinction between discourse uniqueness and absolute uniqueness: an indefinite predicated of an individual topic is necessarily specific or *discourse unique*.[3] An indefinite predicated of a stage topic is, however, not specific but rather unique to the stage upon which it is introduced. I refer to this type of uniqueness as *absolute uniqueness*. I will now examine these claims more carefully.

2.1.1 Introducing objects on stage: absolute uniqueness

The following two sentences have unambiguous focus structures: They must be predicated of stage topics.

(1)   There are dogs in the garden.
        $sTOP_t$ [there are dogs in the garden]$_{FOC}$

(2)   A man came in. (He was wearing a brown hat.)
        $sTOP_t$ [a man came in]$_{FOC}$

Both these sentences are extensional with respect to "dogs" and "a man," i.e., they imply the existence of "dogs" and "a man," respectively.[4] I claimed in chapter 1 (section 1.3) that singular indefinites introduced on stage must be unique in that a sentence such as (2) would be inappropriate if more than one man came in. Similarly, a unique set of dogs, defined by the stage topic, is asserted to exist in the garden according to (1). This is illustrated if we quantify over the stage topic as follows:

(3)   There are always dogs in the garden.

If *always* is interpreted as quantifying over the variable introduced by the stage topic, the sentence will be true at any t index of the stage, i.e., for any time chosen, if there are dogs in the garden then. The most prominent interpretation of (3) is one in which the set of dogs found at t_1 differs from the set found at t_2, i.e., no specific set of dogs is asserted to be on stage.

For (2), the initial intuition is that a specific man must be involved, but this interpretation may result from the implication that if the speaker asserts that a man came in, it might be because s/he has seen this. If indeed the speaker's assertion is based on such visual evidence, this would be represented as an implicit subordinate f-structure "a man I see." Specificity would be a direct result of this subordinate f-structure according to the definition of specificity in chapter 1 (section 1.6.2.3). But, I want to claim, introducing an indefinite NP on stage does not, in and of itself, make the NP specific. All we have to do is devise a context in which the speaker does not perceive the individual in question and the assumed subordinate f-structure will not be valid. Specificity will then not be implied even with a singular indefinite:

(4)   There's a worm in this apple.

No specific worm is assumed here, especially if no worm is in view, but only its traces in the apple. What is assumed is simply a unique worm defined by the stage topic. Clearly, if a following sentence attributes some property of the indefinite introduced on stage (as in the continuation of (2)), this too will make for specificity. In this case the indefinite becomes specific only by means of the entry made by updating according to the *following* sentence.

In chapter 1, section 1.2, an index was given to indefinites introduced on stage and the index of the stage was also incorporated in the heading of the new card. The heading of the new card for "a man" in (2) is:

(5) man_1 [e came in (at) s_t]

This representation makes overt Carlson's (1977) idea that a certain stage of "a man" came in. The index 1 on "man" refers to the particular man on the stage "t", making the index on the new individual dependent on index of the topic stage.

Indefinites introduced on stages are therefore unique, but not specific. I call this type of uniqueness, i.e., uniqueness bound by a stage, *absolute* uniqueness. Absolute uniqueness follows from the nature of stages. What we predicate of a stage is, by definition, a property of that stage. It follows that a stage is defined by its inventory. A stage with one man is different from a stage with two men. A stage with a tall man is different from one with a short man. But the identity or reference of the man is irrelevant to the stage in question. Absolute uniqueness therefore involves attribution, not reference.

I will use example (6) from Heim (1982) to make my notion of absolute uniqueness clearer. In particular I will show contra Kadmon (1990) that Heim's original intuition about this example is correct, yet that Kadmon's view can *also* be made to follow.

(6)   A wine glass broke last night. (It had been very expensive.)

According to Heim the uniqueness implication is restricted to a certain contextually relevant place but she claims no uniqueness for the glass in question, i.e., more glasses could have broken on said evening. Kadmon argues, following Evans (1980), that an expensive glass can be distinguished contextually from all others making it have unique properties.

The only f-structure possible for (6) is one in which the sentence is predicated of a stage topic. The indefinite subject does not qualify as a topic unless it is interpreted generically (see chapter 1) and the generic interpretation is ruled out by the stage-level predicate and the temporal adverb.[5] It follows from my claims concerning indefinites introduced on stage that "a wine glass" must be unique to the stage upon which it is introduced. This stage is defined by the index t on the stage topic. The index in turn although placed in the interval defined by "last night" must be punctual due to the aspectual properties of the sentence. It follows that a unique wine glass broke at time t, which equals some moment included in "last night." The claim of absolute uniqueness is one which is bound by the stage topic. No claim about other glasses breaking at other moments included in "last night" have therefore been made. If absolute uniqueness is uniqueness relevant to a stage, only *one* glass could have been broken at the place/time defined by the stage in (6). But the time interval defined by the stage is narrower than "last night," therefore more otherwise indistinguishable glasses could have been broken during the whole night. I thus assume that the stage topic defines the minimal stage defined by its spatio-temporal parameters. This accords with Heim's position. Contextual clues can, however, involve a subordinate f-structure which will render the glass discourse unique as well. If the glass is contextually distinguished as "the glass that was expensive" or "the glass that affected my mood," a discourse-unique interpretation will indeed be derived.[6]

2.1.2 *Objects introduced by individuals: discourse uniqueness*

Here I examine indefinite objects of transitive, individual-level predicates with subject topics. I show that such objects must be specific. (I use the term discourse uniqueness interchangeably with specificity.) Examine the following well-known example:

(7)   Oscar owns sheep. (Otto vaccinates them.)

According to Evans (1977), the pronoun in (7) refers to *all* of Oscar's sheep or whatever sheep Oscar owns. How does the discourse theory account for this? The f-structure of (7) is

(8)   Oscar$_{TOP}$ [owns sheep]$_{FOC}$[7]

and the new card made out due to the indefinite in the focused constituent has the following heading:

(9)   sheep(pl)₁ [Oscar owns e]

Since "sheep" is plural, the card stands for the set of sheep Oscar owns as required. The set of sheep is a specific set, specified by the predication. Here the predication is of an individual, hence the set of sheep is identified, not by a particular time/place, but by the fact that they are owned by Oscar.

The main topic card shows the following entry after update:

Oscar$_j$

e owns sheep

Note that on this card "sheep" has no index. The assertion that is being evaluated is therefore whether Oscar has the property of being a sheep-owner. The truth value of the sentence does not depend in any way on any properties of the sheep, only on there being some instances of the kind of sheep which belong to Oscar.[8]

To clearly distinguish discourse uniqueness from absolute uniqueness we must examine a singular indefinite in object position.

(10)   a. Oscar owns a sheep.
        b. Peter knows a lawyer.

In chapter 1, I made the following point: when the speaker utters the sentences in (10), he is not saying that the subject owns only *one* sheep or knows only *one* lawyer, respectively, he probably owns or knows many more of each. The utterance made by the speaker does not make reference to those other sheep or lawyers, and no cards are made out for them. The only way these objects are identified is as the unique one introduced in the particular discourse, the one under discussion now. This is why I call this type of uniqueness "discourse" uniqueness.[9]

Carlson (1977: 285) makes the point that the following are odd:

(11)   a. ??Hans adores a dog.[10]
        b. ??The queen of England has a fear of a mouse.
        c. ??This is a dissertation on a unicorn.

These improve significantly if modified:

(12) a. Hans adores a dog I own.
      b. The queen of England has a fear of a mouse which keeps appearing in her kitchen.
      c. This is a dissertation on a unicorn which appears in a certain fairy tale.

These modifiers make the indefinites specific by means of a subordinate f-structure which allows for a new card to be taken out *before* the truth value of the sentence is determined, i.e., the subordinate f-structure is not part of the assertion itself. This subordinate update determines the properties of the dog, mouse, and unicorn in question. Subordinate f-structure thus generates specificity or what I have here called discourse uniqueness.[11] In chapter 1, indefinites were licensed via subordinate update as topics. The subordinate f-structure caused a new card to be made out for the indefinite satisfying the requirement on topics that they be represented by existing cards on top of the file.

A comparison between (11) and (12) allows us to conclude that objects introduced by individuals must be discourse unique (or specific). It follows that the indefinites in (10) must also be interpreted specifically. Note first that although (10b) is acceptable, (13) is odd (on a noncontrastive reading):

(13) ??Peter knows a man.

The difference between (13) and (10b) must therefore be that somehow "a lawyer" on its own can be interpreted easily as a specific lawyer, where "a man" cannot. Note that "a lawyer" can be interpreted as "a person who is a lawyer," i.e., "a lawyer" attributes the property of being a lawyer to a person. This is possible in the context of the predicate *know*. No such analysis is likely for "a man" in (13). Similarly, "a sheep" can be interpreted as "a thing which is an animal" (in the context of the predicate *own*). This is sufficient to allow for a specific interpretation.[12]

Note that stress on the unacceptable indefinite object improves acceptability:

(14) Peter knows a MAN.

In a context in which gender is discussed, the sentence is acceptable with a contrastive interpretation, allowing for the NP to be taken generically. Contrast will be discussed in chapter 3.

The problem with (13) is that it is highly uninformative. Therefore the following context makes it acceptable:

(15)   A: Well, if we want to have a role model for our sons we're going to need
        to find some father figure? Does anyone know a man?
        B: Petra knows a man, I think. She has to meet people for her job.

The natural interpretation for "a man" here is "a man who can be a father
figure." The context here, represented by the implicit subordinate f-structure,
does make "a man" more informative.

In the last two sections I have shown that there are two different ways to
identify an individual to the hearer. The speaker may either place this individual on stage or predicate it of another individual. In the first case absolute
uniqueness ensures identification, in the second case specificity does.[13] Carlson
(1977: 315) makes the point that although existence is not a requirement for
specificity (see for example, (12c)) existence is often associated with specific
NPs. Carlson comments: ". . . it is normally quite difficult to have something
specific in mind that does not exist." Linguistically, existence of X boils
down to there being a card for X. Whether X (or an instance of X) exists in
the "real" world or in some imaginary world is of no significance linguistically, although the distinction is expressible in language.

2.1.3   Objects introduced on "imaginary" stages
I now wish to examine the predictions made so far with respect to opacity-
inducing predicates. The following example receives an opaque (de dicto) as
well as a transparent (de re) reading:

(16)   Bill is looking for a doctor.

I would like to argue that predicates which render this type of ambiguity have
the following f-structure:

(17)   NP V [sTOP$_{sub}$ [NP]$_{FOC-sub}$]^{14}

This f-structure for (16) means something like: Bill is looking for a stage
which has a doctor on it. Note that the subordinate stage topic has *no* index
indicating that this stage does not represent an existing stage, but rather an
imaginary one. Carlson (1977: 193) suggests an analysis of these predicates
in terms of lexical decomposition. *Seek* is analyzed as *try to find* and *want*
as *want to have*. This allows for two predicates, one which introduces the
intensional aspect, the other which introduces a stage. Predicates which introduce indexed stages are *see*, *hear*, *find*, etc. Evidence that intensional predicates select a stage as their complement is the fact that individual-level
predicates are blocked from occurring in the complements of those intensional
predicates which select *indexed* stages (as noted in chapter 1, it is possible

to view individual-level predicates as allowing a generic stage, but not an indexed one):

(18)   a. *John tried to fear snakes.
        b. *John tried to know French.

As pointed out by a reviewer, intensional predicates which select a generic stage as their complement do allow individual-level predicates:

(19)   a. John wants to know enough French to be able to order lunch in Paris.
        b. John wants to own more houses than his father.

Imaginary stages are set up via lexical properties of certain predicates and modals as well as conditionals. I treat the latter in section 2.4.

If *a doctor* in (16) is introduced on a stage, he will be absolutely unique, but not specific, rendering the opaque reading in which *any* doctor will do as the goal of the search. The specific reading results from an implicit subordinate update (derived from discourse). As argued in section 2.1.1, specificity can be induced on stage by additional subordinate f-structure (implicit or overt). This analysis predicts that the specific reading (when there is no overt subordinate f-structure) must be discoursally implied. The transparent reading is therefore the more marked one for these predicates. As noted in section 2.1.2 bare plurals which are analyzed as names do not allow for further specification. This is why the specific reading for bare plurals is excluded in intensional contexts.[15]

2.1.4   *Definites on stage*
In the previous sections I discussed the interpretation of indefinites introduced in the focused part of the sentence and distinguished them according to whether they were introduced on stage or by an individual. Here, I would like to examine the interpretation of Definites in the same cases using the well-known example from Donnellan (1966):

(20)   Smith's murderer is insane.

According to Donnellan, two interpretations of the subject are possible. Under one interpretation, the attributive one, Smith's murderer denotes any person who satisfies the description "is Smith's murderer." This reading does not necessitate the speaker's knowing who Smith's murderer is, although he might. Under the second reading, the referential reading, the speaker intends for the hearer to realize whom s/he has in mind. The latter reading we have referred to as the specific reading. The distinction made above between absolute and discourse uniqueness is applicable to definite descriptions as well.

In the current framework Definites pick out existing cards and the description in the heading of the card is used to select the card in question. In chapter 1, I claimed that any entry on a card can commute to the heading. It follows that a variety of definite descriptions can be used to select the same card. Let us assume that the speaker wants to select a card referring to a man₁ who both speaker and hearer encountered that morning. Moreover, the speaker assumes that s/he and the hearer have the entries on the following card in common:

---

man₁ [we met e this morning]

e was wearing a brown hat
e made important points during our conversation

The speaker could choose to refer to this man as "the man we met this morning," "the man who was wearing a brown hat," or "the man who made important points during our conversation with him this morning." I assume that the reason the speaker has a choice of definite descriptions is that the entries may commute with the heading and that any one of the entries or any combination thereof can be used by the speaker to enable the hearer to pick out the relevant card.

Assume now concerning (20) that the speaker has a particular person in mind (Jones, for example) as he utters the sentence. Since he does not assume that the hearer knows that Jones is the murderer of Smith, he uses the definite description "Smith's murderer." If the context allows the hearer to infer that the speaker has someone in mind, the specific reading ensues from the implicit subordinate f-structure involved as before. The speaker takes out a card via this subordinate update with the heading

(21)   Smith's murderer₂ [A has reference for e]

The restriction on the heading indicates the relevant subordinate f-structure. This restriction signifies to the hearer that since the speaker has such a card, the hearer can ask the speaker to transmit whatever entries he might have on it.

If, however, no subordinate f-structure is discoursally implied, i.e., the case in which no particular murderer is assumed by the speaker, I assume the following f-structure for (20):

(22)   [[sTOP$_{t\text{-sub}}$ [Smith's murderer]$_{FOC\text{-sub}}$]$_{TOP}$ [is insane]$_{FOC}$

The suggested subordinate f-structure is identical to the one proposed for the intensional contexts in (17), with the exception that here the stage topic is indexed. The index is derived from the stage topic of the presupposed proposition "John was murdered" and the card with this index has on it everything the hearer knows concerning said event, including the fact that some person was the murderer of Smith. The main topic, derived from this subordinate f-structure, is the unique person present on the stage upon which Smith was murdered. It therefore follows from this f-structure that Smith's murder is unique (absolutely) but not specific.[16]

Note that nothing has to be added to the discourse theory to account for Definites. The difference between definites and indefinites remains, as Heim (1982) proposed, a difference between existing and new cards.

2.2   Discourse

Discourse is a means of altering the "hearer's" inventory of filing cards as well as the entries on them. "Existing" cards are cards that have come up before (i.e., they have been introduced in the conversation previously). Cards which are on top of the file must have been introduced in the immediately preceding discourse. I claimed in chapter 1 that the topic of a sentence must be selected from the cards which are defined as being "on top of the file." In this section, I would like to pursue the repercussions of this idea for discourse analysis, i.e., I will examine the constraints imposed by this view of topichood on the coherence of sentence sequences.[17]

According to Daneš (1974) there are three types of thematic progression. I will refer to them here as Topic Chaining, Focus Chaining and Restrictive Focus Chaining. Topic Chaining is the simplest case:

(23)   *John* likes to read. *He* is intelligent and industrious and will go far.

In the first sentence in the sequence, *John* must be the topic since the predicate is individual level. In order to utter this sentence the speaker must assume a card with the heading *John* on top of the file. This card remains on top of the file and is therefore licensed as the topic of the following sentence. Topic Chaining can go on forever.

How are new potential topics introduced? This is clear from the file system developed here. Focusing introduces new cards to the top of the file. Focus Chaining occurs when a focused constituent is picked up as the topic of the following sentence:

(24)   a. *A boy* came into the classroom. *He* gave the teacher the book he was holding in his hand.

        b. Fortunately *someone* knew enough French to help us. *He* even lent us his map.

(24a) has a stage topic (which is always available in our system and allows for out-of-the-blue sentences). The subject is focused and indefinite. According to the focus rule, a new card headed *boy*$_i$ is opened and placed on top of the file. The subject pronoun of the following sentence is the topic of its sentence. Coreference will be ensured by the fact that this topic must be selected from the cards on top of the file. (Coreference will be discussed in section 2.3 below.) Similarly in (24b), in which the object *French* provides the topic, *someone* is focused and triggers the introduction of a new card to the topic of the file licensing the pronoun in the following sentence.

It is *not* the case that *any* NP contained in a sentence licenses a topic in the following sentence. Only existing topics or focused NPs which introduce new cards do so. Hence, if an NP does not represent an existing card on top of the file, it must be focused in order to license a future topic:

(25)   The boy gave *the teacher* the book he was holding in his hand. *He* was happy.

He, which is the only possible topic of the second sentence, cannot refer to *the teacher* since this constituent cannot be focused in the first sentence. (See Erteschik-Shir (1979) for arguments to this effect.) *He* can refer to *the boy*, the unmarked topic of the first sentence which can also naturally be interpreted as the topic of the second clause due to Topic Chaining. If, however, contextual clues made *the teacher* the topic of the first sentence, then, of course, the pronoun in the continuation could be interpreted on the card for him/her. If the gender is changed in the second sentence as follows:

(26)   The boy gave *the teacher* the book he was holding in his hand. *She* is happy.

Here *the teacher* is the only possible antecedent of the pronoun. If *the teacher* does not present a card on top of the file from previous discourse, i.e., an available topic card, then, the sequence of these two sentences will lack cohesion.

In the following sequence the focus constituent triggers the placement of two cards on top of the file. The following sentence, in which the topic pronoun could refer to either of these cards, is thus ambiguous:[18]

(27)   sTOP, [The United States invaded Iraq].
         It is an aggressive country.

Does a card on top of the file stay there "forever" while other new cards are introduced. Examine the following sequence:

(28)   John likes to read mystery novels. [They are easily available at the local book store. It has a big selection and the books are inexpensive.] ?He/John is never bored.

In the first sentence in the sequence *John* is the topic. In the following sentence *the mystery novels* are the topic by Focus Chaining. Topic Chaining takes care of the next sentence. The final sentence attempts *John* as the topic again. This is still possible in spite of the intervention of the bracketed sequence. Due to the distance the pronominal form is somewhat strained but the card for *John* must still be on top of the file, otherwise the final sentence in the sequence would not be possible at all. I assume that cards do not stay on top forever. I doubt that it is possible to define how long they do. This depends not only on pure distance but also on the structure of the intervening discourse. Polanyi and Scha (1989) argue for the existence of discourse units and levels of discourse. These interact in interesting ways with Topic Chaining and Focus Chaining. I will not, however, deal with the organization of discourse here.

What about cards introduced by subordinate f-structures? If the new card opened by subordinate update serves as the topic of the sentence, a new card is made available on the top of the file and the status of this card is no different from that of any other card. The card for "a man," in the following example (from chapter 1, section 1.6.2.2), is introduced by the subordinate update enabled by the relative clause:

(29)   [A man *who was wearing a brown hat*], knew enough French to help us.
         He, was extremely friendly.

The claim I am making here is that pronouns must be interpreted on topic cards. Such cards are available *either* by Topic Chaining (and a subordinate f-structure enables the construction of a topic card) *or* by Focus Chaining. Thus an indefinite in a preceding sentence licenses a pronoun if it is in focus.

An important question I have not addressed so far is the status of cards opened as a result of subordinate update which do not serve as topics in the main f-structure in which they occur. It has often been observed that the life span of such cards lasts only till the end of the sentence, whereas cards introduced by the main focus live on beyond the sentence.

(30)   *If a farmer owns *a donkey* he is happy. *It* works hard.

(31)   If a farmer owns *a donkey* he is happy and *it* works hard.

Cards opened due to subordinate update which are not needed to determine truth values must therefore be filed differently from those opened in the update triggered by the main f-structure. I will assume that such "subordinate" cards are *attached* to the main topic cards using the same strategy as was used for restrictive sets in chapter 1. This prevents them from having an independent existence, i.e., from being available as topics of the next sentence.[19]

It is also well known that quantified expressions introduced by subordinate f-structure block singular anaphora in the *same* sentence:

(32)   *A farmer who beat every donkey$_i$ resented it$_i$.

Note that the "attached" card introduced by subordinate update will have as its heading a plural set of donkeys over which the quantifier ranges.[20] Since assessment is not "per donkey," *every donkey* renders the group reading and only plural anaphora is appropriate:

(33)   A farmer who beat every donkey$_i$ resented them.

An interesting test case for the theory of discourse which follows from f-structure discourse theory is given in Heim (1989):

(34)   Almost every child got a cookie. They ate them right away.

The first sentence presupposes a set of children for which a card is available on top of the file. "Almost" partitions the topic set and creates a subset of the set of children, which is "almost" as big as the original set, providing a new card on top of the file. "Every" indicates that assessment must come out true for every member of the partitioned topic set. The partitioned topic card is the one picked up by the subject of the following sentence. How do we get a plural set of cookies? For every assessment in which "a cookie" is introduced in the focus constituent, a "cookie" card is introduced. Each card is placed on top of the file and each has the same entry. Since these "cookie" cards are identical, they can be redefined as a collective set of cookies. This is, in my view, an instance of accommodation and involves, if you will, recognition that each individual cookie introduced is the same as the others. Once this set has been accommodated, the relevant card is available on top of the file and the second sentence can be assessed. Accommodation involves manipulation of the file restricted by the availability of cards introduced via f-structure. Accommodation by extralinguistic context will always be deictic. (See also Heim 1989.) In chapter 1 section 1.6.3.1, the term accommodation was applied to cases in which assessment was extended to the subordinate f-structure. The current case of accommodation is similar in that it also involves the manipulation of the file in order to create a different topic for purposes of assessment. In both cases the accommodated topic depends on extralinguistic context.

Daneš' third type of thematic progression involves derived topics. These topics are derived by subordinate update from a restrictive topic set (Daneš' hypertheme) in the manner discussed in the context of the Restrictive Focus rule in chapter 1. Once a restrictive set has been introduced into the discourse, and the relevant card has been added to the top of the file, any individual member of the set is available as a future (definite) topic.

(35)   Speaker A: Tell me about *your family.*
        Speaker B: *My mother* is a teacher, *my father* works in an office and *my sister* is a student.

Note that each topic in speaker B's sentences belongs to the restrictive set defined by A. However, neither one needs previous mention on its own. It is because speakers know that families are made up of parents, siblings, etc., that these family members can be derived as future topics. This knowledge is represented in the card system as existing entries on cards. I assume therefore that world knowledge as well as knowledge gained from current discourse is represented. The fact that cards exist in the file at the beginning of a conversation acknowledges this view. Determination of truth value also measures up any new utterance with previous knowledge which may have been gained in many ways. I am assuming, therefore, for the previous example, that speakers have, as entries on the generic card for "family," the fact that family "parts" are fathers, mothers, siblings, etc. This generic information can be accessed whenever a specific "family" card is taken up. In addition, Speaker A may have entries on his card for Speaker B's family, information about its members. If Speaker A's card lacks an entry concerning a sister, he may respond:

(36)   Speaker A: I didn't know you had a sister.

The filing system therefore represents world knowledge which is filed on the appropriate cards. Generic cards play an important role in that all generalized knowledge about the category in question is entered on them. This information is represented in an organized fashion. Take "family," for example. The information that families consist of particular family *parts* is represented on the "family" card. Each of these parts, however, also exists as a generic card in its own right. These cards are conceivably filed each in its own subdirectory of the main directory "family." The filing system under this view is organized ontologically and it is only if Speaker A and Speaker B have similarly organized filing systems that the discourse can progress smoothly. It is not my intention, with this illustration, to imply that the only way in which a card such as the "family" card can be introduced is by overt discourse. World knowledge also allows such cards to pop up by association with any speaker since it is also known that we all have families. Manipulation of cards not triggered by overt mention is, as discussed immediately above, an instance of accommodation.

Bolinger (1980: 26) argues that definite generics define subsets:

(37)   a.   Since we are talking about animals, what about the beaver?
       b.   *Since we are talking about trees, what about the beaver?
       c.   Since we are talking about trees, what about beavers?

The reason (37b) is out is that *the beaver* cannot be conceived of as a subset of trees. (37c), with the bare plural generic, does not imply a subset relation between the generic and trees, hence it is sufficient that there be some discoursal relation between trees and beavers for the sentence to be acceptable. In the particular sentence type (37a) made up by Bolinger, the first part of the sentence determines the topic of discourse and the second part suggests a new, but connected, topic. According to the discourse theory, Definites necessitate existing cards. *The beaver* can therefore only be accessed by (partitive) subordinate update on condition that beavers are classified as a subset of the topic (in this case *animals*).

Another illustration is given in (38):

(38)   Speaker A: What do you know about Italy?
       Speaker B: The capital is Rome, . . .

If a country is introduced, then its *parts* can be assumed to be carried to the top of the file with it.

Since "the world" is permanently available around us, it is also represented as a card permanently available on top of the file. World-parts are therefore also permanently available, explaining the occurrence of Definites such as "the sun" and "the moon" in out-of-the-blue sentences.[21]

These basic forms of thematic progression follow from the file-change rules introduced here. It is not surprising that the organization of discourse and f-structure are interdependent. Since f-structure is defined on the s-structures of individual sentences, it is part and parcel of sentence gram-mar. F-structure is, however, also accessible to discourse theory where the rules of thematic progression are spelled out.

2.3 Coreference

Reinhart (1983, 1986) allows pronouns to be interpreted in two ways: a) as bound variables (illustrated in (39) and b) by pragmatic Coreference (illus-trated in (40) from Evans (1980: 337):

(39) a. John loves *his* mother.
      b. Every man loves *his* mother.
      c. John loves *himself.*

(40) a. *He's* up early.
      b. I'm glad *he's* left.
      c. John owns some sheep and Harry vaccinates *them* in the spring.

The former, I argue, are cases of I-dependent pronouns and I discuss them in chapter 6 which deals with I-dependencies in general. The latter, which I refer to as R-dependent pronouns are discussed here. E-type pronouns (as in (40c)) are classified as R-dependent pronouns, since their interpretation follows from the discourse theory defined here by the same coreference rule applied to other pronouns. Therefore it is only necessary to distinguish two pronoun types here.

A pronoun functions to signal Coreference with some discoursally promin-ent NP, namely a card on the top of the file. I claim the interpretation of a pronoun is derived from the heading of the card upon which it is entered. This card may not be referential in any sense of the term. In such a case the pronoun will not be referential either. I use the term coreference for conven-ience, even in cases in which reference proper is not involved.

2.3.1 Coreference licensing

Entering a pronoun (with matching features) on a card is what licenses coreference. This principle can be stated as follows:

Coreference licensing (I):

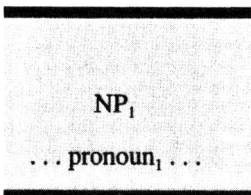

$$NP_1$$

$$\ldots \text{pronoun}_1 \ldots$$

The following case which illustrated topic chaining is repeated here to illustrate the principle of Coreference licensing:

(41)   *John* likes to read. *He* is intelligent . . .

In the beginning of this discourse a card for *John* must be on top of the file. The two sentences change this card as follows:

John$_i$

. . . .   = previous entries
e$_1$ likes to read   = entry (first sentence)
he$_i$ is intelligent . . .   = entry (second sentence)

The pronoun in the second entry gets the same index as the one in the heading and its interpretation is fully derivable from the interpretation of the heading. If a feminine or plural pronoun occurred in the same f-structure, it would simply not receive an interpretation.[22]

Coreference licensing works the same way in cases of focus chaining. The pronoun is interpreted according to the heading of the card upon which it is entered. This is also true for generic cards which are unindexed. Again a pronoun is interpreted according to the heading of the card upon which it is entered. In such a case the pronoun will be unindexed and interpreted generically. Examine the following sequence of sentences:

(42)   I like roses. I have *one* in the garden. *It* is red.

Let us examine our cards at the end of this sequence:

(a)	(b)
roses	roses$_3$
I like e	it$_3$ is red
I have one (of e) in garden	

Card (a) shows the entry on the generic card for "roses" which was put on top of the file by the focus rule in processing the first sentence and the second entry was made by processing the second sentence. Note that *one* is interpreted as a cardinal determiner selecting one arbitrary representative from the generic set of roses, i.e., one arbitrary rose. This instance of subordinate update triggers the initiation of the new card (b) which represents a card for a particular rose (the one I have in my garden), which in turn is asserted to be red. This case illustrates the type of restrictive topic chaining we get with generics.

Let us change the sequence somewhat:

(43)   I like roses. Peter likes *them* too. **It* is red.

In this case the pronoun *them* in the second sentence will be interpreted generically since it is entered on a generic topic card:

roses

Peter likes *them*ROSES too

According to coreference licensing, *them* can only be interpreted to mean the genus "roses." Since no unique rose card has been introduced (as in the previous case), the pronoun in the last sentence in (43) will receive no interpretation.

The E-type pronoun in (40c) is interpreted as follows. The heading for the new card constructed by the Focus rule in the first conjunct is:

(44)   (some) sheep$_i$ [John owns e]

This was discussed in section 2.1.2. Once the second conjunct is processed the following card is derived:

sheep$_i$ {John owns e}

Harry vaccinates them$_i$

The pronoun will therefore refer to the set of sheep that John owns. This result is achieved by the discourse theory defined here and the coreference principle.

The principle of coreference suffices to explain all the cases of pragmatic coreference in the rest of this chapter.

2.3.2   *Backward pronominalization*

According to Reinhart (1986), the condition for backward pronominalization is that the antecedent must be interpreted as the topic of the main clause as in the following (her (27)–(28)):

(45)   a. When he entered the room Max greeted Bill.
        b. When he entered the room Bill was greeted by Max.

(46)   #When *she* entered the room Max was greeted by *Kora*.

(45a) is ambiguous since either *Max* or *Bill* can be the antecedent of the pronoun. This is due to the fact that either one can play the role of topic in the predication rule. (45b) is not ambiguous. Only *Bill* can be interpreted as the topic of the passive and is therefore the only antecedent for the pronoun. It should now be clear why (46) is pragmatically inappropriate.

Reinhart suggests (in a note) that "the function of backward anaphora in actual discourse might be, contrary to common assumptions, that of introducing a new topic into the discourse." This must be correct, since (45b), for example, could not be a response to a request for information about *Bill*, i.e., a card with this heading cannot be available on top of the file. Yet *Bill* is the topic of the main clause indicating that the mechanism of subordinate update must be at work here, making the card for *Bill* available on top of the file by the time the main f-structure is processed. Mittwoch (1983) argues that backward anaphora functions as a marker of pragmatic subordination, i.e., the clause that contains the antecedent must be taken as the main assertion.

Let us examine the f-structure for (45a) with these proposals in mind. We will do so bit by bit, due to its complexity. First note that the *when*-clause provides a (subordinate) stage topic for the main clause (for simplicity, I ignore the main f-structure in the main clause):

(47)   [When he entered the room]$_{sTOPt-sub}$ [Max greeted Bill]$_{FOC-sub}$

The main clause is the one that determines assessment. I show this by applying the lie-test to the sentence:

(48)   Speaker A: When he entered the room Max greeted Bill.
        Speaker B: That's a lie – he didn't.
        = he didn't greet
        = *Max greeted Bill at a different time.

The lie test shows that the sentence is not evaluated according to the stage topic. It follows that the f-structure in (47) must be subordinate as marked. The fact that this f-structure is subordinate makes it irrelevant to assessment but instrumental to the arrangement of the cards. Since the main clause is focused, the cards for the NPs in it must be found (since they are definite) and placed on top of the file. Both are now topic candidates for any subsequent rule applications. This is due to the subordinate f-structure in (47). The main clause can now be processed. Let us select *Max* (one of our accessible topics) as our topic this time. The main clause can now be assessed according to the f-structure

(49) Max_{TOP} [greeted Bill]$_{FOC}$

But we are not done yet. The *when*-clause must still be processed, i.e., it must be entered on the main topic card. The pronoun contained in this entry may now receive the same index as the heading of the card upon which it is entered.

If *Max* were *not* the topic of its clause, there would be no way of retrieving an antecedent for the pronoun from within the sentence itself. Our filing system thus predicts the properties of backward anaphora, namely the fact that the antecedent must be the topic of its clause and the fact that the antecedent must occur in the clause which determines the assessment of the sentence as a whole. Backward anaphora will therefore be possible in cases in which the main clause functions as the focus of a subordinate stage topic and the antecedent is the main topic. If the main clause comes first, and the antecedent is in the subordinate clause, backward pronominalization will be blocked:

(50)   #*He* greeted Kora when *Max* entered the room.

This follows if we assume that the *when*-clause cannot play the role of (stage) topic unless it is preposed. The preposed *when*-clause also allows "forward" pronominalization:

(51)   When *Max* entered the room *he* greeted Bill.

This, in turn, follows from the fact that the *when*-clause is not precluded from functioning as the main topic of the assertion.

(52)   Speaker A: When Max entered the room he greeted Bill.
        Speaker B: He didn't = at that time/place the event of Max greeting Bill
               didn't take place

Here the lie-test identifies the stage topic as the one that determines assessment. The stage topic is therefore processed first, positioning *Max* on top of
the file as an available topic for the processing of the main clause, thus
licensing the pronominal topic of this clause.

We have seen that *when*-clauses provide suitable stage topics. So do locative
prepositional phrases, as in the following examples from Reinhart (1983)
(with coreference intended):

(53)   a. Near him, Dan saw a snake.
        b. In her kitchen, Zelda cooks dinner.

The f-structure is parallel to the previous one:

(54)   [Near him]$_{sTOPt-sub}$[Dan$_{TOP}$ [saw a snake]$_{FOC}$]$_{FOC-sub}$

Again the main f-structure involves the clause without the stage topic and the
stage topic provides a subordinate f-structure with the clause as its focus. The
card for the subject *Dan* is introduced via this subordinate update, making a
card with this heading available as the topic of the main f-structure. At this
point the content of the locative phrase must be entered on the only available
card, namely the card with the heading *Dan*$_i$. The pronoun receives the index
of the card upon which it is entered.[23] Compare (also from Reinhart):

(55)   *Near Dan$_i$, he$_i$ saw a snake.

Here coreference is blocked. If the f-structure of (55) is taken to be (54), then
the problem arises when we enter the content of the locative on the card with
the index *i*. This must be ruled out. If it is assumed that no two cards may
share an index, a rather obvious assumption, then it follows that this entry
cannot be made with the indexing assumed in the following card:

    *   he$_i$

       Near Dan$_j$, e saw a snake

The card for *he*$_i$ must be available on top of the file, the card for *Dan*$_j$,
however, must be retrieved from the stack. It follows that two different cards
are involved, hence the same index could not be assigned to both.

Why isn't (55) licensed (as in the similar (51)) by taking the stage topic as the *main* topic of the f-structure? In this case we would get the following card:

[Near Dan$_j$]$_t$

he$_i$ saw a snake

Here the pronoun cannot pick up its index from the heading, since the heading is a stage with a stage index and, although the heading includes a proper antecedent for the pronoun, this is not sufficient for coreference licensing.[24] (55) is therefore ruled out whether the stage topic or the subject is selected as the main topic.

The following case, with two R-expressions, is similarly ruled out:

(56)   *Near Dan$_i$, Dan$_i$ saw a snake.

The violation here can be made less severe by destressing the first occurrence of the R-expression and contrastively stressing the second. This would allow for a different type of f-structure to be discussed in chapter 3. This option is not available for (55) since stressing the pronoun would make it deictic rather than contrastive.

It therefore follows from the discourse theory associated with f-structure that R-expressions must be free. Principle C of binding theory thus becomes superfluous. Let me illustrate this in the following simple cases:

(57)   a. He$_{TOP}$ [criticized Max]$_{FOC}$
       b. TOP$_i$ [he criticized Max$_i$]

Since pronouns must access cards from the top of the file, i.e., they must be topics, the only f-structures available for these sentences are the ones indicated. In both cases, coreference between the R-expression and the pronoun topic is blocked as before since the former is contained in the focus constituent and the latter must be the topic, i.e., each must represent a different card. Since the cards for *he* and for *Max* have been shown to be different, their indices must be different as well.

The notion that R-expressions are referentially independent, i.e., they come with their own index, is retained from Binding Theory. R-dependent pronouns differ from R-expressions in necessarily retrieving their index from a card on top of the file.

(58a), also from Reinhart (1983), is ruled out in the same fashion:

(58)   a. *In Ben's picture of Rosa, she found a scratch.[25]
         b. In Ben's picture of Rosa, she is riding a horse.

Although Reinhart discusses aspects of the f-structures along similar lines to the ones expressed here, she accounts for the difference between (58a) and (58b) structurally. The PP in (58a) (and in the previous cases) modifies the VP, and the one in (58b) modifies the sentence. She argues that this structural difference also shows up in the preposed versions. In cases such as (58a) the preposed PP is in the structural domain of the subject. This is not the case for preposed sentential PPs which is why the coreference in (58b) is not blocked.

The difference between these sentences can be accounted for by f-structure. The f-structures of the sentences in (58) (with only main f-structures indicated) follow:

(59)   a. In Ben's picture of Rosa, she$_{TOP}$ [found a scratch]$_{FOC}$
         b. [In Ben's picture of Rosa]$_{sTOP}$ [she is riding a horse]$_{FOC}$

In (59b) the stage-level topic is responsible for the *main* predication. Rosa's riding a horse is a property of the picture, not a property of Rosa herself. The focused constituent is therefore entered on the card for the stage topic and nothing prevents coreference. Note that the same sentence with backward pronominalization does receive the f-structure in which *Rosa* is the topic of the main f-structure as in the previous cases:

(60)   In Ben's picture of her, Rosa is riding a horse.

(60) thus differs from (58b) in f-structure even though the only difference is in the order of the R-expression and the pronoun. This may be correct, not only because this f-structure correctly enables the backward pronominalization, but also because (60), but not (58b), is a possible answer to:

(61)   What is Rosa doing?

It follows that sentences with preposed sentential PPs are ambiguous with respect to f-structure. The f-structure (59b) must, however, be blocked for sentences with preposed verb-phrasal PPs as in (58a). Let us examine this sentence with the acceptable backward pronominalization:

(62)   In Ben's picture of her, Rosa found a scratch.

Rosa's finding a scratch cannot be interpreted as a property of the picture. The main topic must therefore be found in the main clause as indicated in

(59a). It follows that (58a) with this f-structure is ruled out because the stage topic including the coreferent R-expression would have to be entered on the topic card for *Rosa*. Is this interpretive fact due to the structural position of the PP in each case? Reinhart herself (1983) presents the following cases which cast strong doubt on her hypothesis:

(63) a. *In Zelda's letter, she spoke about butterflies.
      b. In Zelda's latest letter, she speaks about butterflies.
      c. In the letter Dr Levin got from Zelda, she spoke about butterflies.

Reinhart argues that the PP in (63a), but not in (63b) and (63c) must be interpreted as verb phrasal. When the preposed PP is "lengthened," the rest of the sentence is more easily interpreted as a statement about this PP. This, according to Reinhart, warrants the structural difference. Note that these cases are not surprising in the system set up here. Let us examine the difference between "Zelda's letter" and "Zelda's latest letter." The latter involves a subordinate f-structure in which a particular letter is selected from the set of Zelda's letters.[26] This set is contextually available and provides us with a topic card with the heading "Zelda's letters." The content of the rest of the sentence is predicated of this topic, as Reinhart argues, but not because of the length of the preposed PP, but because of the subordinate f-structure which derives a topic set. A parallel argument can be made for (63c) since it has already been argued that relative clauses necessarily involve a subordinate f-structure. The definite head is what ensures the creation of a set of letters in this case as well.

In this section I showed that f-structure gives us a powerful tool to explain what Reinhart has named "pragmatic coreference." The principle of coreference licensing is very much in the spirit of Reinhart's work since its raison d'être is derived from the function of pronouns: to enable coreference where coreference licensing is governed by the heading of the particular card upon which an entry is made.

2.3.3 Crossover

Lappin (1982) argues that the following cases of weak crossover involve f-structure (italics = intended coreference):[27]

(64) a. *The woman who loved *him*, kissed *someone*.
      b. *The woman who loved *him*, kissed *a man*.
      c. The woman who loved *him*, kissed *the man*.
      d. The woman who loved *him*, kissed *some man I was talking to*.
      e. *The woman who loved *him*, kissed JOHN.
      f. The woman who loved *him*, KISSED John.

Lappin argues (based on Wasow's (1979) insight that determinateness, i.e., referentiality, is involved) that those NPs which are necessarily interpreted as foci cannot be interpreted as coreferential with the pronoun. (64e), in which the NP is stressed, hence focused, makes this clear. Destressing *John* as in (64f) suffices to enable coreferentiality. A brief examination of the NPs indicates that the relevant property is whether or not the NP is interpreted as the topic of the sentence. If it is, coreferentiality is possible, otherwise not. (64a) and (64b) illustrate NPs which cannot be topics as shown in chapter 1. In (64c) the topic is appropriately definite and in (64d) subordinate update allows the indefinite to be interpreted as the topic of the sentence. If the NP in question is the topic of the sentence, then the rest of the sentence is entered on the card with this NP as its heading. Coreference licensing allows the pronoun to receive the same index as the heading on the card. If, however, the NP is not taken as the topic of the sentence, then the principle of coreference licensing will not be available to enable coreference. Strong quantifier antecedents warrant further examination:

(65)   a. *The woman who loved *him* kissed *everyone*.
        b. The art historian who was looking for *them* finally located *every Rembrandt he was writing about*.

(65b) indicates that if the strongly quantified constituent is interpreted as a topic, it can form the antecedent for a plural pronoun, i.e., the topic is the set of Rembrandts, hence the plural. (65a) with the singular pronoun would have to receive an interpretation in which a separate instance of predication occurred for every member of the topic set. Such cases will be defined as I-dependencies in chapter 6 and (65a) will be ruled out by the Subject Constraint, a syntactic constraint on f-structure introduced there.

2.4   Donkey sentences in the light of f-structure

2.4.1   *Implicit contingencies*

Faber (1987), in a fascinating discussion of accentuation of intransitive sentences, notes sentences such as the following:

(66)   TRESpassers will be PROsecuted. (i.e., "if there are any")

(67)   SPELLing mistakes will be PENalised. (i.e., "if you make any")

What is the topic of these sentences? This sentence type can only be evaluated if the conditionals (*if there are any*, *if you make any*) hold, i.e., the implicit conditional functions as the topic of the overt sentence which is in focus.[28] *If*-clauses are analyzed as restrictive clauses (cf. Heim 1982 etc.) and topics have been identified here as the restriction in tripartite structures. Further, we have seen that topics can be implicit, in the case of stage topics at least. Let us therefore examine overt conditionals within our framework, to see how they are interpreted and then proceed to an analysis of the implicit conditionals in (66) and (67).

Heim (1982: 182–3) argues for a syntactically unrealized necessity operator in bare conditionals. According to Heim, the same necessity operator, when restricted by an indefinite, renders the generic reading discussed in chapter 1. There I argued that the implicit operator need not be stipulated, but rather falls out of the proposed discourse theory. Let us examine whether this can be argued for conditionals as well. Remember that TOPIC instructs the hearer to locate on the top of his file an existing card with the relevant heading and index. How does the "if-clause" accomplish this?

(68)   If my party wins the election, I'll be happy.

(69)   If it'll rain, I'll take an umbrella.

In (68) the conditional functions as a generic stage or situation with respect to which the consequent is evaluated. There are many kinds of possible situations, just like there are many kinds of things. The conditional sets up a stage card with the propositional heading: "my party wins the election." This card is generic in that it refers to a kind of situation, not a particular instance in which the situation actually takes place. The consequent appears as an entry on this card. The interpretation is that for any instance of a situation in which the proposition in the heading holds, the consequent also holds. This follows from the fact that according to the predication rule, the entry must be evaluated with respect to the heading on the card.[29]

Back to (66): the implicit conditional "(if) there are trespassers," must appear as the heading of a generic stage card in order for a truth value to be assigned to the sentence. The f-structure of (66) is:

(70)   sTOP [trespassers will be prosecuted]$_{FOC}$

The heading of the (implicit) stage topic defines a situation kind and therefore no additional index is required.[30] The discourse theory defined here so far makes available an indexed stage topic, indicating the here and now, on top of the file, but not a generic one. This topic is constructed by subordinate update. The only possible candidate for the triggering of subordinate update here is the generic subject which is contained in the focus constituent, i.e., a new card must be made out with the heading "trespassers." But since this new card is made out due to a subordinate f-structure, the sentence is assessed for each occurring instance of "trespasser," in the generic set of trespassers. It follows that the focus constituent is predicated of each existing trespasser, exactly the interpretation that Faber assigned. This interpretation, then, follows from a focus structure with an implicit generic stage topic.

2.4.2　When-*clauses vs.* if-*clauses*

I mentioned in chapter 1 (section 1.6.3.2), following Kratzer (1989a), that *when*-clauses with individual-level predicates must have indefinite topics. Unquantified conditionals are not constrained in this way. Compare:

(71)　a. *When the farmer owns the donkey, he beats it.
　　　　b. If the farmer owns the donkey, he beats it.

This follows from the fact that *when*-clauses form unindexed stage topics, and conditionals may or may not do so. The f-structure for a conditional construction with indefinites involves an unindexed stage topic as follows:

(72)　[a farmer owns a donkey]$_{sTOP}$ [he beats it]$_{FOC}$

In the previous section the conditional was shown to function as a generic stage or situation with respect to which the consequent is assessed. The conditional sets up a stage card with a propositional heading. This card is generic in that it refers to a kind of situation, not a particular instance in which the situation actually takes place. The consequent appears as an entry on this card. The interpretation is that for any arbitrary representative instance of a situation in which the proposition in the heading holds, the consequent also holds. This follows from the fact that, according to the predication rule, the entry must be assessed with respect to the heading on the card, i.e., the topic defines the range for predication. Since assessment necessitates evaluation with respect to an arbitrary representative instance of the "stage," let us assign an index t to the arbitrary stage topic chosen for evaluation. Once this index is assigned, we must assign indices to the NPs within the heading as well, since a particular "stage" must have particular actors, not generic ones. Once the NPs in the heading are indexed, the pronouns in any entry we make, following the coreference principle, may be assigned coreferential indices. (The pronouns may, of course, also receive different indices from the context.) The following structure results:

(73)　If [a farmer$_i$ owns a donkey$_j$]$_{sTOPt}$ [he$_i$ beats it$_j$]$_{FOC}$

We now get the interpretation we want, namely, that it is a property of a stage *t* in which "a farmer$_i$ owns a donkey$_j$," that "he$_i$ beats it$_j$." (The "farmer$_i$" and the "donkey$_j$," are representative instances of their kind.)

This is also the f-structure and interpretation assigned to *when*-clauses, which necessitate assessment with respect to a range of times. What would happen if the topic inside the initial clause were definite? In that case we would not get a set of kinds of situations or stages, but one specific stage, the stage in which a specific farmer owns a particular donkey. But a specific stage must be identified with a specific time and place, i.e., the initial clause would have to be associated with an indexed stage topic. Indexed stage topics are, however, not available for individual-level predicates. A definite topic in a *when*-clause would therefore make the sentence uninterpretable. This explanation is very similar to the one offered in Kratzer (1989a). Kratzer argues that (individual-level) *when*-clauses must contain at least one indefinite, otherwise quantification would be vacuous. Here quantification is associated with topichood. A stage-level *when*-clause with no indefinites presents no problem. There the topic is an unindexed stage-level topic which generates a set of situations which in turn provide a stage topic for the consequent:

(74)   When[sTOP [the man meets the woman]$_{FOC}$]$_{sTOP}$ [he faints]$_{FOC}$

Chierchia (1992a) argues that certain stage-level predicates must also be excluded from the *when*-clause, casting doubt on Kratzer's generalization:

(75)   a. *When John dies, he is unhappy.
         b. *When John destroys this house, he destroys it thoroughly.
         c. *When John kills this rabbit, he kills it cruelly.

I agree with Chierchia that these must be ruled out for the same reason individual-level *when*-clauses with no indefinites are ruled out. This follows from the fact that these stage-level predicates are "uniterable" (you can't die twice, neither can you destroy the same house twice). It follows that the *when*-clause provides a nongeneric stage. The consequents in (75) get individual-level readings (the latter two because they are in the present tense), which in turn blocks the indexed stage topic. A context which allows for iteration, for example, if *John* is an actor in a play, makes these sentences good. (See also de Swart 1991.)

Condoravdi (1992) shows that individual-level predicates such as *hesitant, serious, decisive* can occur in *when*-clauses:

(76)   When John is serious/decisive/hesitant, his proposal usually gets accepted.

These predicates behave like individual-level predicates with respect to all other diagnostics. What licenses these predicates in this construction is their stage-level interpretation: "behave in a serious/decisive/hesitant manner." This reading does not, however, license:

(77)   *There were politicians serious/decisive/hesitant.

Although existential sentences require a (main) stage topic, the (subordinate) topic relevant to the adjectival predicates is an individual one (politicians). It seems that an overt stage topic must be accessible in order to get the "behave" reading of the adjectives:

(78)   At the meeting John was decisive.

Without the overt (or contextually prominent) stage topic the interpretation will be individual level with John as the (dead) topic.

Conditionals, but not *when*-clauses, allow another f-structure as well:

(79)   If [a farmer owns a donkey]$_{TOP}$ [he beats it]$_{FOC}$

The difference between (72) and (79) is that in the latter the main topic is an individual and not a stage.

Note that indexing proceeds in the same manner as before, since the main focus "he beats it" is entered on a card with a heading defined by the antecedent. The interpretation here differs somewhat: the property "he beats it" must be predicated of an individual. In the next section we shall see that the "individual" derived depends on the internal f-structure of the antecedent.

The f-structure in (79) would be equally well formed if the subject inside the initial clause were definite. In that case the individual topic of the main f-structure would pertain to a referential rather than a generic topic.

2.4.3   Donkeys on stage

Heim (1989) recognizes that pragmatic factors are involved in the interpretation of donkey sentences. She poses the following question quite succinctly: "... why should topic-focus structure have any effect on the way we tend to individuate situations?" It is my intention to propose an answer to Heim's question here.

Chierchia (1992a) identifies two different interpretations for donkey sentences, the $\exists$ reading and the $\forall$ reading of the dependent "donkey" variable. Chierchia argues that the classic donkey sentence (80) can get both readings:

(80)   If a farmer owns a donkey, he beats it.

The existential reading is made more salient, according to Chierchia, if we imagine a context in which frustrated farmers are given the sentence "Every farmer who owns a donkey should beat it" as advice by a psychotherapist. In this context the sentence will be true even if each farmer does not beat all of his donkeys. (Neither is it necessary that a special donkey gets beaten each time.) The universal reading is the one in which a farmer who owns more than one donkey necessarily beats them all.

I will show that this ambiguity shows up only with a consequent with a stage-level predicate. An individual-level consequent forces the universal reading as in Heim's (1989):

(81)   Every man who owned a slave, owned its offspring.

This sentence would be falsified if someone did not own the offspring of all the slaves he owned. Chierchia notes that (81) cannot get the $\exists$ reading but does not offer an explanation for this fact. He assumes that both readings are generally available.

The difference between consequents with stage-level and individual-level predicates shows up in focus structure which is what explains this difference. Further, the f-structure of the antecedent plays a role in interpretation, as we shall see below. Chierchia, following Kadmon (1990), incorporates the latter point in his Dynamic Type Theory. The f-structure dynamic theory proposed here starts with the assignment of f-structure, making the interpretation of donkey sentences sensitive not only to the f-structure of the antecedent, but to the complex f-structure of the whole donkey sentence. This approach also allows for a unified interpretation of anaphora in such sentences: all anaphora is interpreted by means of the rule of coreference licensing introduced above.

Let us now examine (80). Remember that the existential reading is made more salient, according to Chierchia, if we imagine a context in which frustrated farmers are given the sentence "Every farmer who owns a donkey should beat it" as advice by a psychotherapist. In this context the sentence will be true even if each farmer does not beat all of his donkeys. The context forces a reading in which the antecedent *if*-clause functions as a stage topic for the consequent. Metaphorically, if a farmer has a donkey on the "stage" with him, the psychotherapist says it would be good for him to beat it. The universal reading in which a farmer who owns more than one donkey necessarily beats them all, would follow if the antecedent is interpreted as an individual topic, namely a donkey-owning farmer. In that case the interpretation would be that a donkey-owning farmer has the property of beating his donkeys, i.e., all of them. In the consequent *beat* is a stage-level predicate.

As discussed in chapter 1, stage-level predicates occur in two different f-structures: one in which the topic is a stage, the other in which it is an individual. (80) therefore has two different f-structures: the ∀ reading is represented in (82), and the ∃ reading in (83):

(82)   If [a farmer owns a donkey]$_{TOP}$ [he beats it]$_{FOC}$

(83)   If [a farmer owns a donkey]$_{sTOP}$ [he beats it]$_{FOC}$

First I am assuming that propositions form topics, both individual topics as in (82) and stage topics as in (83). An individual topic is formed from a proposition by the subordinate f-structure (and resulting subordinate update) as I show in detail below. A proposition may form a stage topic interpreted as the stage defined by the proposition, i.e., the stage upon which the situation defined by the proposition takes place.[31]

In (82), the *if*-clause provides an individual topic, i.e., the consequent receives an individual-level interpretation with respect to the antecedent. This f-structure derives the ∀ reading in which quantification is over individual donkey-owning farmers. In (83) the *if*-clause provides a stage topic. It follows from this f-structure, together with the idea that quantification is over topics, that the ∃ is derived by quantification over stages composed by placing a unique farmer with a unique donkey on stage.

Let us examine the details of how this works for (82). Note first that the antecedent in the conditional functions as a topic (in this case an individual topic) with respect to which the consequent is assessed. It follows from the fact that these conditionals include only indefinites that the individual antecedent topic must be a generic one. The f-structure in (82) thus consists of an individual generic topic which has the internal f-structure in (84). This will be a subordinate f-structure since the antecedent is not assessed by itself.

(84)   a farmer$_{TOP-sub}$ [owns a donkey]$_{FOC-sub}$

The function of subordinate update is only to construct and rearrange cards. Since the topic is indefinite, it must be generic. We therefore have a topic card with the following heading:

(85)   farmer [e owns donkey]

The subordinate focus "owns a donkey" also triggers the construction of a new card with the generic heading in (86):

(86)   donkey [farmer owns e]

Singular generics are assessed with respect to an arbitrary representative member of the relevant generic kind, in this case any instance of (85). This farmer may have one donkey, two donkeys or many donkeys. If more than one donkey is owned, the consequent will apply to them all, since the object of "beating" is defined by (86).

How does the f-structure assigned derive the ∀ reading for (81) (repeated in (87))?

(87)   Every man who owned a slave, owned its offspring.

The antecedent clause presents us with a slave-owning-man. But here (in view of the individual-level predicate in the consequent) the consequent is interpreted as a property, not of a stage, but of an individual. So we get the interpretation that it is a property of a slave-owning man that he owns slave offspring. Why don't we get a unique slave? Well, this is because there is no stage upon which a unique slave, or any slave for that matter, will appear. Due to its f-structure, which cannot have a stage as the antecedent, an individual-level consequent blocks the existential interpretation. The f-structure assigned will therefore be:

(88)   Every[man$_{TOP-sub}$ [who owned a slave]$_{FOC-sub}$]$_{TOP}$ [owned its offspring]$_{FOC}$

The ∀ reading is generated from this f-structure as follows: the function of subordinate update is to construct and rearrange cards. Since the topic is indefinite, it must be generic. We therefore have a topic card with the unindexed entry "man." The predicate "own a slave" is entered on the generic card for "man." Subordinate f-structures on generics, as argued in section 2.1, define new generics, subsets of the original ones, in this case the set of slave-owning men. The new card generated by subordinate update therefore has the heading "slave-owning man". The sentence is now assessed with respect to an arbitrary slave-owning man$_i$. This man may have no slaves, one slave or many slaves. The sentence itself is *not* only about men who own unique slaves, and if more than one slave is owned, the consequent will apply to them all, rendering the universal reading. According to the f-structure (88), the card with the heading "slave-owning man" provides the main topic card and *every* will range over this topic, selecting a representative arbitrary "slave-owning man$_i$" from the generic set for each assessment, entering "e owns its offspring" on the main topic card each time.

Appropriately, Kadmon (1990) argues for the universal reading for the sentence (her (44)):

(89)   Most women who own a dog are happy.

She argues, however, that this follows not from the individual-level predicate in the consequent but rather from a missing pronoun or definite NP in the consequent. According to Kadmon's view uniqueness follows from the occurrence of a definite anaphoric NP, rather than properties of the indefinite antecedent as claimed in section 2.1. According to the view argued for here, this interpretation is necessarily associated with individual-level consequents and, indeed, the occurrence of a pronoun in a consequent with an individual-level predicate does not change the ∀ reading:

(90)   Most women who own a dog like it.

In (90) the existential reading is not available in spite of the pronoun. None of the examples offered by Kadmon to argue her point involve individual-level predicates with the relevant pronouns included in the consequent.

Not only does the addition of a pronoun in examples with individual-level predicates in the consequent not make the existential reading available, this reading is still available in stage-level conditionals even if no pronoun is present:

(91)   Every man who sees a snake, runs for his life/runs away.

My predictions thus differ from Kadmon's in two ways: 1. I allow both readings for stage-level consequents. 2. The ∀ reading is derived as the only reading for individual-level consequents. The occurrence of pronouns in the consequent is not relevant to this issue. Most importantly (as opposed to Chierchia), I offer clear predictions for which readings are available in each case.

2.4.3.1   The f-structure of the antecedent: placing individuals on stage
Before examining the existential reading (repeated in (92)) in detail it is necessary to add some observations which involve the internal f-structure of the antecedent of the conditional.

(92)   If [a farmer owns a donkey]$_{STOP}$ [he beats it]$_{FOC}$

Chierchia gives several examples (his (6)) which, he argues, get only the ∃ reading:[32]

(93)   a. Every person who has a credit card, will pay his bill with it.
       b. Every person who has a dime will put it in the meter.
       c. Every person who has a hat will wear it to go to the stadium.

In each of the cases only one credit card, dime or hat will be used, even if more are available. The f-structure I assigned here gives this interpretation as follows: the consequent is predicated of a generic stage topic formed by the antecedent clause which places a person with a dime, say, on the stage.[33] Could the relevant person have more than one dime in his pocket? The answer is yes, but the sentence does not say anything about these "other" dimes since only one dime is asserted to be on stage. Remember that indefinites introduced onto a stage are *absolutely* unique. It follows that (93b) gets the interpretation that if the "stage" has a person with a dime on it, he puts this dime in the meter. The analysis I just gave assumes an f-structure in which the antecedent forms a stage topic for the consequent. This is possible since the consequent contains a stage-level predicate.

So far the subordinate f-structure of the antecedent has been ignored. For the existential interpretation I assumed a stage-topic antecedent, but I did not specify the subordinate f-structure of this antecedent. Assume that the internal f-structure of the antecedent also involves a stage topic. This would give us the complex f-structure outlined in (94):

(94) $[sTOP [\ldots]_{FOC}]_{sTOP} [\ldots]_{FOC}$

The subordinate f-structure would put *one* person and *one* dime on stage. This stage then provides the stage topic for the consequent.

Heim's problematic bishop example (her (23)) can be assigned the same f-structure:

(95)   If a bishop meets another man he blesses him.

The problem raised by this example is that the "other" man could be a bishop too. (Heim calls this the "problem of indistinguishable participants.") If the "other" man is also a bishop we would have a stage in which this man counts as a bishop and the bishop plays the role of "other man." This would also fit the subordinate f-structure of the antecedent, requiring a blessing to take place. Here we get the appropriate interpretation by deriving two separate stages, each with its separate blessing. This is intuitively satisfactory.

In principle, an individual topic should also be available for the sentences in (93) as it is for any stage-level predicate. Why does the universal reading then seem to be blocked? Note that slight alterations of the context of (93b), for example, allow different readings:

(96)   a. Every kid who has a dime puts it in his piggy bank.
        b. Every man who has a dime puts it in his pocket.

(96a) can be interpreted to mean that a representative kid who has a dime puts it in his piggy bank. If he has more than one dime, they all go in the piggy bank. What happens next time the kid has a dime or more? He goes back and puts them in the piggy bank. I.e., stages can be reiterated as we saw in the "bishop" case. An f-structure which gives the correct result for (96a) is outlined in (97):

(97)   [TOP [. . .]$_{FOC}$]$_{sTOP}$ [. . .]$_{FOC}$

It works as follows: the subordinate f-structure in the antecedent identifies a dime-owning kid. (The kid is the topic and "have a dime" is predicated of him, giving the dime-owning kid as before.) But here is an innovation: this dime-owning kid (who, as you may remember, could have one or more dimes in his possession) is now placed on stage.[34] If a unique man can be placed on stage, so can a unique dime-owning kid. Nothing can prevent that. The unique dime-owning kid (who may have several dimes) now proceeds to put the dimes he brought with him on stage into his piggy bank. What happens next time said kid gets hold of a dime or two? Well, that would be another case of the same stage type and the operation of putting the dimes into the piggy bank will be repeated.

(96b) can mean that a dime-owning man has the property of always keeping his stock of dimes in his pocket. This is the f-structure outlined in (98):

(98)   [TOP [. . .]$_{FOC}$]$_{TOP}$ [. . .]$_{FOC}$

Here an individual dime-owning man is taken to form the individual topic of the consequent. This is the individual-level reading usually open to stage-level predicates (given the right context) and the *only* f-structure open to individual-level predicates. If the consequent contains a stage-level predicate, all three f-structures will be available. If, however, the consequent contains an individual-level predicate, the stage-topic reading will be blocked, since individual-level predicates must take individual topics. All the examples in which the $\exists$ reading is available have stage-level predicates in the consequent. In these cases, context will determine which of the three possible readings we get, although all three readings are in principle possible. The reason the "piggy bank" context allows for a different f-structure from the parking meter is that it is assumed that, whereas the kid will naturally deposit his dimes in his piggy bank whenever he has any, this would be an unnatural relationship to have with a parking meter. Similarly, it is possible to envision that someone might have the property of keeping dimes in his/her pocket, whereas someone else, for example, has the habit of keeping them in a wallet.

I have made the assumption that f-structure is contextually restricted. When several f-structures are available in a particular context, each f-structure will generate a different reading. The preferred reading will in turn be determined by world knowledge. I do not take a stand here on how such world knowledge interfaces with semantic structure, although in principle a file system, which accesses cards with entries representing available world knowledge, could provide a plausible framework for this task.

Finally it is important to note that (99) is not a possible f-structure:

(99)   *[sTOP$_t$ [. . . .]$_{FOC}$]$_{TOP}$ [. . .]$_{FOC}$

(100) illustrates a case in which the consequent is individual level, and the antecedent is most naturally interpreted as a stage (otherwise we'd create an individual man who has the habit of bumping into women), i.e., the f-structure in (99) must be assigned to it:

(100)   *If a man bumps into a woman, he loves her.

This f-structure must be ruled out:[35] To get an interpretation for it, we must "type shift" a stage into an individual. The reverse type shifting was done by taking an individual and placing it on a stage. I cannot imagine any way to make an individual into a stage. This mechanism is therefore not available, correctly ruling out the f-structure in (99).[36]

2.4.3.2   Asymmetries
Kadmon (1990) recognizes both symmetric and asymmetric readings of donkey sentences such as the following:

(101)   a. Mostly, if a woman owns a dog, she is happy.
         b. Mostly, if a woman meets a dog, she is happy.
         c. Mostly, if a woman OWNS a dog, she talks to it.

Kadmon claims that in (101a) the asymmetric reading is dominant. The other two examples only receive symmetric readings due to the choice of verb and prosodic clues. The asymmetric reading of (101a) goes as follows: the sentence is true if, for most dog-owning women, the woman is happy. This is the same reading we get in

(102)   Most women who own a dog are happy.

According to Kadmon, in these asymmetric cases, quantification is over the subject and the predicate specifies a property of the woman. Kadmon calls the element quantified over the "boss" and the predicate the "dependent." It should be quite clear by now that the relevant notions should be Topic and Focus, respectively. Moreover, our theory accounts for the distribution of symmetric and asymmetric readings in Kadmon's examples. In (101a) the antecedent contains an asymmetric individual-level predicate for which the most straightforward f-structure takes the subject as a topic and the predicate as the focus. (The only other option would be to take the object to be the topic.) This matches Kadmon's analysis. In (101b) the stage-level predicate allows for a stage-level topic which in turn gives us the symmetric reading, which follows, in this case, since quantification is over "stages" i.e., situations for which the whole conditional clause holds. Finally, (101c) comes out symmetric due to the subordinate f-structure of which the object is the topic as we saw in chapter 1, section 1.6.3.1. The truth value of conditionals is thus determined according to the subordinate topic inside the antecedent.

In view of the fact that there are two general f-structures available for donkey sentences, one in which the antecedent plays the role of a stage topic and another in which the antecedent is an individual-level topic, it is necessary to see how these two f-structures interact with the different internal f-structures of the antecedent. In order to simplify matters, I will start with a case which is f-structurally unambiguous. This is the case with a relative clause antecedent and an individual-level consequent. Relative clauses, as discussed in chapter 1, form subordinate f-structures on their heads. This excludes a stage topic for these cases and, as recognized by Kadmon, allows only an asymmetric reading.

Chierchia (1992a) recognizes that asymmetric readings follow from topic selection and that quantification is over topics. His Dynamic Type Theory (DTT) operates on structures which are T-marked (for topics). Chierchia's system therefore has some form of f-structure built into it. My purpose here is to argue that an account of the phenomena dealt with here falls out of a well-developed theory of f-structure, which is independently necessary. Distinguishing f-structure properties from pure semantic properties allows both components to remain maximally simple. I am not able to discuss the details of DTT here. Neither is this the place to review all the contributions to the discussion of the various problems involved with donkey anaphora. I refer the reader to Chierchia and Heim (1989), who review many of these contributions.

2.4.3.3 Anaphora in donkey sentences

It is now time to worry about the details of the anaphoric links. I illustrate with examples (87) with the universal reading and (93b) with the existential reading, repeated below:

(103) a. Every man who owned a slave, owned its offspring.
       b. Every person who has a dime will put it in the meter.

In (103), the subordinate f-structure in the antecedent forms a new generic card, which, as specified in section 2.1, is the subgenus defined by the predicate. This is how we got the slave-owning man. In order for the truth value of the sentence to be determined, the predication rule applies and update results in an entry on an arbitrary representative topic card as follows:

> **man$_i$ [owns a slave]**
>
> **he$_i$ owns its offspring**

The pronoun "he" in the consequent is licensed, according to coreference licensing, since its index matches the heading of the arbitrarily chosen topic card and it correctly refers to an arbitrary slave-owning man. The "slave" pronoun "it," is similarly not problematic. The object ("a slave") in the subordinate focus constituent triggers the selection of the generic card for *slave*. In section 2.2 I argued that such "subordinate" cards are *attached* to the topic cards of their main predication for reasons having to do with the life-span of subordinately introduced referents:

> man$_i$ [owns a slave] $\rightarrow$ slave$_i$ [man$_i$ owns t]
>
>   he$_i$ owns it$_i$s offspring
>
> he$_i$ owns it$_j$s offspring

The card on the left defines the main topic for verification. The entry made on the main card is copied onto the attached card which therefore represents an arbitrary member of the genus man-owned-slave. Update enables each pronoun to be interpreted in accordance with the heading of their respective cards. *It* will therefore take as its antecedent any arbitrary slave owned by man$_i$.[37]

The following cards illustrate the existential case with the stage topic (see the f-structure in (94)):

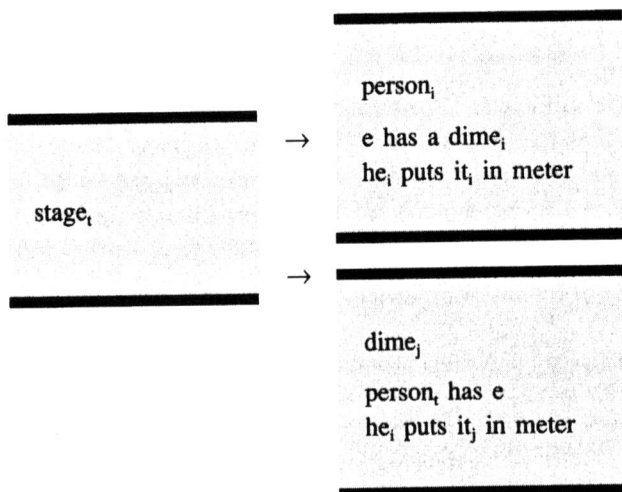

The "person" card and the "dime" card are both attached cards as before, but here they are introduced by predication of a stage topic. This means that there is no way to get person-owned dimes or dime-owning persons. These could only be derived by f-structures with individuals as topics. Instead, according to absolute uniqueness, one representative of each is placed on stage. Once our representative $person_i$ and $dime_j$ cards are available on stage, the pronouns in the consequent get their indices from these cards according to the coreference principle. The sentence is assessed as true if for each arbitrary stage t, in which a person has a dime, the person will put the dime in the meter.

This chapter concluded with an account of the various interpretations of donkey sentences. I showed that the distinction between absolute uniqueness (relevant to stages) and discourse uniqueness (relevant to objects predicated of individuals) is what explains the occurrence of both the existential and the universal reading of donkey sentences. I have also shown that coreference explains donkey anaphora. Donkey sentences have provided an excellent test case for the f-structure-theoretical discourse theory argued for here.

3 Negation, questions, and contrast[1]

The main purpose of this chapter is to analyze negation in terms of f-structure and to show that many well-known issues concerning negation receive a natural explanation once the array of f-structures associated with negative sentences has been elucidated. Among the issues to be discussed are sentential negation (does it exist?), the distribution of *any* and association with focus. To clarify the particular f-structural properties of negative sentences, it is useful to demonstrate their interaction with questions. I therefore analyze questions in terms of f-structure in this chapter as well. I conclude by showing what it is "affective" operators have in common.

3.1   Negation

Horn (1985, 1989) distinguishes three kinds of negation: Predicate denial, term negation and metalinguistic negation. Here, these distinctions are made in terms of the f-structure assigned to the negative sentence allowing for a simple analysis of negation itself, i.e., I uphold a uniform interpretation of the negation marker in all cases. This does not deny the possibility of languages that distinguish different negation markers for each kind of f-structure.

3.1.1   Term negation

The effect of negation on the filing system will be examined first. Examine (1):

(1)   Peter isn't bald.

If the subject of (1) is taken as its topic (i.e., we are talking about Peter and his card with the index 1 is on top of the file), then all B has to do is to add the entry "e_1 is not bald" to the card.

Peter₁

e is not bald

I have treated (1) in the same way as its nonnegative counterpart and it is therefore assigned the following f-structure:

(2)   Peter$_{TOP}$ is [not-bald]$_{FOC}$

No previous context is assumed (beyond the necessity for "Peter" having been introduced and placed on top of the file). The sentence is assessed as any nonnegative sentence. If it is assessed as true a new entry will be made to the effect that "e isn't bald." Negative affixes form the same negation type. The analysis would be no different if the predicate were "unhappy." Term negation is of little interest here in that it does not interact in any interesting way with f-structure. I will therefore not discuss the constraints on term negation here.[2]

3.1.2   *Predicate denial*
Another likely context for (1) is as an answer to a yes/no question such as the following (any other context that sets up the cards in a similar way would do):

(3)   Is Peter BALD?

This question can be answered either *yes*, or *no* (as in (1)). In choosing one of these answers, A not only asserts baldness or nonbaldness of Peter, he also eliminates the other possibility from consideration. I have here adopted Ryle's "elimination-within-a-disjunctive set" analysis of negation reported by Horn (1989). Note that the reply "Peter is bald" is totally parallel to the negative answer. In the context of a yes/no question, there is no difference between assertions and negations – in each case one of the two possibilities is eliminated by the answer. The difference between negation and assertion lies in the fact that negations of this sort are limited to a yes/no context, whereas assertions are not.

How is this fact formalized in our filing system? Let us look at B's file at the point he asks (3). His card for Peter₁ is on the top of his file and it looks as follows:

$$\text{Peter}_1$$
$$\text{e} \begin{Bmatrix} \text{is bald} \\ \text{is not bald} \end{Bmatrix}$$

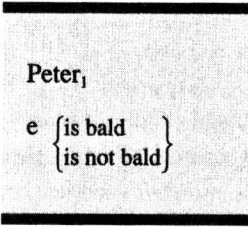

The curly brackets indicate a disjunctive set. B's question arises due to the presence of this disjunction, in which each member of the set contradicts the other. A's (1) eliminates the positive option and leaves B with a well-formed entry on his card. Here, negation operates on a restrictive set (contained in the curly brackets) and eliminates one member of this set. The f-structure of (1) assigns the subject to the topic and the VP to the focus. The operations on the file are:

1. the card with the relevant topic heading is selected (according to the topic rule).
2. rather than making an entry on this card, the card is scanned for an existing entry that can be eliminated.

I.e., with a negative predicate we do not assert the truth of the negative statement, but instead *eliminate the parallel positive statement from consideration*. This reading for negative sentences requires an assumed yes/no question in the context, represented on the card by two (contradictory) entries, one of which will be eliminated. A card in this state is referred to here as a card in a state of disequilibrium. The f-structure for this reading is complex. It involves a subordinate f-structure in which $Peter_1$ is the topic and the VP is focused, but in the main f-structure, the whole sentence functions as the topic and the focus is the negative element itself. Evidence for this view of the f-structure of negative sentences is the fact that the answers to yes/no questions generally take the form of either *yes* or *no*, rather than a complete sentence. If the sentence as a whole (minus the negative element) is taken as the main topic and if we assume that topics need not be reiterated in question–answer pairs, then it is predicted that the negative element "No" will suffice to answer the question. (Similarly, "Yes" suffices in case the answer to the yes/no question is positive.) The f-structure assigned to answers to yes/no questions thus explains their form.

The truth conditions for predicate denial in which a disjunction is set up between the positive and negative predicate are the following: the sentence is assessed as FALSE in exactly those cases in which the positive sentence would be assessed as TRUE or vice versa, it is assessed as TRUE in those cases in which the positive sentence would be assessed as FALSE.

Another context type can also produce predicate denial. Assume that Joan went out for the evening and that she planned to either go to the movies, have coffee with a friend or go eat pizza. In this context if someone were asked about Joan's evening, the answer might be:

(4)   Joan didn't go to the movies.

This answer, by eliminating the possibility that Joan went to the movies, leaves two of the three options still open. Note that without a restrictive context, i.e., a context in which two or more options are assumed, predicate denial is not possible. An overt or implied alternative question is required. (4), for example, cannot be an answer to

(5)   What did Joan do last night?

unless some restrictive context is conjured up. Since the context is duly entered in the file, the eliminative function of negation is not hard to represent in the file discourse theory defined here.

In an example in which a subconstituent of the predicate is focused, the restrictive set is formed with the focus constituent as one of its members:[3]

(6)   Joan didn't eat the PIZZA.

Again a restrictive set is contextually required. A possible context would again be a yes/no question. Another possible context follows: Joan's brother prepared a meal which included pizza and several other delicacies. (6) eliminates "pizza" as a member of the set of foods that Joan may or may not have eaten rendering the following f-structure:

(7)   Joan$_{\text{TOP}}$ didn't [eat $\left[\begin{array}{l} \left[\begin{array}{l} \text{[the PIZZA]}_{\text{FOC}} \\ \left\{ \begin{array}{l} \text{delicacy}_1 \\ \text{delicacy}_2 \end{array} \right\} \end{array} \right]_{\text{TOP}} \end{array} \right]_{\text{FOC}}$

Negation, in each of these cases, functions to eliminate one of the members of a restrictive set. The restrictive set is constructed on the focused constituent of the negative utterance forming a subordinate f-structure in which the implicit subordinate topic is the contextually specified restrictive set and the overt focus represents the negated member of this set. This is what it means for negation to be "associated" with the focus. In section 3.3, I show how negative polarity *any* interacts with restrictive sets.

3.1.3   Negation and stage topics

An issue which arises repeatedly in discussions of negation is whether there is such a thing as sentential negation. (Horn (1989) reports on a variety of views on this issue.) Sentence negation translated into focus theoretical terminology would mean that the negative sentence would be assessed with respect to a stage topic. This type of reading is generally blocked. Take, for example, the f-structure

(8)   sTOP$_t$ [The United States didn't invade Iraq]$_{FOC}$

which is interpreted as follows: "It is false (or not a property) of a certain time/place that the U.S. invaded Iraq." This kind of statement is pragmatically odd in that a stage is generally not characterized by a certain event *not* taking place there.

For restrictive negation, one would have to assume that the constantly available stage topic card has on it a disjunctive entry consisting of the positive and negative versions of the focus constituent, i.e., the whole sentence. This state of affairs arises only in the case of metalinguistic negation to be discussed in section 3.3 below in which the restrictions on this construction are defined.

There are cases, however, for which negated sentences have stage topics. The following are relevant illustrations:

(9)   a. It isn't snowing.
           b. The King of France isn't sitting in the chair to your right. (Horn 1989: 488)

Sentence (9a) can only be assessed as a predication of a stage topic. No other topic is available for assessment. (9b) can be assessed as predicate denial, but also as predication of a stage. Horn says of (9b): "if I note that the designated chair is empty, I am far less inclined to grant that you have presupposed the existence of the King of France." In f-structural terms, the locational phrase provides the stage topic of which the rest of the sentence is predicated. These cases all exemplify restrictive negation in which the whole sentence is negated, i.e., eliminated from the relevant stage card. This is evidenced by the fact that these sentences cannot be asserted out-of-the-blue as an answer to "What's happening?". They are restricted to the context of a yes/no question or the equivalent. In cases which have an overt stage topic, or with weather verbs that must be interpreted with a stage topic, so-called sentential negation may occur. This is because the predicate and the sentence are coextensive.

Zucchi (1990) makes a similar point. He argues that negative sentences have much in common with statives. Most negative sentences are blocked from occurring in *while*-clauses as are statives ((10a) is from Zucchi (his (3b)):

(10)   a. ??While Mary didn't eat the cake, John washed the dishes.
       b. *While Mary knew French, John washed the dishes.
       c.   While Mary was sleeping, John washed the dishes.

(10b and c) exemplify a stative and nonstative *while*-clause, respectively. Let us assume, with Zucchi, that negated sentences "do not describe an eventuality" (p. 21). In our terms this would mean that a negated sentence cannot be predicated of a stage, nor can it define one. If it is assumed further that a *while*-clause introduces a new stage, providing a topic for the rest of the sentence, it follows that a negated sentence is akin to a stative in that it cannot constitute such a clause. Zucchi notes the following exception to this generalization (his (25)):

(11)   While John wasn't at home, Mary washed the dishes.

Note that the locative provides an overt stage topic as above, and the sentence can therefore be predicated of it.[4] The weather verbs predictably are also licensed here:

(12)   While it wasn't raining, Mary took a walk.

Negative sentences with stage topics are therefore limited to a small well-defined class of predicates. A reviewer suggests that the well-known example due to Partee refers to a particular situation:

(13)   I didn't turn off the stove.

Since (13) is an appropriate response to *What happened?*, an f-structure with a stage topic should indeed be appropriate. Note, however, that (13) does not communicate what happened, but rather indicates to the hearer the *cause* of a possible (disastrous) event. Further, the sentence cannot be assessed as true or false by examining the situation defined by the spatio-temporal parameters of the stage. This type of negative sentence can therefore not be assigned a (main) f-structure with a stage topic.

The f-structure of negative sentences is restricted further as indicated by the following examples:

(14)   a. *A man doesn't like Mary.
       b. *A man didn't read the book.
       c. *A man hadn't arrived.
       d. *A man wasn't available.

The fact that (nongeneric, noncontrastive) indefinite subjects are blocked in negative sentences indicates that the subject, in these cases, must be assigned the topic role.[5] In other words, not only can't negative sentence be predicated of implicit stage topics (except for weather verbs), the object is not a possible topic with negation either. We will see that the same constraints on f-structure hold for sentences with *only* as well. In chapter 6 this asymmetry is accounted for by regarding negation and *only* as operators that form I-dependencies. There a constraint on I-dependencies (including multiple *wh*-dependencies, binding dependencies, and *wh*-trace dependencies) is formulated which blocks object topics.

3.2   *Wh*-questions: two f-structures

It is well known that the predication rule, when applied to *wh*-questions, cannot involve assessment for truth values. Instead it can be viewed as an instruction to fill in those individuals for which the predication would come out true. In other words predication "interprets" *wh*-questions as asking for the values of some variable x, such that those values will make for a true assertion. The following gives a formalization of the predication rule for *wh*-questions:

(15)   a. What did Sue eat t?
        b. $(?x) \{x | P_x (Sue_1)\}$

Let us briefly examine how the formalization in (15b) relates to the filing system model. (15b) "asks" for the values of x, such that P (of x) (of Sue) is true, where P_x indicates that the predicate is parameterized by x. (15b) assumes a context in which *Sue* is the topic of (15a). P_x indicates that the predicate has a variable in it. The state of the speaker's file as he asks (15a) is that on top of his file is the following card:

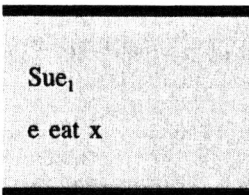

The speaker's card is in a similar state of disequilibrium as it was when he asked question (3), but he is in even worse shape, because instead of a set of options of which he must select one, the range of x is unlimited, restricted only to edibles. The hearer is asked to fill in the value of x. The variable x is "located" by reconstruction to *wh*-t position.[6] I have argued elsewhere (Erteschik-Shir (1973), Erteschik-Shir (1979) etc.) that such variables are limited to constituent positions which allow (nonrestrictive) focus interpretation. We can now reformalize this idea to say that parameterization necessitates reconstruction to the position of the trace and reconstruction is limited to focus-internal positions.[7] Reconstruction depends on f-structure and feeds the rule of predication. I therefore argue that it is a semantic rule. The constraints on reconstruction, I argue in chapter 6, account for the restrictions on *wh*-movement.

There exists an alternative interpretation of (15a) in which the *wh*-word is taken to be the topic of f-structure:

(16) $(?x) \{x| P (x)\}$

(16) asks for the values of x, such that P of x is true. The topic is identified with the *wh*-phrase, i.e., x must range over a restrictive set. Under this interpretation the top of B's card file has a set of (attached) cards, each headed with a different kind of "food." The following card illustrates such a card:

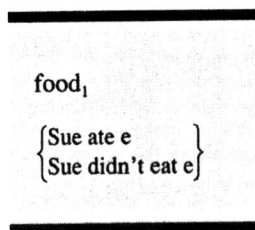

food$_1$

$$\begin{cases} \text{Sue ate e} \\ \text{Sue didn't eat e} \end{cases}$$

A's answer will allow B to eliminate one member of the disjunctive set on each card included in the set.

It follows that (15a) is ambiguous in that it can be asked in both restrictive and nonrestrictive contexts. Individual-level predicates with only one argument allow only the restrictive interpretation of *wh*-questions. Compare:

(17)   a. ?Who is intelligent?
        b. Who is available?

(17a) receives an interpretation only if the context makes available a restrictive set of *who*s and the question asks for a partitioning of this set into intelligent and nonintelligent individuals. This type of question is a request to decide for each individual student in the topic set, whether or not s/he is intelligent. In effect we get a list of yes/no questions, one for each individual within the set. Without a context, in which a set of students is defined, the question makes no sense. *Who* differs from indefinites such as *a man* in that it allows for a contextually specified referent. Note that replacing *who* with *which students* or *which one of your students* improves the question considerably:

(18)   a. Which students are intelligent?
         b. Which one of your students is intelligent?

These partitive question forms make overt the context set and the fact that a partitioning of this set is called for. They involve subordinate update in which a set of students is the topic, and the subordinate f-structure triggers a scanning of this set.

This view of the interpretation of questions, as well as the distinction between two question types, was inspired by Frampton (pers. com., 1991, 1992). According to Frampton, traces can be interpreted either via chains or as variables in operator-variable structures. The former case is represented in (15b), the latter in (16).

3.2.1   Negative wh-*questions*

We are now ready to examine negative *wh*-questions. But first I'd like to take you on a trip to Greece and back. Imagine that upon your return I ask you:

(19)   What did you see on your trip?

It is very likely that you will answer by giving me a list (probably partial) of the things you saw. Imagine now that, instead of (19), I ask you the question in (20a):

(20)   a. What didn't you see on your trip?
         b. Which sights didn't you see on your trip?
         c. Which of the famous sights you were told to see didn't you see on your trip?

In order for you to answer (20a) at all, you must assume that, in asking you this question, I have some expectation or knowledge concerning the relevant sights that you either intended to see, or that are generally seen by tourists to Greece. If you answer:

(21)   I didn't see the Parthenon.

then *the Parthenon* is eliminated from the set of sights under discussion. The sights you didn't see on your trip to Greece must therefore necessarily be interpreted as a subset of the sights you were expected to see. There is no interpretation for (20a) unless such a set of sights is invoked. It turns out that focusing and *wh*-questioning have the same effect in negated sentences, they force a restrictive set reading. In order to answer a restrictive *wh*-question, it is necessary to scan this restrictive set and to partition it into two subsets according to whether the negative or positive option in the disjunctive set is to be eliminated. It follows that negative questions can only be interpreted as in (16) above. (Often so-called d-linked *wh*-phrases, such as "which-N," "which of the-N" in (20b and c), are used to ensure the restrictive reading of the question.) One could probe a little further into this phenomenon and ask how the question in (20a) could make sense without the restrictive set context. Without such a context (20a) would be asking for the elimination of members of an infinite set. Any answer would leave one with an equally infinite set of possibilities, a situation Grice, for one, would be quite unhappy with.[8]

A good illustration of a restrictive context is a rhetorical question or a test question situation. An example (from an anonymous reviewer) follows:

(22)   A: What doesn't dissolve in water?
        B: OIL doesn't dissolve in water.
           OIL doesn't.
           OIL.

Here the existence of a set of correct answers (possibly consisting of only one) is contextually specified. What A is asking is whether B can produce this set. *What* in the question thus ranges over this set and a correct answer such as B's produces part or all of this set. The subordinate f-structure of B's answer again selects a subordinate focus from a discourse-specified topic set:

(23) $$\left[\begin{Bmatrix} [\text{oil}]_{FOC} \\ \text{everything else} \end{Bmatrix} \right]_{TOP}$$

It is plausible that this question type belongs to the category of metalinguistic phenomena to be discussed in section 3.5.

What I have established so far is that *wh*-questioning in negative sentences is limited to what I refer to as restrictive questioning, i.e., the question involves a request for the partitioning of an existing topic set. I therefore predict that *wh*-questioning over negation will be blocked if

   a) the questioned constituent cannot be a topic and
   b) no context set is available for partitioning.

I return to this issue in chapter 6.[9]

3.3   Focus on *any*

In Kadmon and Landman (1993), the following generalization is made concerning the function of *any*:

(A)   *any CN* = the corresponding indefinite NP *a CN* with additional semantic/ pragmatic characteristics (widening, strengthening) contributed by *any*.

FC (Free Choice) *any*, according to Kadmon and Landman, is treated in the same way, but receives a generic interpretation. They offer the following illustrations (their (26), (28)):

(24)   a. I don't have potatoes.
       b. I don't have any potatoes.

(25)   a. An owl hunts mice.
       b. Any owl hunts mice.

They argue that what *any* contributes to the meaning of the indefinites is a "reduced tolerance of exceptions." In (24), for example, rotten potatoes may be excluded from consideration in (a), but not in (b). Similarly, for sick owls in (25). This is what is meant by widening. *Any* contributes this widening along some contextual dimension. If the context implies that the potatoes are needed for cooking, rotten potatoes are indeed irrelevant and may not even be included, even in the example with *any*. The widening incurred by *any* is along some contextually defined dimension. The f-structures of the two sentences in (24) follow. They differ only in the effect of *any* on the restrictive focus set:

(26)   a. I_{TOP} don't [have $\left[\left\{\begin{matrix} \text{potatoes} \\ \text{"other" potatoes} \end{matrix}\right\}\right]_{TOP}$ $]_{FOC}$

       b. I_{TOP} don't [have *any* $\left[\left\{\begin{matrix} \text{potatoes} \\ \text{"other" potatoes} \end{matrix}\right\}\right]_{TOP}$ $]_{FOC}$

In (26a) "potatoes" are eliminated from the restrictive set, leaving the potential for having "other" irrelevant potatoes. The function of *any* (following Kadmon and Landman), eliminates *both* members of the restrictive set. "Other" potatoes, depending on context, can be "rotten" potatoes, "sweet" potatoes, etc. Focusing on *any* has an interesting effect. When *any* itself is stressed, the effect is to eliminate *all* "other" potatoes, i.e., elimination occurs along all contextual dimensions, leaving no possible exceptions. *Any* can thus be seen as an operator which effects the elimination of the "other" member of the restrictive set available in negative sentences. When *any* itself is focused, the "other" is no longer contextually limited and *any* effects the elimination of all possible contextual extensions. The analysis of negation as providing restrictive sets of the sort illustrated in (26) provides a natural way of incorporating Kadmon and Landman's view of the function of *any* into the f-structure model developed here. It also explains why PS (Polarity Sensitive) *any* occurs under negation.[10]

It has frequently been noted that an indefinite in the scope of negation does not set up a discourse referent:

(27)   Sue didn't eat any PIZZA. *It was delicious.

A focused indefinite normally triggers the construction of a new card in the file. However, due to negation, the instruction here is to eliminate an entry on a card, *not* to open a new one which would be necessary for the continuation of (27).

Specific indefinites introduced in the scope of negation *do* set up discourse referents. The following example from Carlson (1977: 19) illustrates this:

(28)   John didn't see a (particular) spot on the floor.
        It was tiny.

The continuation is possible only if the speaker has a particular spot in mind. The f-structure of the specific reading involves an implicit subordinate f-structure as argued in the previous chapters. It is this subordinate f-structure which allows for the construction of a new card. Once the new card is constructed and positioned on top of the file, further reference to it is possible since subordinate update operates independently of the elimination of the positive entry on the card.

Kadmon and Landman's idea that Free Choice *any* is generic is based on the observation that this *any* has the same distribution as generics. These are here viewed as cases in which *any* operates on the topic constituent. Since topics necessarily provide restrictive sets, they provide the proper environment for *any* to operate on. Indefinite topics must receive a generic interpretation according to the definition of topics given in chapter 1. Viewing Kadmon and Landman's analysis of *any* within a f-structural framework thus provides further evidence for their analysis that there is only one *any*. It also provides another argument in favor of the f-structural framework argued for here.

3.4   *Only* or *Even*: association with focus[11]

3.4.1   Only

Taglicht (1984) assigns three different interpretations to the following example, although he assumes a unique f-structure for it, in which the underlined constituent is the focus:

(29)   John only <u>phoned Mary</u>.
     a. He took no other action. (*only* has scope over the VP)
     b. He phoned no one else.
        (*only* has scope over the NP, MARY is stressed.)
     c. He did not write to her for example.
        (*only* has scope over the V, PHONED is stressed)

Taglicht claims that there are two types of focus, a syntactic–semantic one and a contextual–pragmatic one. In (29) the syntactic focus is the VP, but *only* is associated with the pragmatic focus as indicated in (a)–(c). In (29b) the pragmatic focus is narrowed due to the backgrounding of the verb. Similarly, in (29c) the NP is backgrounded, and the verb is left as the pragmatic focus. The pragmatic focus is also what determines the intonation.

Selkirk (1984) discusses examples similar to Taglicht's, and calls his pragmatic foci, embedded foci. The embedded focus is contained in a focused constituent in which the remaining constituents are old. Selkirk would assign the same f-structure to (29b) as Taglicht did, since all three interpretations answer the question: "What did John do?" She would consider the NP an embedded focus, and the V-constituent old information. Selkirk's view is thus identical to Taglicht's.

Rooth (1985) introduces the notion of p-sets: the sets of alternatives under consideration in the discourse. This set of alternatives is defined by replacing the focused constituent with a variable. The set of alternatives under consideration in (29b) would be:

(30)   John phoned y
     y ranges over a set of individuals under consideration in the discourse.

And its interpretation, according to Rooth, would be:

(31)   If a proposition of the form "John phoned y" is true, then it is the proposition "John phoned Mary."

Similarly, (29c) would get the interpretation (see Rooth 1985: 43)

(32) $\forall Q[[Q\{j\} \ \& \ C(Q)] \rightarrow Q = \text{phone}']$

where C is the characteristic function of the set of relevant properties distinct from phone$'$. *Only* thus quantifies over a contextually relevant set. This agrees with Taglicht's interpretation, giving "write" as an example of a member of this contextually relevant set.

Let me start with (29b and c). Both answer the question:

(33)   What did John do?

Hence they both have the f-structure:

(34)   [John]$_{TOP}$ [only phoned Mary]$_{FOC}$[12]

If both sentences have the same f-structure then they should not have different interpretations. Neither should they have different intonation patterns. Clearly, there must be more to it. Note that the interpretation for (29b) is:

(35)   John phoned $\begin{cases} \text{Mary} \\ \text{no one else.} \end{cases}$

i.e., the sentence will only be true if it is true that "John phoned Mary," and that "John phoned nobody else," i.e. the "silent" member of the set {Mary, everyone else} is eliminated. Taglicht (1984) argues that both these propositions are in effect asserted. Horn (1969) claims that the proposition *John phoned Mary* is presupposed and the assertion is *John phoned no one else*. Here I propose that what is presupposed is the existence of a context-specified set which *only* operates on. I assume that only the overt predication is asserted but achieve Taglicht's effect by assigning the following f-structure to (35):

(36)   [John]$_{TOP}$ [ONLY phoned $\left[\begin{cases} [\text{Mary}]_{FOC} \\ \text{everyone else} \end{cases} \right]_{TOP}$]$_{FOC}$

(*Only* is in small capitals to indicate that it is an operator.) The set consisting of {Mary, everyone else}[13] is the topic of a subordinate f-structure, i.e., we are "talking about" *Mary* and the alternative persons. The focus of this subordinate f-structure is [Mary]$_{FOC}$, i.e., Mary is the focus of this set of alternatives (of which she is a member).[14] The operator *only* is similar to the negation operator in that it too "eliminates" a member of a restrictive set. For *only*, the eliminated member of the set is the one that is the complement to the focus, rather than the focused member of the set. With negation one member of a restrictive set is eliminated, narrowing down the number of choices by one set member. *Only* eliminates the whole complement set, fully identifying a single member of the set relevant to the application of the predication rule. Eliminating too many members of the topic set would render the sentence false. Under this analysis *only*, like *negation*, associates with a focus, namely a focus of a subordinate f-structure.

Let us now examine example (29c). Note that the interpretation should come out:

(37)   John $\begin{cases} \text{phoned Mary.} \\ \text{did nothing else (with respect to Mary)} \end{cases}$

We can now get this result, by assigning a subordinate f-structure as before. Remember that Taglicht, as well as Rooth, assume that the interpretation should be: "phoned, not wrote," or some other contextually relevant options. This aspect of the interpretation follows from the requirement that *only* must operate on a contextually defined restrictive set. The interpretation given in (37) is peculiar simply because it is unlikely that John did nothing but phone Mary in some time interval. In the following sentence it makes perfect sense that all other actions are eliminated:

(38)   John only slept.

Here, a contrastive set of "actions" could be set up too, but the sentence is interpreted naturally without it. The type of restrictive topic set is therefore dependant on context as well as the meaning of the sentence itself.

The context can also define a scaled set. Assume that among our friends it is customary to send faxes, second best is to send an e-mail message and the only thing worse than phoning is not communicating at all. In that context *only* limits the range of possibilities to the focused item and everything below it on the scale. Taglicht (1984: 92) calls this use of *only* the "limiting *only.*" If a real scalar item is focused by *only* then this function is more prominent:

(39)   He only phoned THREE friends. (no more than THREE)

This function of *only* can be defined in f-structural terms as follows: *only* operates on a restrictive set and eliminates all members of the set except the focused one. This renders the result that no more than three friends were phoned in (39), but does not exclude that "he phoned two friends" is true. The restrictive set can be formed in a variety of ways, depending on the context. This variety reflects the types of restrictive sets that can be contextually formed.

I have claimed that *only* associates with subordinate foci. A strong argument for this position can be derived from the following fact:

(40)   Only JOHN is intelligent.

I argued above that the subject of an individual-level predicate such as this one must be interpreted as the topic of the main f-structure. It follows that although the subject is stressed in (40) it cannot be the main focus of the sentence. Nothing stands in the way of a subordinate f-structure in the position of the subject, however:

(41)   ONLY $\left[\begin{bmatrix} \left\{ \begin{matrix} [\text{John}]_{\text{FOC}} \\ \text{everyone else} \end{matrix} \right\} \end{bmatrix}_{\text{TOP}} \right]_{\text{TOP}}$ [is intelligent]$_{\text{FOC}}$

Note that the main f-structure of this sentence has as its topic the set {John, everyone else}.[15] This f-structure is adequate only if the topic is a well-defined restrictive set placed on top of the file. That is why the interpretation here must involve the elimination of a set of individuals who together with *John* form a restrictive topic set. This restriction on the range of *only* is required only when the subordinate f-structure is on the main topic constituent, contrary to Rooth's claim.

Finally, *only* may associate with the whole VP as in (29a). The interpretation in this case is that "John phoned Mary and did nothing else." This is the interpretation one would get from the f-structure:

(42)   John$_{TOP}$ [only [phoned Mary]$_{FOC}$]

Since such an interpretation often makes little sense, alternate set formations are often called for.

Although *only* can associate with the subject if it precedes it, this is not the case when *only* is positioned between the subject and the VP:

(43)   *JOHN only loves her.

(44)   *JOHN only came.

(45)   *JOHN is only intelligent.

In other words, *only* is excluded from the following S-structures, respectively:

(46)   TOP$_i$ [John]$_{FOC}$ ONLY loves her$_i$

(47)   sTOP$_t$ [John ONLY came]$_{FOC}$

(48)   [[{ [John]$_{FOC}$ }]$_{TOP}$ [is ONLY intelligent]$_{FOC}$
        [{ everyone else }]$_{TOP}$

A pragmatic account might be feasible for (47) in which *only* is associated with the focused sentence and not just with the subject. (47) excludes any other activity, except for John's coming, from a certain "stage." An unlikely situation. (46) and (48), are, however, both semantically and pragmatically possible, since that is the interpretation we get when *only* precedes the subject. This interpretation must therefore be ruled out structurally. Jackendoff (1972) and Rooth (1985), among others (the latter with some hesitation), argue that *only* (as opposed to *even*) cannot be a daughter of S and therefore does not c-command the subject. In chapter 6 I apply the Subject Constraint on I-dependencies to sentences with *only*, thus providing a structural account which rules out all three problematic f-structures (46)–(48).

Partee (1975) notes that the following sentence is ambiguous, receiving both a bound variable, and pronoun-of-laziness interpretation:

(49)   Only John expected that he would win.
         a. x expected that x would win ("John" binds both variables)
         b. Only John expected that John would win.

The bound variable interpretation results from taking the topic set of the subordinate f-structure as the "antecedent" for the pronoun, i.e., "everyone." Interpretation (b) follows from taking the topic of the main f-structure (*John*) as the antecedent. The existence of the bound variable interpretation is evidence for an f-structure which includes the subordinate f-structure argued for. Partee also notes that "scalar" *only* does not result in ambiguity:

(50)   Only one man expected that he would win.

Here the subordinate update involves a scaled set out of which *one* is picked at random. The main f-structure does not provide an indexed topic antecedent for the pronoun. The main topic is the contextually defined set of men which is available as an antecedent if the pronoun is appropriately plural:

(51)   Only one man expected that they would win.

Finally, Partee argues for two different analyses of the following sentence, in spite of the fact that it is not ambiguous:

(52)   John expected that he would win.
         a. JOHN expected that he would win.
            (Who$_i$ expected that he$_i$ would win?)
         b. John expected that HE would win.
            (Who did John expect would win?)

But (52) *is* ambiguous or rather can be assigned two different f-structures, as can be seen by examining (52a and b). The stressed constituents trigger subordinate updates in which *John* and *he*, respectively, are selected from context-specified sets rendering answers to two different questions. The bound variable interpretation thus follows from an f-structure in which the main topic is focused, resulting in a subordinate update involving a context-specified set from which this topic is selected.

Taglicht (1984) gives several examples to show that *only* is scopally ambiguous in complex sentences such as the following (from Rooth (1985: 83)):

(53)   We are required to study only SYNTAX.

He notes further that this ambiguity disappears when *only* is adjoined to either of the VPs.

(54)   a. We are required to only study SYNTAX.
        b. We are only required to study SYNTAX.

The account presented here extends naturally to these facts if we assume that *only syntactically* adjoins to focus, either to the main focus or the subordinate one. (53) receives the following two f-structure analyses (only the main f-structure is shown):

(55)   a. [We]_{TOP} are required to [study ONLY SYNTAX]_{FOC}
        b. [We]_{TOP} are [required to study ONLY SYNTAX]_{FOC}

In (55a) *require* is outside the focus constituent, hence assessment is for "study only syntax." In (55b) the focus constituent includes *require*, and assessment is for the larger VP. F-structure again automatically predicts the correct scopal interpretation. No further (semantic) rules are necessary to account for these facts. The f-structures for (54a and b) are identical to the ones in (55a and b), respectively, except for the position of *only*. The syntactic position of *only* fixes which VP must be taken as the focus, as mentioned above.[16, 17]

3.4.2   Even: *interpretation and structure*
The analysis of *even* is very similar to the analysis of *only*. The meaning of *even* differs, however. *Even* operates on the exact same set defined for *only* and the f-structure for (56) is (57):

(56)   John even phoned Mary.

(57)   [John]_{TOP} [EVEN phoned $\left[\left\{ \begin{array}{l} [\text{Mary}]_{\text{FOC}} \\ \text{everyone else} \end{array} \right\}_{\text{TOP}} \right]_{\text{FOC}}$

Even operates on this set as follows: the focus [Mary]_{FOC} is again selected, but not by eliminating the other member of the set as with *only*, but instead by interpreting "Mary" as the least likely (among the members of the set {Mary, everyone else}) to be phoned by John.[18]

   Even differs from *only* in one other significant way. *Even* takes scope over the subject (compare (43)–(45)):

(58)   JOHN even loves her.

(59)   JOHN even came.

(60)   JOHN is even intelligent.

Even is therefore not excluded from the following S-structures as is *only*:

(61)   TOP$_i$ [John EVEN loves her$_i$]$_{FOC}$

(62)   sTOP$_i$ [John EVEN came]$_{FOC}$

(63) $\left[\left[\begin{Bmatrix} \text{[John]}_{FOC} \\ \text{everyone else} \end{Bmatrix} \right]_{TOP} \right.$]$_{TOP}$ [is EVEN intelligent]$_{FOC}$

I argued that the interpretation of (62) would not make sense for *only*. This is, however, not the case for *even*. With *even* the complement set is not eliminated, merely relegated to the category "more likely than the focused constituent." Therefore, the focus will not appear as the only possible entry on the relevant card, the situation argued against for *only*. The fact that all three f-structures are ruled out for *only* and licensed with *even* does not, as we have seen, receive a comprehensive pragmatic explanation. In chapter 6 I show that association with focus with *only* and negation is subject to a syntactic constraint on f-structure ruling out association with subject for these operators. This constraint does not apply to cases of association with focus involving *even*, due to the different semantic properties of this operator.[19]

Only, *even* and negation may also associate with a focused element within a topic set. In this case, however, the operator must be syntactically adjoined to the topic itself, i.e., it precedes the topic:

(64)   a. Only JOHN likes pizza.
         b. Even JOHN likes pizza.
         c. No one   like(s) pizza.
            No people
            None of my friends

(64a and b) involve a subordinate restrictive f-structure on the topic set. In (64c) the whole topic set is eliminated by the negation operator.

In view of the fact that *even* can associate with the subject both when it precedes the subject and when it follows it, the question arises as to whether the following two sentences can or must be assigned the same f-structure:

(65)   a. JOHN even likes pizza.
         b. Even JOHN likes pizza.

A variety of f-structures can be assigned here, but it seems that (65a) but not (65b) can be used as an answer to *Who likes pizza?* indicating that when *even* precedes the subject, an f-structure such as the one suggested for (64b), in which the subject forms the main topic, is required.

To summarize, the three operators under discussion associate with either the topic or the focus constituent. There is, however, an important difference between *even* and the other two operators. Although *even* operates on restrictive sets, it does not eliminate one of the members of the set, the way *only* and negation do. In section 3.4, I showed that *any* operates on restrictive sets in which one of the members is eliminated. I therefore predict that PS *any* can be triggered by *only* and negation, but not by *even*. This follows from the function of these operators as well as the function of *any* and can be seen as a basis for understanding the notion "affective" operator introduced in Klima (1964).

Although only one main f-structure is allowed per sentence, the number of subordinate ones is not limited. It should therefore be possible, to the extent that the interpretations make sense, to have more than one operator per sentence. Taglicht (1984: 168) discusses such examples:

(66)   Only Paul speaks even Mohawk.

(67)   Only John ate only rice.

I have limited the discussion of operators such as *even* and *only* here to a demonstration of the general line of analysis which follows from the theory of f-structure presented.[20]

It is now possible to point out some basic differences between Rooth's (1985, 1992) theory of focus interpretation and the one defined here. I pointed out above that Rooth (1985) introduces the notion of p-sets: the sets of alternatives under consideration in the discourse. The focus semantic value of a phrase, under this view, is "the set of propositions obtainable from the ordinary semantic value by making a substitution in the position corresponding to the focused phrase" (Rooth (1992: 76)). In von Stechow (1989a: 42), Rooth (1985) is criticized for not indicating how the alternatives under consideration in the discourse are to be restricted. Rooth (1992) uses the focus semantic value to constrain C, the domain of quantification. This makes Rooth's notion of focus equivalent to the notion of restrictive focus defined here. Most of Rooth's applications of his notion are cases which are considered restrictive here as well. There is, however, one notable exception, namely his analysis of question–answer pairs. Rooth (p. 84) argues that the function of "focus in an answer is to signal other propositions which are potential answers in the context of the question. Or if we wanted to speak in terms of contrast, we could say that focus in an answer expresses contrast between the asserted answer and other potential answers." This view of question–answer pairs would fit only the restrictive questions defined above. It seems that Rooth does not allow for nonrestrictive question–answer pairs or else he does not allow for a clear distinction between restrictive and nonrestrictive foci, a distinction I argue is semantically significant and without which an account of the constraints on *wh*-questions is not obtainable.

3.5   Metalinguistics

Horn (1985, 1989) distinguishes metalinguistic negation from regular negation. Horn (1985: 136) argues that negation is neither semantically nor scopally ambiguous, but rather pragmatically ambiguous as follows: "It can be a descriptive truth-functional operator, taking a proposition *p* into a proposition *not-p*, or a metalinguistic operator which can be glossed 'I object to *u*', where *u* is crucially a linguistic utterance rather than an abstract proposition." Metalinguistic rectification denies the *assertability* of the proposition (along with any associated implicata) conveyed in the context of the utterance. If Horn's perspective is correct we must assume a separate metalinguistic level within which logical operators are used to predicate "ABOUT the object language rather than WITHIN it" (Horn 1985: 162).

3.5.1   Metalinguistic negation
Observe the following two intonation patterns:

(68)   Bill didn't catch TWO FISH[21]

(69)   Bill didn't catch TWO FISH

(68) and (69) exemplify what has been considered to be internal and external negation respectively. What would be an appropriate context for (68)? Imagine that Bill has an aquarium with five fish in it. He needs to clean it and must catch all the fish but two of them escape.[22] (68) is fine in this context. The same sentence would be very awkward if Bill were returning from a day of fishing. But this is exactly as it should be. It follows from our claim in section 3.1.2 that only restrictive foci are licensed under negation. Sentences such as (68) are therefore good to the extent that a restrictive context can be imposed on them.

   The focus structure of (69) necessitates some further elaboration. Note first that this sentence does not render a downward entailing environment and does not license *any*:

(70)   *Bill didn't catch ANY fish, he caught three.

(69) does not entail (as does (68)) that Bill didn't catch even *one* fish. He might not have caught any. It doesn't follow, however, that the focus here is not restrictive.

(69), according to Horn, is an example of metalinguistic negation. The negation here does not negate the Proposition that Bill caught two fish. It rather functions metalinguistically to reject the implicated upper bound associated with the assertion of the proposition involving a scalar predicate (namely that Bill caught *only* two fish).[23] Horn (1989) calls cases such as these the "not X but Y" construction and describes them as involving "rectification." I argue that <not X, yes Y> form elements of a restrictive set.

In the following example, we return to "the King of France," but this time with metalinguistic negation:

(71)   The KING of FRANCE isn't BALD,
        because there is no King of France.

The intonation of this sentence, as we shall see in chapter 4, is that of an out-of-the-blue sentence, i.e., a sentence which is predicated of a stage topic. (Overlaid on this general stress pattern is also a distinct tune, also to be discussed in chapter 4.) One possibility is then that the "stage" in this case is the utterance being objected to, since the topic is the locus of all the contextual information. The interpretation of a metalinguistic utterance of (71) is:

(72)   Concerning the King of France being bald, it isn't so.

Similarly, (69) is interpreted as

(73)   Concerning Bill's catching two fish, it isn't TWO.

Metalinguistic negation has the effect of sentence negation. It is important to distinguish it from regular negation in order to account not only for the special intonation involved, but also for its semantic properties which differ from those of "regular" negation, some of which were noted above.

Another characteristic of metalinguistic negation is that it applies to parts of constituents (Horn 1989: 435):

(74)   I'm advocating PROsecution, not PERsecution.

I refer you to Horn for many more examples and diagnostics that distinguish metalinguistic from descriptive negation. Horn makes another important point, namely that there are other logical operators that function on the metalinguistic level and also on the descriptive one. Horn includes metalinguistic uses of *but*, inclusive disjunction, and conditionals. Echo-questions, according to Horn, are simply metalinguistic questions. Incredulity questions can be added to the list. In view of the fact that all the metalinguistic phenomena observed so far come with characteristic intonational patterns (see chapter 4), it is important for future research to address the issue of whether a separate metalinguistic component of f-structure should be defined.

I have adopted Horn's view which extends the notion of a metalinguistic utterance, beyond what is usually accepted, to a class of phenomena which can be associated with distinctive semantic and intonational properties. Although these phenomena form a natural class which includes phenomena that have traditionally been called "metalinguistic," it is possible that a more appropriate term than the one suggested by Horn can be found.

3.5.2 *Contrast*

Contrast is by definition metalinguistic:

(75)   Speaker A: You saw Susan at the party.
          Speaker B: No, I didn't see SUSAN, I saw PETER.

Speaker B can deny speaker A's utterance by simply denying it as in the first part of his reply. Speaker B may also add an alternative candidate to fill the slot that is being objected to as in the second part of the response. Note that if PETER is to be interpreted contrastively, {Susan, Peter} must be members of a contextually defined set. Contrast is the metalinguistic equivalent of a restrictive focus. These metalinguistic foci occur both with and without negation. In either case a previous utterance (possibly implied) is being objected to.

Before leaving metalinguistics, let me briefly address an issue I left hanging in my discussion of topics. I noted there that indefinite topics must be ruled out unless they are interpreted generically or contrastively. Take for example:

(76)   A MAN is intelligent.

If interpreted contrastively, this would mean something like "a man, not a woman, is intelligent." I suggest the following f-structure:

(77) $\left[\begin{bmatrix} \begin{Bmatrix} \text{a man}_{FOC} \\ \text{a woman} \end{Bmatrix} \end{bmatrix}_{TOP}\right]_{TOP}$ [is intelligent]$_{FOC}$

The second line of the f-structure indicates the other member of the contrast set (which is, of course, not overt). This constituent plays a role in the discourse theory and in assessment and must therefore be present in f-structure. In addition it *could* be made overt by adding "not a woman." The overt version can also be reversed: "a woman isn't intelligent, a man is."

What is represented here is on a par with the previous interpretations of metalinguistic foci:

(78)   Concerning a man/a woman being intelligent, pick "a man."

Note that the topic of the individual-level predicate in the subordinate f-structure is a restrictive set, i.e., a possible topic type. In the main f-structure, "a man" is not analyzed as the topic of the individual-level predicate, but rather as the focus of the subordinate f-structure. This is what gives us the correct stress pattern, as well as the correct interpretation and this analysis of contrast does not involve the interpretation of simple indefinites as topics. The sentence is assessed as follows: The main f-structure is assessed with respect to the "man" card ("be intelligent" is entered). The subordinate update eliminates "a woman" excluding the assessment TRUE for the predicate on this card. Note that (76), by itself, has no reference to "a woman." Therefore, the sentence is not interpretable unless the contrastive set is available in the context, or can be inferred from it. The distinctive contrastive intonation forces a contrastive interpretation even if the context does not make such a set available. Certain lexical items may contain an unmarked contrastive interpretation. There may, for example, be an unmarked contrast in the man/woman pair. Similarly, for good/bad etc. In the cases of scalar predicates (such as the latter), either the contrast involves the extremes of the scale (if there are any) or else another contrast involving individual members of the scale must be contextually evoked. Thus,

(79)   Bill caught TWO fish.

can be used contrastively to deny that Bill caught any other number of fish that someone might suggest.

Metalinguistic foci are a subcategory of restrictive foci, but metalinguistic restrictive sets are distinct in that they have exactly two members. In the case of contrast, for example, two individuals are contrasted. If the restrictive set summoned up from context (scalar or not) has in it more than two members then the contrast is defined between the contrasted element, and all the other individuals in the restrictive set, which form a group individual for this purpose.

Metalinguistic f-structures will be further discussed in chapter 4, where metalinguistic intonation will be defined, and in chapter 6, where the interaction of metalinguistic negation and metalinguistic extraction (i.e., clefting) will be discussed.

3.6   Semantics? Pragmatics?

The discourse theory advocated here introduces the context into the semantics by the front door, via the notion topic. But the type of "context" involved is needed in any semantics which deals with reference. Hence, this part of the theory of f-structure is not a problem for purists. Metalinguistic aspects of the theory of f-structure might not fare as well. Here the whole story depends on context and not only linguistic context at that. The metalinguistic component of f-structure is therefore situated smack in the middle of pragmatics. It follows that f-structure is interpreted both by the semantic component and by the pragmatic component. The "main" f-structure is interpreted by the predication rule which involves assessment with respect to truth values. The metalinguistic aspects of f-structure are processed by subordinate update. The restrictive sets upon which these rules operate cannot be derived directly from context. Inferences must be made as to which type of set is involved: contrast, emphasis, etc. The metalinguistic component which interprets those aspects of f-structure associated with contrast, etc., is, in my view, pragmatic.

The model I have presented in the last three chapters shows how f-structures are processed by the Topic, Focus, Predication and Update rules. My worry here has not been to provide an explicit semantics, only to present those aspects of f-structure which provide the input to the semantics, thus removing from the latter some of its burdens. In view of the fact that a separate level of f-structure (derived from s-structure) is necessary to derive intonation, this level is an obligatory part of the model. Chapter 4 demonstrates how intonation is derived from f-structure.

4 *The phonological interpretation of f-structure*

4.1 Under stress

In the previous chapters the level of f-structure was characterized as a projection of s-structure marked for Topic and Focus constituents. In those chapters f-structure was fine-tuned to take into account a variety of semantic properties. Three levels of f-structure were defined. 1. The main level of f-structure to which the rule of predication applies. 2. Subordinate f-structure that involves only the manipulation of the cards in the filing system, not assessment. 3. Metalinguistic f-structure that involves a different application of the predication rule. These three types of f-structure, however, have in common that they prompt the same operations on the file according to the rules of Topic, Focus, and Update.

In this chapter I propose *one* Phonological Form (PF) stress rule to account for intonation in English sentences:

(1)   Assign *stress* to the focus constituents.

(Duration, amplitude and pitch combine to give the effect of perceived stress.[1]) This rule does not distinguish focus types and can be viewed as a simple linguistic marking of the focus rule: to place a new or existing card on top of the file. This, as I claimed in chapter 1, is tantamount to saying that the hearer's attention is drawn to the intension of the heading of this card. The stress rule reflects the fact that the speaker stresses what he intends the hearer to attend to. The stress rule applies to every focus in sentences with complex f-structures.

In proposing this rule to account for sentence stress, I side with those linguists who argue that sentence stress cannot be derived from s-structure alone. (For example, Bolinger, Halliday, Selkirk, etc.) I argue that the level of f-structure, mediating between s-structure and PF, enables a maximally simple account. Since the level of f-structure has been well defined in the preceding chapters, and its raison d'être established as the input to the semantics, intonation falls out for free. In addition, the syntactic "link" is maintained in that topic and focus assignment in f-structure applies to syntactic constituents only.

Once I have established how the stress rule applies to the three kinds of focus argued for in the preceding chapters, I offer an account of the lack of stress on "colorless" or "light" constituents in terms of subordinate f-structures. I then proceed to derive stress in complex f-structures with multiple occurrences of the stress rule.

In addition, I show that a variety of "tunes" argued to have independent meanings, can be naturally associated with the properties of f-structure already developed (cf. Pierrehumbert and Hirschberg 1990).

I conclude with a review of alternative approaches to intonation, choosing four representative theories: Selkirk (1984), Jacobs (1991, 1994), Cinque (1993), and Steedman (1991). (Ladd (1980) is discussed in the context of the review of Selkirk.)

4.1.1 Main f-structure

The application of the stress rule to a complex f-structure may result in a complex intonational structure. To simplify the presentation, I abstract away from subordinate and metalinguistic f-structure and examine the intonation of the main f-structure first.

In Erteschik-Shir and Lappin (1983b) we argued for a rule (the sentential stress rule) essentially identical to the stress rule in (1). The following f-structures (from chapter 1) are assigned stress according to this rule.[2]

(2) a. [the children]$_{TOP}$ [ate the candy]$_{FOC}$
                    H*   H*
     b. TOP$_i$ [the children ate [the candy$_i$]]$_{FOC}$
                    H*   H*
     c. sTOP$_t$ [the children ate the candy]$_{FOC}$
                   H*   H*   H*

Following Pierrehumbert (1980), I associate high pitch accents with H*. Stress is thus assigned to the major constituents within the focused constituent (i.e., stress is not assigned to "little words": functional categories, prepositions, etc.) In (2b) the stress rule ignores the topic constituent contained in the focus. As mentioned in chapter 1, section 1.5, the coindexing of object topics is a notational variant of taking the focus to include a variable bound by the topic. In (2b) the focus is in effect *[the children ate x]* and the stress rule applies correctly.

I assume a "rhythm rule" which operates in fast speech. This rule applies to the three pitch accents in (2c) roughly as follows:

(3)   sTOP, [the children ate the candy]_FOC
         a.   2   3   1
         b.   3   1

I use 1 to indicate the relatively highest accent, 3 the lowest, and 2, an intermediate level. (3b) shows the minimal "effort" necessary to indicate out-of-the-blue intonation.[3] Similarly (2a) may be produced as either (4a) or (minimally) (4b).

(4)   [the children]_TOP [ate the candy]_FOC
         a.   2   1
         b.   3   1

The beginning of the focused constituent is minimally marked with a low accent, the end of this constituent with a high accent. (The difference between (a) and (b) is that in (b) the accent on the verb is lower relative to the accent on "candy" than in (a).) Intermediate accents can be lowered to a minimum down to nothing. Note that "stressing" the focused constituent according to the stress rule means stressing the whole constituent in the manner indicated, not merely its last subconstituent as proposed in Chomsky (1971) among others. The fact that out-of-the-blue sentences such as (2c) are assigned a sequence of high pitch accents on each of the major constituents is recognized. (For example, Schmerling 1973, Steedman 1991: 286, his (61)). These can be perceived by the bare ear: if the two first pitch accents in (2c) were removed, the sentence would be hard to interpret as out-of-the-blue. For shorter focus constituents such as the VP in (2a), the initial rise on the verb is much harder to perceive. Compare the f-structures and their intonations in the contexts of the relevant questions in the following:

(5)   What did the children do?
         [the children]_TOP [ate the candy]_FOC
                              3   1

(6)   What did the children eat?
         [the children]_TOP ate [the candy]_FOC
                                    1

That the stresses assigned in (5) and (6) are appropriate in the contexts of the questions given seems right. The question is whether reversing these stress patterns does not give equally good results. Until experiments have been undertaken to test this, the issue cannot be decided. I will assume that the distinction between (5) and (6) is real until it is proven otherwise, i.e., that the actualization of the proposed stress rule in (1) is correct. The validity of the rule itself is not in question, since stressing a focused constituent could be actualized as simply stressing the final major category as in the traditional nuclear stress rule.

I assume that the rule that lowers initial and middle stress of a complex focus constituent is a *rhythm rule* which is sensitive to the rapidity of speech. It is beyond the scope of the current work to examine the actualization of assigned stresses any further. (But see also the discussion immediately below and section 4.7.3.)

Selkirk (1984: 225–30) notes that the verb is unstressed in German focused VPs in which the verb is in final position, although final prominence is (generally) the rule for other constituents:

(7)   Er hat ein BUCH betrachtet.
        he has a   book looked at
        "he has looked at a book"

According to Selkirk only focused *arguments* (in English as well as German) are necessarily "new," but this is not so for verbs. Hence an unstressed verb is ambiguous with respect to its information status. My view here has been that the stress on verbs within focused constituents is lowered due to the rhythm rule which applies equally to all constituents. It is possible that further research across languages will show that stress on verbs is indeed different from stress on arguments.[4]

(2b) requires some attention since it is not obvious from what has been said so far that the stress rule will assign pitch accents correctly here. From the point of view of the stress rule the indexed topic "behaves" as though it were in the position of TOP outside the focus constituent, i.e., no pitch accent is assigned to it. This is in fact the point of the coindexing. Another way of achieving the same result would be to move topics to the front in f-structure, leaving a variable behind. A possible advantage of the latter approach might be that "topicalization" is available as a movement rule in the syntax. The structure I propose has the same advantage since it has an initial topic and is therefore isomorphic with a structure in which topicalization has occurred. In favor of the indexed structure is the fact that topics can be metalinguistically focused, hence stressed. If an object topic left a variable in f-structure, one would not expect stress in this position under any circumstances. Although I favor the indexed structures for these reasons, I will not decide this issue here and take the two approaches to be notational variants.

The f-structures in (2) are appropriate in the context of the following questions, respectively:

(8)   a. What did the children do?
        b. What happened to the candy?
        c. What happened?

The f-structure of the questions sets up *the children* and *the candy* as topics of the first two and a stage as the topic of the third. There are other possible questions for which the sentence "the children ate the candy" can provide an answer rendering a variety of f-structures:

(9)   a. What did the children eat?
        b. Who ate the candy?
        c. Did the children eat the candy?

The f-structure for the answer to (9a) has already been given in (6). The topic of (9b) is *the candy*, rendering the following f-structure for the answer:

(10)   TOP$_i$ [the children]$_{FOC}$ ate the candy$_i$
          I

The f-structure of the answer to (9c) is identical to (2a) although the operations on the file differ. In (2a) the focus constituent is entered on the topic card with the heading *the children*. The yes/no question (9c), as discussed in chapter 3, sets up a disjunctive set on the topic card:

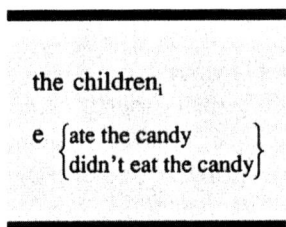

the children$_i$

e { ate the candy
     didn't eat the candy }

The answer eliminates one of the members of the disjunctive set, in this case the negative one. Pierrehumbert and Hirschberg (1990) (=P&H) show that the operation of set elimination is intonationally marked in that a different tune is assigned in each of these cases. I will return to this issue in section 4.6.

4.1.2   Short answers

In the previous section, I embedded one sentence in a variety of interrogative contexts. This created extremely artificial, albeit possible discourse sequences. The natural way to answer *wh*-questions is to pronominalize where possible and to respond with the focus constituent itself, leaving out the rest of the sentence. The fact that the focus constituent has a life of its own in such "short" answers is further evidence for the f-structures assigned. The short answers to the questions in (8) and (9), respectively, follow:

(11)   a. What did the children do? They ate the candy.
                                   *Ate the candy.
       b. What happened to the candy? The children ate it.
       c. What happened? The children ate the candy.

(12)   a. What did the children eat? The candy.
       b. Who ate the candy? The children/ The children did.
       c. Did the children eat the candy? Yes/Yes, they did.

The only case in which it is not possible to answer exclusively with the focus constituent is (11a) in which the focus is the whole VP. Languages that allow topic drop would allow the second response to (11a). In English, however, topic drop is highly restricted, and therefore excludes this short answer. In the answers in (11b and c) the focus contains the whole sentence, therefore no sentence parts can be left out. In (11b) the topic is pronominalized in accordance with coreference licensing discussed in chapter 2. (12a and b) allow for one-constituent answers; in each case the answer is the focused constituent. Finally, in (12c), the short answer is *yes*. An f-structural explanation for this short answer was proposed in the previous chapter. The alternative semi-short answer to the yes/no question allows the pro-verb(phrase) *do* indicating the focused constituent. In the presence of a proform for the VP, the topic again cannot be left out. (12b) also offers a semi-short answer. In this case the pro-verb is left in addition to the focused constituent. A simple principle is thus involved in generating short answers: a focus *answers* a *wh*-question. Assigning pitch accent to the focus and using the focus alone to answer *wh*-questions serve the same purpose.

Note that when a speaker opts for a full-sentence answer, in which constituents present in the question are repeated, a weakened version of the stress contour appears, especially if that part of the answer is long. It is possible that the reason for this is to disambiguate contrastive answers from noncontrastive ones. In cases of contrast, as I show below, the only stress in the sentence is the one associated with the contrastive focus. (13) follows by way of illustration:

(13)   Who is available for the job?
       sTOP$_t$ [The children]$_{FOC}$ are available for the job.
            I   3   2

Remember that the repeated portion of the sentence is presupposed, hence present, as an entry on the card. (The focus constituent replaces the variable on the topic card.) The stress rule will assign prominence to the focus constituent and in so doing will lower (to the extent possible) the stresses on the presupposed constituents inherited from the question.[5]

Partee (1992, 1994) raises the problem of what she refers to as deaccented foci (see also Rooth (1992) among others):

(14)   A: Eva only gave xerox copies to the GRADUATE STUDENTS.
        B: No, PETR only gave xerox copies to the graduate students.

In theories in which focus assignment is derived from intonation the phrase *graduate students* cannot be marked as a focus since it is not accented. In view of the fact that *only* still associates with this phrase, it clearly functions as a focus semantically. Here the deaccented result will be derived exactly as in (13):

(15)   No, PETR *only gave xerox copies to the graduate students.*
                 | |
                 1   2

Partee only recognizes the accent on the subject. The secondary accent on the "inherited" focus is, however, perceptible to the ear. Here again the italicized part of B's contrastive response is presupposed and exists as an entry on an existing card. I assume that existing entries are semantically fully interpreted and that subordinate f-structures involved in interpretation are still available. This will derive both the correct association for *only* and the correct (lowered) accent on the "inherited" focus.

This type of example provides a challenge to any theory which derives focus assignment from accent, but not for a theory such as the one proposed here which derives accent from focus assignment.

4.1.3   *Answers to restrictive questions*

In the previous section, the yes/no question (9c) was again analyzed as setting up a restrictive set of two alternatives, one of which is eliminated by the answer. The following questions (answerable by our sentence or similar ones) also involve restrictive sets in the discourse:

(16)   a. Which child ate the candy? Charlie (ate it.)
        b. What candy did the children eat? (They ate) the toffee.
        c. Who ate what? The children ate the candy.

Questions such as (16a and b), as discussed in chapter 3, involve subordinate f-structures in which topic sets (in this case a potential set of "eaters" and a

set of kinds of candy, respectively) are available from context, and the subordinate f-structure triggers a scanning of this set: the question is "asked" for
each individual within this set. (16a), for example, can be asked when a card
for a certain set of children$_i$ is available on top of the file. The question "asks"
for a scanning of this set in order to select (focus) the member of this set
which "answers" the question. The NP which is selected is thus the focus
of the answer and is stressed accordingly. The answer to a single restrictive
wh-question differs f-structurally from the answer to a nonrestrictive one only
in the added subordinate f-structure:

(17)   TOP$_j$ [[Charlie$_{FOC-sub}$]$_{TOP-sub}$]$_{FOC}$ ate [the candy]$_j$
          H*

The subordinate topic is the set of children, specified by the question.

The subject of the multiple question (16c) is also analyzed in this manner. Available is a contextually defined restrictive set (the set of potential
"eaters"). This set provides a subordinate topic. For each individual within
this set, a new *wh*-question is asked. This is how we get a list question. The
answer will therefore consist of a list of answers for each individual within
the topic set. This analysis derives the following f-structure for one of the
answers in this list:

(18)   [[The children$_{FOC-sub}$]$_{TOP-sub}$]$_{TOP}$ ate [the candy]$_{FOC}$

The focus structure of (18) is therefore similar to that of (6) except for the
subordinate f-structure on the subject. The stress rule will apply to both foci
in (18), since the subject as well as the object is marked as a focus, rendering
the following stress pattern:

(19)   the children ate the candy
              H*   H*

This stress pattern is actualized very much like the out-of-the-blue pattern
since the fast-speech rhythm rule will lower the initial accent, making the two
cases very much alike out of context.

4.1.4   Restrictive enumeration

In chapter 1 (section 1.6.2.3), a restrictive focus was characterized as a
focused set. This set can be introduced as a plural NP, or it can be enumer-
ated either conjunctively or disjunctively. The following illustrations are from
Erteschik-Shir and Lappin (1983b):

(20)   a. I invited JOHN, MARY, and SAM to the party.
        b. Bill CAUGHT the fish, CLEANED it, FRIED it, and then SERVED it.
        c. Mary dusted UNDER the table, on TOP of it, and BESIDE it.
        d. The department will schedule the exam for TODAY or TOMORROW.

In these sentences all the listed expressions receive equal high pitch accents (indicated here by capitals for convenience). Each list constitutes the conjunctive enumeration of the elements of a set which defines this set and triggers the opening of a new (set) card on top of the file. The new card for (20a), for example, contains the cards for *John, Mary,* and *Sam.* In Erteschik-Shir (1987, in prep. b) I argue for an account of coordination as parallel-formatted structures.[6] This account allows for a view of coordinate constituents, such as the ones in (20), as "vertical" lists. Such lists will receive stress by the stress rule:

(21)   I invited |John | to the party.
                  |Mary |
                  |Sam |
                    H*

Vertical stress actualization simply means that the stress is distributed equally on each element of such a set. Linearization of the structure takes place in PF to allow for the sequential pronunciation of coordinate structures. The rhythm rule will naturally lower the initial accents, leaving the highest stress on the final conjunct.

4.2   The intonation of questions

In the previous section I examined restrictive questions, noting that the *wh*-phrase in these cases involved a subordinate f-structure made available by a restrictive topic set in the context. Stress follows from the f-structure as follows:

(22)   TOP$_i$[Which$_{FOC\text{-}sub}$child$_{TOP\text{-}sub}$]$_{FOC}$ ate the candy$_i$.
            H*

Similarly, the f-structure and intonation of multiple *wh*-questions follow:

(23)   [[Who$_{FOC\text{-}sub}$]$_{TOP\text{-}sub}$]$_{TOP}$ ate [what]$_{FOC}$
            H*   H*

    In Erteschik-Shir (1986a), I showed that restrictive *wh*-phrases, including contrastive and incredulous (metalinguistic) ones, are the only *wh*-phrases which constitute foci, and receive stress independently. Other *wh*-phrases are *not* separately focused, but receive stress as part of the focused constituent they occur in. The unmarked stress on *wh*-questions follows from an out-of-the-blue f-structure:

(24)   a. sTOP$_t$ [who ate the candy]$_{FOC}$
                 H* H*   H*
         b. sTOP$_t$ [what did the children eat]$_{FOC}$
                 H*   H*   H*
         c.   2   3   1

Stress is actualized (by the fast-speech rhythm rule) with reduced medial and lowered initial accent as in the parallel assertion rendering the accents in (c). The other f-structures are also available for questions.

(25)   a. TOP$_i$ [who ate the candy$_i$]$_{FOC}$
                 H* H*
         b. TOP$_i$ [what did the children$_i$ eat]$_{FOC}$
                 H*   H*

Yes/no questions also allow for a wide range of f-structures. According to P&H (1990), "the items made salient by H* accents are to be treated as 'new' in the discourse," adding the proposition to "the hearer's mutual belief space." The L* accent, however, "marks items which S (the speaker) intends to be salient but not to form part of what S is predicating in the utterance." It follows that L* accents (stressed low pitch tones), but not H* accents appear in simple yes/no questions in which the focused phrase is eliminated from an entry on the topic card, not added to it. According to P&H, the fact that yes/no questions do not involve predication is indicated by L*. I agree, and associate L* with a request to choose between the two entries on the topic card (rather than adding a new entry). *Wh*-questions differ in this respect from yes/no questions in that they request the hearer to supply an entry, and entry-making is associated with H*. I illustrate a variety of yes/no f-structures in (26):

(26)   a. did sTOP$_t$ [Peter laugh]$_{FOC}$
                         L* L*
         b. did he$_{TOP}$ laugh$_{FOC}$
                         L*
         c. did he$_{TOP}$ [see Susan]$_{FOC}$
                         L* L*
         d. did TOP$_i$ [Peter see her]$_{FOC}$[7]
                         L* L*

Questions have the same f-structures as assertions and are stressed by the same stress rule. The fact that these are questions must be indicated in f-structure in view of the characteristic tune associated with them. Those f-structures (yes/no questions among them) which are associated with L* pitch accents rather than H* must also be distinguished in some manner. I will return to these issues in section 4.6.

4.3   Metalinguistics and intonation

In chapter 3, I argued for a metalinguistic level in the discourse theory. Metalinguistic foci were shown to evoke contrastive sets that provide the topic for the subordinate (metalinguistic) f-structure. I repeat an illustration of this phenomenon:

(27) $\left[\begin{array}{c}\left[\begin{array}{c}\left\{\begin{array}{c}\text{the man}_{FOC} \\ \text{the woman}\end{array}\right\}\end{array}\right]_{TOP}\end{array}\right]_{TOP}$]$_{TOP}$ [is intelligent]$_{FOC}$

The following two properties were associated with metalinguistic phenomena: first, the metalinguistic predication is additional to the assertion of the sentence itself and second, the content of the sentence is qualified by a process whereby one of the two members of the context-generated set is eliminated. Remember that the second line of the f-structure is contextually supplied and is not (necessarily) overt, therefore the stress rule will not apply to it. It is not clear from what has been said so far how the stress rule will apply. I suggested in the previous chapter that metalinguistic focusing overrules regular focusing with respect to stress. This is indeed the case:

(28)   the man is intelligent.
            H*

The pitch accent on "the man" is derived by applying the stress rule to the subordinate focus. The problem is to block the application of the stress rule to the main focus ("be intelligent"). Metalinguistic f-structures are distinctive in that a nonovert member of a set is overtly presented in f-structure. This is what makes for the distinct operation of the discourse rules as well. The characteristic f-structure also presents a way of distinguishing these f-structures for the purposes of PF and the application of the stress rule there. A constraint must be imposed to the effect that in sentences with metalinguistic foci, the stress rule is applied only to the metalinguistic foci, to the exclusion of the other foci. Other subordinate f-structures do not have this effect as was seen in (18).

What could be the reason for this constraint? The focal stress on the contrasted element is the only overt marking of the contrast operator which triggers the construction of the contrastive set.[8] It is therefore crucial that this marking be univocal. Stressing the main focus as well would cause ambiguity in that such a stress pattern yields a paired focus reading. It follows that *not stressing the main focus prevents ambiguity.* The reason often given for the fact that no stresses occur on the noncontrasted part of the sentence is that it is presupposed (alternatively, given or old). This explanation is not available for the following reasons: first, the discourse theory defined here demands that the predicate in (27) be a focus in f-structure for purposes of assessment. Second, presupposed constituents are often focused, especially metalinguistically. (28), following the assertion of the same sentence, would be taken to mean that the utterer of the sentence didn't believe it (i.e., an incredulity question), and "the man," although stressed, would be part of the presupposition.

Note that if the contrasted element is overt, parallel stress is assigned to it, again with no stress on the main focus:

(29)   a. The man is intelligent, not the woman.
           H*   H*
    b. The woman isn't intelligent, the man is.
           H*   H*

The f-structures of these sentences coincide with the f-structures in which the contrasted element is covert. Here we make use of the parallel structures introduced in (21):

(30)   [|the man $_{\text{FOC}}$|]$_{\text{TOP}}$ [is intelligent]$_{\text{FOC}}$
             not |the woman$_{\text{FOC}}$|

The stress rule will again apply to the contrastive constituent, excluding the main focus. The stress is actualized in parallel to each of the elements in the "vertical" factor. Linearization applies in PF to derive (29a). The linearization rule is sensitive to the nature of the vertical constituent. Coordinate parallel constituents differ from contrastive ones (marked by negation).[9] The f-structure assigned to (29b) is more complex and involves gapping. A discussion of gapped sentences would take us too far afield. Important for the current issue is that the stress rule again applies to the parallel format in which the two foci form one "vertical" constituent.

As was mentioned in chapter 3, metalinguistic foci are not limited to constituents. This again distinguishes these foci from the others. The stress rule, however, applies here too:

(31)   a. I am advocating PROsecution, not PERsecution.

b. I$_{TOP}$ [am advocating |pro$_{FOC}$| secution]$_{FOC}$
                     not |per$_{FOC}$| secution
                          H*

This focus structure gives the correct interpretation and also the correct stress assignment. Note that although the vertical factor is built on a syllable, syllables cannot stand alone in structures. That is why the whole constituent which contains the focused syllable must appear. Linearization will therefore apply correctly to the whole constituent. Note further that a larger constituent chunk could have been chosen rendering the following alternatives:

(32)   a. I am advocating PROsecution, not advocating PERsecution.
        b. I am advocating PROsecution, I am not advocating PERsecution.

Full-sentence foci (predicated of stage topics) can also be used contrastively (see also chapter 3):

(33)   a. The United States DIDn't invade Iraq.
        b. The United States DID invade Iraq.

Do is used to carry the metalinguistic pitch accent signaling that the contrast is between the positive and negative option.

4.4   Subordinate f-structure and stress

So far, we have seen that restrictive subordinate foci are assigned stress by the stress rule. This stress is additional to the stress assigned to the main focus if the two do not coincide. Metalinguistic foci (involving subordinate metalinguistic restrictive f-structures) are also assigned stress by the stress rule, but in this case assignment of stress to the main focus is blocked. It remains to examine the stress assigned to nonrestrictive subordinate f-structures. We have encountered two different types: modifiers, such as restrictive relative clauses, and subordinate topics. I will examine each in turn. Then I examine the f-structures associated with nouns and verbs that are not "focusable" and show that the lack of stress on such lexical items follows from the subordinate f-structure which must be assigned to the constituents in which they occur.

4.4.1   *Subordinate f-structure: modifiers*
In chapter 1 (1.6.2.2) subordinate f-structure was discussed in the context of topics of individual-level predicates. Topics, which are not assigned stress by

the stress rule, provide good test cases for stress assignment to subordinate foci since the only possible source of stress on these constituents is the subordinate f-structure.

(34)   a. A friend of mine is intelligent.
        b. A certain student likes linguistics.
        c. A student who I know likes linguistics.
        d. A man who was wearing a brown hat knew enough French to help us.

The f-structure assigned to (34c), for example, is:

(35)   [[a student]$_{FOC-sub}$ [who I know]$_{TOP-sub}$]$_{TOP}$ [likes linguistics]$_{FOC}$
              L*   H*   H*
              2   3   1

The stress rule applies to the main focus to assign the two final pitch accents and a further pitch accent is assigned to the subordinate focus. (In section 4.6, I discuss the phrasing of this f-structure and will show that the subordinate f-structure can induce independent intonational phrasing.) In view of the fact that the subordinate f-structure does not involve assessment for truth value, the stress on the subordinate focus should be L, according to P&H. I suspect that this is correct, but experimentation on sentences with subordinate f-structures of this sort would have to be done to verify this. For those speakers for whom a relatively low pitch accent is perceived on subordinate foci an explanation in terms of f-structure could be provided. The rhythm rule cannot account for the low pitch accent here since the subordinate f-structure constitutes a separate intonational phrase.[10]

Subordinate f-structure is also at stake in the classic sentence pair (Newman 1946):

(36)   a. I have INSTRUCTIONS to leave. (I am to leave instructions.)
        b. I have INSTRUCTIONS to LEAVE. (I have been instructed to leave.)

The focus structures of these sentences are represented in (37) and (38), respectively:

(37)   I$_{TOP}$ [have [[instructions]$_{FOC-sub}$ [to leave]$_{TOP-sub}$]]$_{FOC}$
                              H*

(38)   I$_{TOP}$ [have instructions to leave]$_{FOC}$
                      H*   H*

(37) is assigned a subordinate f-structure. The subordinate topic is "PRO to leave t" which means that it is presupposed that I am to leave something.

The focus associated with this topic is "instructions" rendering the correct intonation. Note that since the subordinate focus is also a constituent of the main focus H* is assigned. (38) is the simple case, in which no subordinate f-structure is involved, and the VP or the object is focused.

4.4.2   *Subordinate f-structure: subordinate topics*

In chapter 1 (1.6.3.1) f-structures of the following type were discussed:

(39) $TOP_{i\text{-sub}}[He_{TOP}$ [loves her$_i$]$_{FOC}]_{FOC\text{-sub}}$
                    H*

This f-structure is assigned if the sentence is asserted in the context of questions such as

(40)   a. What is the relationship of John to Mary?
        b. How does John feel about Mary?

Although assessment applies to the main predication for which the subject "he" provides the topic, the sentence is also "about" Mary for whom a card is also available on top of the file. In this case the stress rule applies just as it did in (2b) in which the object provided the main topic. It follows that subordinate topics are no different from main topics with respect to the stress rule. This is as it should be if, as we have seen above, the stress rule applies to the subordinate f-structure in the same way it applies to the main f-structure.

4.4.3   *Focusability: colorless nouns*[11]

Little work has been done on focusability and the lexicon although observations have often been made to the effect that focusability depends on the nature of the particular lexical item. Function words, in particular, have been assumed to be unfocusable as have pronouns and other anaphoric elements. I have argued that the fact that pronouns must be topics accounts for their not being focusable. If (nondeictic) pronouns function as the main or subordinate topic, it follows that they are not focused (and therefore not stressed). Bresnan (1971: 271) characterizes words like *people* and *things* as semi-pronouns. Bolinger (1983: 108) refers to these as "intrinsically colorless" and gives the following illustration:[12]

(41)   Why don't you come right out and say so?
        Because I don't want to emBARrass any of the *people*.
                                            anybody

Bolinger says that "the fact that [*people*] can be deaccented shows its semantically lean status." He characterizes *people* as "a noun whose content barely exceeds [+Human]." I would like to show that these so-called semi-pronouns also function as topics when they are destressed. It is exactly the fact that they are semantically "lean," i.e., almost contentless, that allows these words to play the role of topic. Selkirk (1984: 233) selects a few examples from Bolinger (1972) to make a related point:

(42)   My GERANIUM plant is almost dead.

(43)   There were CRAWLING things all around.

Bolinger, as just mentioned, relates these facts to "relative semantic weight" and "predictability." The former is a lexical property of the item in question, the latter is derived from context. Selkirk captures these intuitions by the Redundant Focus Rule:[13]

(44)   If a constituent is *redundant* in S_j, it may be a focus in S_j.

Redundant is a well-defined notion (see Selkirk's definition 5.56): the redundant item does not add anything content-wise. Since intonational prominence, in Selkirk's system, is interpreted as focus, this rule is necessary to explain why these elements are not intonationally prominent, yet part of the focus constituent. In the current framework the opposite problem arises. Here it is not obvious why pitch accents are not assigned to semantically empty nouns contained in focused constituents. The following partial f-structures for (41)–(43) resolve this problem:

(45)   Because I don't want
        [TOP$_{i\text{-sub}}$ to emBARrass [any of the people]$_{iFOC\text{-sub}}$]

(46)   There were [CRAWLING$_{FOC\text{-sub}}$ things$_{TOP\text{-sub}}$] all around.

(47)   My [GERANIUM$_{FOC\text{-sub}}$ plant$_{TOP\text{-sub}}$] is almost dead.

(45) and (46) are of a kind. In both we have "semi-pronominals" which must be argued to be interpreted as subordinate topics. No other interpretation is possible since these elements cannot be (nonmetalinguistically) stressed. First, it is possible to demonstrate that these empty items are not focusable when unmodified:

(48)   A: Who/what do you like?
        B: *I like people/things.

It can also be shown that they can function as main topics:

(49)   a. People are intelligent.
         b. Things can be ugly.

Since they cannot be foci, new cards cannot be opened with headings such as "people" or "things." It follows that such cards must be generally available in order for the sentences in (49) to occur. In this sense these nouns are just like generics as they were characterized in chapter 1. They differ from other generics, however, in that they cannot be focused. I follow Bolinger in claiming that focusability depends on semantic weight. The nouns under discussion are, as Bolinger claims, close to meaningless. For such nouns I claim that permanent generic cards are available on top of the file. Since they are almost meaningless, they can only be used if the sentences in which they occur imbue them with meaning. The way this is done is by subordinate update that applies in (46), for example, as follows:

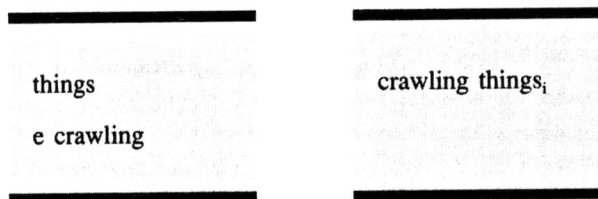

things e crawling	crawling things$_i$

The card on the left has the unindexed heading *things*. The subordinate f-structure in (46) induces the entry "e crawling" which in turn defines the card on the right.[14] This is how nouns which are semantically empty take on more heavy guises via subordinate update. Calling them semi-pronouns is therefore a misnomer.

Consider now (47) which is slightly different. *Plants* differ from *people* and *things* in that the former *can* be focused. (Replace *things* with *plants* in (49b).) It is only in the context of *geranium* which is marked [+plant] in the lexicon that the work loses its meaning. This is the kind of evidence Selkirk adduces for her Redundant Focus Rule and so far the only advantage of my approach is that no special rule is needed to handle these cases. Subordinate update is available to do the job. Let us now try a little exercise and reverse the subordinate f-structure as follows:

(50)   My [GERANIUM$_{TOP-sub}$ plant$_{FOC}$] is almost dead.

This exercise renders the following ill-formed card sequence:

geranium_i	geranium plant_i
e plant	

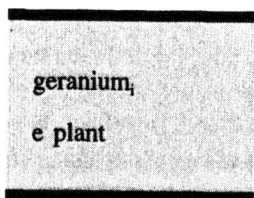

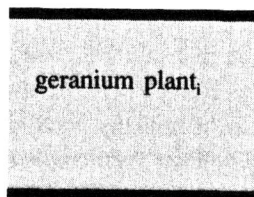

This card sequence is ill-formed for two reasons. First, the sentence does not depend on *geranium* having been brought into the conversation, hence the card on the left is not available as a topic. Second, assuming that we did introduce the card for *geranium_i*, the entry on this card is vacuous in view of the fact that *geranium* is already marked with the feature [+plant] as part of its lexical content. Therefore, (50) is an impossible f-structure assignment. Note that (47) renders a well-formed card sequence:

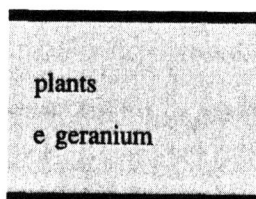

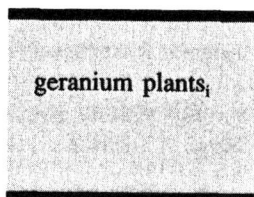

plants	geranium plants_i
e geranium	

Other examples given by Selkirk illustrate the same point (her 5.59):

(51)   a. I'm going over to the DOCTOR's place.
       b. I'm doing it for JOHN's sake.

These she compares to Bolinger's:

(52)   a. I'm going over to the DOCTOR'S BARN.
       b. I'm doing it for JOHN'S WELFARE.

In (51), according to Selkirk, *place* and *sake* are redundant, hence destressed, in spite of their being contained in focused constituents. In my framework they are subordinate topics on a par with *plant* in the previous example. Evidence for my position comes from the examples in (52), in which, according to Selkirk, *barn* and *welfare* are not redundant. Note, however, that these can be destressed if the context introduces them as subordinate topics:

(53)   a. A: Whose barn are you going to?
          B: I am going to the DOCTOR's barn.

       b. A: For whose welfare are you doing it?
          B: I am doing it for JOHN's welfare.

Selkirk could, of course, argue that these nouns have been made redundant by context, and that would be true. However, this is exactly the kind of case for which subordinate f-structures were set up; namely, when more than one of the nouns in the sentence could be associated with a card on top of the file. Assigning subordinate f-structures to semantically empty nouns in the fashion conveyed above seems preferable to adding an additional redundancy rule with basically the same effect. No additional machinery is required here in view of the fact that subordinate f-structures come for free: they are parasitical on main f-structures needed independently for the determination of truth values.

There is another type of semantically empty nouns exemplified by *someone* and *something*. These are similar to the previous ones in that they are not focusable but differ in that they cannot be topics of a main f-structure:

(54)   a. Who/What do you like? *I like SOMEONE/SOMETHING.
        b. *Someone is intelligent./*Something is dirty.
           SOMEONE is intelligent./SOMETHING is dirty.

Here again we must explain why these elements do not get stressed when they are contained in focused constituents:

(55)   A: Why are you behaving so strangely?
        B: i. I am in love with someone.
                 *SOMEONE
           ii. I am worried about something.
                 *SOMETHING

The explanation is similar to the one given for *people* and *things* above, but (54b) shows that the explanation can't be quite the same. Let us examine the following hypothesis: *someone* and *something* are generic proforms. Each represents a member of the set of *people* and *things*, respectively. Generics were shown in chapter I to function either as names or as indefinites. These proforms only have the latter use. The cards for *someone* and *something* (i.e., the cards for *people* and *things*, respectively) are available on top of the file at all times. Evidence for this view is the fact that the proforms cannot be "raised" to the top of the file:

(56)   *As for someone/something, he/it is dirty.

The explanation for the fact that these elements do not get stressed inside focused constituents is thus the same as the one given for the other semantically weightless nouns. It is, however, not apparent why they must be stressed when they function as main topics as in (54b). First, the unstressed cases are ruled out because the generic proforms cannot be used as the name of the genus, hence they cannot be used as main topics. The stressed versions receive the following explanation: the topic card is in fact the card representing a set of people or things in the discourse. In such a case the proforms can be used as topics, but since they represent a *member* of the set defined by the card for which they provide a proform, they are derived by a restrictive subordinate f-structure, generating the stress indicated in (54b).

Selkirk also gives one example with an indefinite:

(57)   a. He was arrested because he KILLed a man.
        b. He was arrested because he KILLED a POLICEMAN.

The story for (57a), in which *a man* is almost as semantically colorless as *someone*, is the same as the one just given. *A policeman*, however, has enough potential weight to satisfy the requirement for heading a card. If policemen have been contextually introduced, however, destressing will occur according to the same analysis in terms of subordinate f-structure. Selkirk mentions (p. 437, note 19) that replacing *a man* with *a woman* or *a child* requires stress on the NP as in (57b). Selkirk posits that this shows that there is "some implicit reference to (possibly) shared assumptions about the nature of the world at large." Instead, I suggest that this gives some indication of what is at stake in defining semantic weightlessness. A plausible tack to take is to say that for each semantic class, the noun with the least *positive* features is the basic unmarked member of the class. This will also be the (semantically) leanest one. If this is correct, it follows that *man* has one +feature less than *woman*:

(58)   man   [+human], [−female]
        woman [+human], [+female]

Metalinguistic focusing of *a man* will bring the negative features up, giving the effect that *man* is contrasted with *woman*, say. For some classes, the semantically leanest may not be weightless. Although a feature analysis of nouns in the light of their focusability and stressability is intriguing, such issues will take us too far afield.

4.4.4   Light verbs

Jespersen (1954: VI, 117–18) refers to "light" verbs and characterizes them as "insignificant verb(s)," to which the marks of person and tense are attached, before the really important idea. In his discussion of Predicatives (1933: XIII,

124–31) he refers to the verbs that take predicatives as approximately "empty" and "colorless." Verbs that have been recognized as "light verbs" are among others *be, have, do, become, put, take, make, give*, etc. (Dowty 1979, Grimshaw and Mester 1988). These are then the verbal parallel to the colorless nouns described in the previous section. As with the nouns, it is not difficult to determine the extreme cases: *be*, for example, is "completely colorless," according to Jespersen (1933). As an introduction to the topic, I would like to discuss some examples given by Bolinger (1972) to argue that the semantics of lexical items determines sentence accent(s). A part of the discussion deals with Newman's classic cases which were discussed in section 4.4.1. I allowed for two different f-structures for those cases, repeated here for convenience:

(59) I_{TOP} [have [[instructions]$_{FOC\text{-}sub}$ [to leave]$_{TOP\text{-}sub}$]]$_{FOC}$
        H*

(60) I_{TOP} [have instructions to leave]$_{FOC}$
        H*   H*

The following are Bolinger's (pp. 633–4):

(61)   a. The end of the chapter is reserved for various problems to compúterize.
        b. The end of the chapter is reserved for various próblems to solve.

(62)   a. I have a point to émphasize.
        b. I have a póint to make.

(63)   a. I can't finish in an hour – there are simply too many topics to elúcidate.
        b. I can't finish in an hour – there are simply too many tópics to cover.

According to Bolinger, the speaker's "choice of the semantically richer verb" equals a choosing "the operation rather than the thing" as "the point of information focus." It is not hard to see that the verbs in the examples (a) are more complex than the parallel ones in (b). Moreover, it could be argued that the verbs in (b) are redundant. Bolinger argues that relative semantic weight is at stake.

Whether the f-structure type in (59) or (60) is chosen therefore depends on how likely it is for the infinitive to be interpreted as a topic: the semantically more empty verbs will be the most likely candidates for topichood.

What we see from the above is that a careful examination of the lexical semantics of verbs and nouns sheds further light on properties of f-structure and stress.

4.5 Who's the boss?

In section 4.3 I showed that stress on a metalinguistic focus suppresses stress on the main focus. I have yet to show the interaction of metalinguistic focus stress and other focus types. The following illustrates a metalinguistic focus within a subordinate f-structure.

(64)   (No,) a man who was wearing a GREEN hat stood at the door.

The sentence could be used as a response to someone saying:

(65)   A man who was wearing a brown hat stood at the door.

The f-structure of (64) is:

(66)   [[a man]$_{FOC\text{-}sub}$ [who was wearing a $\left[\begin{smallmatrix}\left\{\begin{smallmatrix}\text{green}_{FOC}\\\text{brown}\end{smallmatrix}\right\}\\\text{H*}\end{smallmatrix}\right]_{TOP}$ hat]$_{TOP\text{-}sub}$]$_{TOP}$ [stood at the door]$_{FOC}$

In this rather complex f-structure the stress rule is again only applied once – to the contrastive focus. The sentence also illustrates a case in which the metalinguistic focus is contained in a presupposed constituent. But this, as we saw in section 4.3, is not unusual.

There are, however, cases containing metalinguistic foci that require additional applications of the stress rule:

(67)   [[a man]$_{FOC\text{-}sub}$ [who was wearing a $\left[\begin{smallmatrix}\left\{\begin{smallmatrix}\text{green}_{FOC}\\\text{other}\end{smallmatrix}\right\}\\\text{H*}\end{smallmatrix}\right]_{TOP}$ hat]$_{TOP\text{-}sub}$]$_{TOP}$ stood at [the door]$_{FOC}$
H*

The difference between this f-structure and the preceding one is that (67) is contextualized in a different way. This sentence could be a response to a question such as the following if the context provided a set of men, each wearing a hat in a different color:

(68)   Where did each man stand?

The paired focus answer in (67) is just one of a list of answers, each taking as a topic one of the members of the set of men. The metalinguistic focus identifies each of the men by eliminating all the others ("other" in the f-structure stands for "other color"). Another major factor distinguishes the f-structure of this sentence from the previous one: the intonation assigned conveys not only that a set of men (wearing colored hats) is available but also a set of places to be at. If such a set is not available in the context "the door" will not get stressed. The f-structure in (67) is therefore inaccurate. A contrast set must be supplied for "the door" which is also metalinguistically focused. That is why the application of the stress rule is not suppressed. It turns out that if one of the elements of a restrictively paired focus is metalinguistically identified, then the other is too. The examination of this sentence has produced the following result. The stress rule can reply iteratively to several metalinguistic foci, but applications of the rule to other foci will be suppressed as before.

4.6   Tunes

Up to now I have discussed the assignment of pitch accents to f-structures and have shown that a simple stress rule accounts in a straightforward way for rather complex stress patterns. F-structure also contributes to the understanding of the intonational contours associated with them.

P&H argue that tunes or intonational contours contribute to the interpretation of discourse. They argue that this contribution is compositional in that each element of a tune can be associated with a different "meaning." They apply the theory of intonational description first proposed in Pierrehumbert (1980). In this framework tunes are composed of pitch accents, phrase accents and boundary tones. A distinction has already been made (following P&H) between L* and H* accents. They suggest that L* is used when no predication is involved and relate their suggestion to the L* in yes/no questions. I have adjusted their proposal to fit the current framework. L* has been associated with subordinate f-structures as well as with cases in which the focus structure triggers elimination of entries in the file change semantics (as in yes/no questions). Other candidates for L* as opposed to H* are foci of negation and metalinguistic foci, both of which involve set elimination as opposed to new entries. I leave open for future research whether this line of investigation will prove fruitful. In this section I discuss some of the tunes examined in P&H and correlate them with the types of f-structure proposed here.

4.6.1   The declarative tune

According to P&H, tunes are composed of pitch accents as well as phrase accents and boundary tones. Phrase accents are marked by H and L indicating high and low tones respectively. Boundary tones are marked by % and can also be either high or low. The canonical declarative tune is H* L L% illustrated in (69):

(69)   The train leaves at seven.
         H*   H*   H*   L L%

According to P&H the phrase accent L makes it unlikely for the phrase to be interpreted as a unit with a *phrase* that follows. Similarly, the boundary tone L% makes it unlikely that the sentence will be interpreted as a unit with a *sentence* that follows.[15]

4.6.2   The interrogative tune

Whereas *wh*-questions use the same tune as declaratives, yes/no questions have a distinct interrogative tune (P&H, their (16)):[16]

(70)   Do prunes have feet?
            L*   L* H H%

The low-pitch accents indicate, as shown before, that the focus (the whole sentence) is not to be entered on a card, but that an entry representing it or its opposite is to be eliminated from an existing card.[17] The high boundary tone (roughly) conveys that (70) is to be interpreted as a unit with a following utterance – in this case the answer to the question. An anonymous reviewer suggests that alternatively the utterance following (70) (implicitly) should be "or not" (as in cases of restrictive foci in (73a and b) below).

P&H do not elaborate why it is that *wh*-questions typically are uttered with L%. They propose that "an L boundary tone may be used when S wishes H to interpret his/her utterance with greater attention to preceding utterances. An H boundary tone, on the other hand, indicates that S wishes H to interpret his/her utterance with particular attention to subsequent utterances." If this is meant to explain the H% in yes/no questions, it is not clear how the L% in *wh*-questions is to be explained. P&H mention that there is an asymmetry between L% and H%: the former can occur even if the intonational phrase in which it appears need not be interpreted with respect to what has come before. This does not resolve the issue under discussion here.

4.6.3   Restrictive list tunes

Compare the following two f-structures:

(71)   a. Fred$_{TOP}$ ate [the beans]$_{FOC}$
                              H*   L L%
         b. [[Fred$_{FOC-sub}$]$_{TOP-sub}$]$_{TOP}$ ate [the beans]$_{FOC}$
                H*   L   H*   L H%

The following two questions provide possible contexts for these sentences, respectively:

(72)   a. What did Fred eat?
         b. Who ate what?

(71a) has a typical declarative intonation contour in which the object focus receives the pitch accent. (72b) is one of a series of answers, each pertaining to an individual member of the topic set. Each of these answers will receive the intonation contour indicated, except the last one, to which an L% boundary tone will be assigned to mark the end of the list. The L phrasal tones, according to P&H, emphasize the separation of the current phrase from the subsequent one. Thus the low phrasal tone intervening between the two pitch accents emphasizes the separation of the two foci, each part of a separate list.[18]

The H phrasal tone marks exhaustiveness in cases of restrictive enumeration. P&H provide the following illustrations (their (48), (50)):

(73)   a. Do you want apple juice   or orange juice?
                            H*   H   H*   L L%
         b. Do you want apple juice   or orange juice?
                            H*   L   H*   L L%

In (73a) a restrictive set is generated consisting of "apple juice" and "orange juice." The card for the restrictive set (which contains attached cards for each type of juice) may receive the heading "available juices," for example. In (73b) separate cards for each type of juice are constructed by the focus rule, but not a common set card.

4.6.4   The tune for subordinate f-structures (modifiers)
P&H do not give examples from which I can extrapolate to these cases. In section 4.5.1 I assigned the following f-structure and pitch accents:

(74)   [[a student]$_{FOC-sub}$ [who I know]$_{TOP-sub}$]$_{TOP}$ [likes linguistics]$_{FOC}$
            L*   H*   H*
            2   3   I

It is perceptually clear that a high phrasal tone marks the end of the relative clause modifier connecting the complex topic to its focus:

(75)   [[a student]$_{FOC-sub}$ [who I know]$_{TOP-sub}$]$_{TOP}$ [likes linguistics] $_{FOC}$
            L*   H   H*   H*
            2   3   I

It is this phrasal tone that gives the feeling of independent intonational phrasing for these subordinate f-structures.

4.6.5   *The fall–rise tunes*[19]

4.6.5.1   L*+H

In Ward and Hirschberg (1985, 1986) a Fall–Rise intonation is assigned the following contour in Pierrehumbert's framework: L*+H L H%. This contour contains the complex pitch accent L*+H and a low phrasal tone followed by a high boundary tone. They claim that this contour conveys "lack of speaker commitment" to a proposed (partially ordered) scale or scalar value. This generalizes two cases: an uncertainty reading and an incredulous reading. In the former, lack of speaker commitment concerning the proposed scale is conveyed, in the latter, lack of speaker commitment to a particular scalar value. P&H revise this proposal as follows. First, they claim that what characterizes the interpretation proposed by Ward and Hirschberg is the complex pitch accent L*+H by itself and that changing the phrasal and boundary tones does not change the basic interpretation. Second, they propose that the interpretation of this pitch accent conveys an evocation of a scale as well as lack of predication. The evocation of a partially ordered scale is characteristic of restrictive focusing (in my terminology). A few illustrations from Ward and Hirschberg follow (their (25), (26); \/ marks the relevant pitch accent):

(76)   A: Did you read the first chapter?
        B: I read the first \half/ of it.
        B: I read the whole disser\ta/tion.
        B: I read the \third/.

(77)   A: How do I get back to Manhatten from Roosevelt Island?
        B: You take the \tram/way.

B's responses in (76) evoke a set of dissertation parts. B's use of the particular intonation contour indicates further that s/he is uncertain that the evoked set is appropriate in the context of A's question. Similarly, in (77) a set of modes of transportation is evoked and B professes uncertainty about whether the one he proposes is the best one. Whereas, cases of incredulity clearly do not involve predication, it is hard to understand P&H's claim with respect to the uncertainty cases. The fact that both the incredulity and the uncertainty cases can be associated with lack of speaker commitment as claimed by Ward and Hirschberg is what makes both of these cases metalinguistic. If we associate the intonation contour solely with the metalinguistic aspect of the interpretation, it signals the addition of an "uncertainty" marker to the focused constituent which is present as an entry on an existing card. The tune does not indicate whether the entry is made via the update rule involved in the processing of the sentence itself, or whether it is presented by a previous utterance as in the case of incredulity.

In these cases a restrictive set (scalar or not) is evoked. In the metalinguistic type of phenomenon discussed here, a member of this set is introduced without the speaker being committed to it (or the evoked set).

4.6.5.2   Contrast: L+H*

P&H claim that correction and contrast are conveyed by the L+H* pitch accent. They associate this contour with an evoked scale as well as predication. This then is the pitch accent associated with metalinguistic negation, contrast, etc.

The following examples are from P&H (their (31), (32), (35)):

(78)   A: It's awfully warm for January.
        B: It's even warm for December.
                        L+H* L H%

(79)   A: I wonder if they're supposed to be married.
        B: No, I don't think they're married. If they were married, he wouldn't be kissing her hand.
                        L+H* L H%

(80)   Mother: It's Raymond and Janet on the phone. They want to know if we can come for dinner.
                        L+H* L H%

These three illustrations are typical of restrictive focusing as described in chapter 3. In (78) the set of cold months is evoked and "December" is asserted to be less likely than "January" to be warm. (79) illustrates metalinguistic negation. A set of body parts is evoked and "her hand" is eliminated from consideration as a likely body part to kiss for a married couple. Finally, P&H suggest that (80) elicits a set of possible invitations, a set of possible ways to spend the evening, or a set of possible queries. Adapting their suggestions to the current framework, each of these set elicitations would be based on a different f-structure in which the focus would be either "for dinner," "come for dinner" or "if we can come for dinner," respectively. In either case all other members of the relevant sets are eliminated by the metalinguistic utterance.

P&H also use Jackendoff's (1972) classical example to illustrate this contour:

(81) TOP_i Fred_{FOC} ate $\begin{bmatrix} \begin{Bmatrix} [\text{the beans}_i]_{\text{FOC}} \\ \text{other foods} \end{Bmatrix} \end{bmatrix}_{\text{TOP-sub}}$

             H*   L   L+H*   L H%

The context assigned is the question:

(82)   What about the beans? Who ate them?

In addition P&H claim that a set of salient foods is evoked. The fact that "beans" are selected from a set of foods and the "other foods" are eliminated is what renders the characteristic metalinguistic pitch accent.

Finally, let us anticipate the discussion of negation and quantified subjects in the next chapter. I note there that Jackendoff assigns the B-accent (fall–rise) to the following example:

(83)   ALL the men didn't go. (not all the men went)

Ward and Hirschberg (1985: 73) assign the following intonation contour to this sentence:

(84)   \All/ the men didn't go.
         L+H*   L H%

In this case the reading will depend on context. If the restrictive set is formed by contrasting "all the men" and "subset of the men" we get the not-all reading. Ward and Hirschberg provide the following context: "In the context of a rehearsal for a men's choir, the choirmaster might ask his subordinate whether all the singers had attended some rehearsal." (84) taken as metalinguistic negation eliminates "all" as the correct value of those who attended and allows for any subset of the men to have attended. Ward and Hirschberg claim that the fall–rise intonation indicates the speaker's uncertainty about whether the choirmaster was interested in a simple yes/no question, or whether he wanted to know what portion of the singers had missed practice. Metalinguistic negation necessitates a contextual assumption or question as to whether *all* the men went. What is negated, then, is the value of the metalinguistically focused *all*.

Ward and Hirschberg give another context for the sentence with the fall–rise intonation which results in the all-not reading (their (75)):

(85)   A: The foreman wants to know which union meeting some of the men missed.
         B: \All/ the men didn't go to the last one.

Here *some* is eliminated as the incorrect value of relevant men and it is replaced by *all*. Since this is a case of contrast the required result is obtained. Note that metalinguistic restrictive sets are elicited by the sentence combined with the context. This is why a variety of such sets can be set up. It follows that getting both wide and narrow scope readings with metalinguistic fall–rise intonation is to be expected.

4.6.6   How f-structures indicate tune

The stress rule accounts for the assignment of pitch accents. F-structures of yes/no questions and other constructions, to which L* pitch accents are assigned, are distinct in view of the presence of the restrictive set in the f-structure. Subordinate f-structures are also clearly marked. Finally, meta-linguistic f-structures are distinct in that the contrast set is marked. Once the theory of tune assignment is fully developed, it should not be difficult to match tunes with f-structures. They come with all the necessary equipment for this purpose.[20]

4.7   Other perspectives on intonation: brief review

In Erteschik-Shir and Lappin (1983) several approaches to intonation were reviewed. These will not be repeated here. Instead I limit the discussion to four. The first is Selkirk (1984) who gives an encompassing theory of the Prosody-Focus Relation and I will give particular attention to her work. In this discussion I also integrate a discussion of Ladd (1980). The second is Jacobs (1991, 1994) which bears certain affinities to my own. The third is Cinque (1993) who represents a relatively recent contribution arguing for a syntactic analysis of stress in which the stress on the focus is superimposed. Finally I briefly examine Steedman (1991) who offers a syntactic analysis based on Combinatory Categorial Grammar. This should suffice to place the approach argued for here within the perspective of current theory. For thorough reviews of preceding theories see also the other sources referred to in this chapter.

4.7.1   Selkirk (1984)

For Selkirk (1984: 200) "the set of assignments of the property of *Focus* to the constituents of a sentence is what we will call its *focus structure*." Focus structure representation is surface structure labeled for focus. There are two major differences between Selkirk's focus structures and mine. 1. Hers are not marked for topic. 2. Whereas I derive stress from f-structure, her focus is derived from stress assignment by the Basic Focus Rule which says that "a constituent to which a pitch accent is assigned is a focus" (p. 207). There are also several similarities:

  1. Selkirk's system does not assume any notion of normal stress allowing free assignment of intonational structures to surface structures.

2. Selkirk allows for contrastive foci.[21] Selkirk also discusses metalinguistic focusing but limits it to cases in which the focus is on a syllable or affix that has no independent meaning. (As in, for example, "I said COFFIN, not COFFEE" (p. 271).)

3. Selkirk's system is sensitive to argument structure. This is expressed by the Phrasal Focus Rule: a constituent may be a focus if (i) or (ii) (or both) is true:

(i)   The constituent that is its *head* is a focus.

(ii)   A constituent contained within it that is an argument of the head is a focus.

A property of the Phrasal Focus Rule is that it allows for embedded foci. This is one of Selkirk's innovations, one that I have adopted (my subordinate foci). Since Selkirk does not make use of the distinction between main foci, which are involved in assessment, and subordinate ones, which are involved only in file manipulations, her system and mine make different predictions.[22] In addition she does not develop her Phrasal Focus Rule to relate to differences in argument types. Selkirk (p. 219) examines one of Ladd's (1980) examples in which the VP is focused, but only the verb is stressed without an associated contrastive interpretation:

(86)   A. Has John read *Slaughterhouse Five*?
        B. No, John doesn't READ books.

B's response presents a problem for those theories that associate normal stress with broad focus and contrastive stress with narrow focus as argued by Ladd. Here the intonation shows narrow focus and the interpretation is not contrastive. According to Selkirk, B's response receives the following focus structure:

(87)

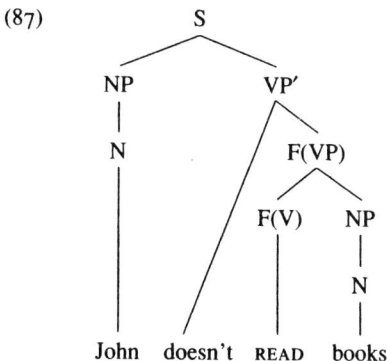

Selkirk's Basic Focus Rule combined with the Phrasal Focus Rule allows the focus to project up to the VP (due to the prominence on the verb). According to Selkirk, the focus must be interpreted as new. The interpretation would come out wrong if the verb were interpreted as the focus, since the verb is not new here. Selkirk is thus able to derive the correct intonation and yet view the VP as focus. Ladd (1980) introduces the following Focus Rule:

(88)   Accent goes on the most accentable syllable of the focus constituent.

According to Ladd, accent falls on READ in (86) because the NP object is deaccented. Ladd (p. 98) claims that deaccenting occurs to signal the relation of the deaccented item to the context. He goes on to show how this contextual relation shows up in an array of examples.

Selkirk raises a conceptual problem with Ladd's analysis in that he does not distinguish between "accentability" and "focus." It follows that deaccenting in Ladd's system is the same as not assigning focus. If, however, "deaccenting" is associated with the notion of Topic (the analysis I propose for cases such as these), Selkirk's conceptual problem disappears and advantage can be taken of the contextual relation in Ladd's analysis. Taking this route would render the following f-structure for the sentence discussed:

(89) $TOP_{i\text{-sub}}$ [John$_{TOP}$ doesn't [read books$_i$]$_{FOC}$]$_{FOC\text{-sub}}$
                      H*

This is the analysis I assigned (in chapter 1) to sentences in which truth value is determined according to the main focus structure, but the card for the subordinate topic "books" is also available on top of the file.[23] It follows that the subordinate f-structure is also involved in the processing of the sentence. The pitch accent is assigned according to the stress rule achieving the correct results, both with respect to f-structure and with respect to stress. The only requirement is that "books" are contextually accessible, i.e., that the mention of *Slaughterhouse Five* summons up the relevant card for books. This type of accommodation is quite common. Ladd mentions that deaccenting is not obligatory in this context and that "books" could equally well be accented. This follows here from the fact that accommodation is not required. I thus take a position quite similar to Ladd's, without evoking degrees of accentability as he does, but still maintaining his ability to account for how context and so-called deaccenting go hand in hand. Selkirk's attempt to manage with just the one notion – focus – does not suffice, it seems, although she is able to derive the correct array of stress assignments. Selkirk (p. 223) offers the following example to argue that default cases occur discourse-initially (this would pull the rug from under Ladd's feet since he only allows deaccenting via context):

(90)   I SAW her again today.

Selkirk says that this intonation pattern depends merely on the referent for "her" being clear enough to the interlocutor, but adds that "it could be spoken upon entering the house, in reference to a particularly strange bag lady who inhabited the neighborhood . . ." Translating Selkirk's (nonlinguistic) "context" into my terminology, it suffices that a card for "her" be accessible on top of the file for the sentence to be uttered, i.e., "her" is a potential (here subordinate) topic.

To argue for her Phrasal Focus Rule Selkirk shows that only heads and arguments can "project" focus to a higher constituent. She gives the following example (her 5.49):

(91)   JOHN bought a RED shirt.

Since "red" is neither a head nor an argument of the VP, or of the NP included in it, Selkirk predicts that the focus cannot project up to the whole sentence. The stress on "red" must, therefore, be taken to be contrastive. This result (and others argued for by Selkirk) also follows from my f-structure analysis of the sentence. (92) illustrates the paired focus structure which must be assigned to (91) due to the accented subject and (93) is the f-structure assigned to the same sentence without stress on the subject. (92) is a possible answer to "Who bought which color shirt?" or "Who bought a shirt of which color?" (93) answers "Which color shirt did John buy?"

(92) $[[\text{John}_{FOC}]_{TOP\text{-}sub}]_{TOP}$ bought a $[\text{red}]_{FOC}$ shirt.
         H*   H*

(93) John_{TOP} [bought a $\begin{bmatrix} \begin{Bmatrix} \text{red}_{FOC} \\ \text{other color} \end{Bmatrix} \\ \quad \text{H*} \end{bmatrix}_{TOP}$ shirt]$_{FOC}$

A crucial advantage of the current approach is that it captures the relation between intonation and interpretation in context. This Selkirk does not do. Selkirk's Phrasal Focus Rule is meant to ensure contrastive interpretation on nonheads and nonarguments. This also falls out of the current theory in which intonation follows from f-structure and not vice versa. The only type of focus that can be assigned to a constituent such as "red" above is paired focus or metalinguistic focus. If we assigned a different f-structure to either of these sentences, we could not derive stress on the adjective. For example, if we assigned the following f-structure instead of (93), all the major categories of the focused constituent (the VP) would be stressed:

(94)   John$_{TOP}$ [bought a red shirt]$_{FOC}$
        H*   H*   H*
         2   3   1

The two major differences between Selkirk's approach and mine (deriving focus from intonation and not vice versa, not allowing for Topic marking in focus structure) make it hard to make a clear comparison. Although Selkirk's intuitions concerning focus interpretation are very much on the mark, her system does not allow for much prediction in that realm. The theory of f-structure I propose is geared to predict interpretation as well as intonation and thus relate the two. I believe this is where its strength lies.

4.7.2   Jacobs (1991, 1994)

Jacobs (1991), who discusses German stress, does mark both topic and focus on syntactic structure. The topic is a designated constituent in SPEC,CP. Focus features are marked on syntactic trees. Jacobs does not distinguish different types of focus but does allow for more than one focus assignment per sentence. His assignment of topic and focus to syntactic trees therefore bears some resemblance to the current system. Jacobs introduces a complex set of rules to account for the derivation of sentence stress in German from his annotated syntactic trees. One of these rules governs the "integration of sister-constituents" (p. 18) which is necessary to explain, for example, the lack of stress of a verb in the vicinity of an argument as mentioned in section 4.1.1. The integration rule proposed by Jacobs is based on the notion "informational unit" which is sensitive not only to adjacency, the focus feature, assignment of the feature [-ns] (not neutrally stressable) and the topic-comment boundary, but also to argument status: "Non-arguments of head constituents in most cases behave like separate information units and therefore cannot be integrated into the head" (p. 19). Jacobs compares the following two examples in German (simplified from Jacobs, pp. 18–20):

(95)   obwohl er in MÜNCHEN wohnt
        although he in Munich   lives
        "although he lives in Munich"

(96)   obwohl er in MÜNCHEN EINKAUFT
        although he in Munich   shops
        "although he shops in Munich"

In (95) the prepositional phrase is an argument of the verb, but not in (96), hence integration of sister constituents has taken place in the former and not in the latter, allowing the different stress patterns.[24] Although the word order makes the data clearer in German, these distinctions in intonation are also noticeable in English. Assume VP focus in the following three examples:

(97)   She lives in Tel-Aviv.
                      H*

(98)   She shops in Tel-Aviv.
              H*   H*

(99)   They inhabit Tel-Aviv.
              H*   H*

The important point to note is that destressing the verb totally does not induce contrast in (97), whereas it does so in the other two examples. Since the object in (99) *is* an argument of the verb, and since none of the other factors listed by Jacobs (1992) is at stake here, his intricate system does not supply a sufficiently accurate account. The approach outlined here, however, can only offer the following solution: the verb in (97), but not in (99), is a light verb, hence the difference in stress. Whether this is sufficient, or whether argument structure is at stake as well, will be left as an open question, a question which should most probably be examined in a language such as German in which the distinctions are much easier to discern.

Jacobs (1994) offers a more refined account of Informational Autonomy which potentially offers a solution to the problematic (99) (for which an equivalent German example should not be hard to find). Jacobs suggests that argument integration is sensitive to whether the argument has a typical θ-role (in the sense of Dowty 1991). It can easily be argued that the object of *inhabit* does not bear any proto-patient properties, hence integration is blocked and the correct result achieved.

Informational autonomy and f-structure are related, I believe, and for many of the phenomena discussed by Jacobs an account in terms of subordinate f-structures can be provided. It would, however, take us too far afield here to do so especially in view of the fact that the problem with Jacobs' approach is not that it cannot derive correct stress assignments, but rather, as Jacobs himself admits, "that it is based on a complex condition consisting of several more or less unrelated parts" (p. 130).

One of the strengths of Jacobs' proposal is that "it explains without additional assumptions the difference between the stress patterns in head-final and non-head-final constructions or languages" (p. 117). This follows primarily from the fact that the non-autonomy of heads is marked by destressing. An integrated VP consisting of a verb and a direct object will have stress on the direct object since the head verb will be destressed. In a verb-final language this will result in stress on the preverbal object. If the verb precedes the object, however, the stress will occur on the last element of the phrase. This distinction surfaces only in cases of non-autonomy, allowing for stress on non-integrated verbs, for example.

4.7.3   Cinque (1993)

Cinque (1993) proposes a purely syntactic approach to stress assignment, the "null theory." Stress assignment on focus constituents is achieved by a separate discourse grammar procedure which determines that stress on focused constituents wins out (relatively) over stress on presupposed constituents. Cinque argues for a separation of the two procedures (syntactic stress assignment and the discourse grammar procedure) by showing that the syntactic stress rule applies not only to focused constituents, but also to presupposed constituents. The example Cinque uses to argue for this conclusion follows (his (46), p. 258):

(100)   a. (Any news of John?)
         [$_{NP}$ Our poor chîld] [$_{VP}$ is in bed with a 'flú].
         b. (Who's in bed with a 'flu?)
         [$_{NP}$ Our poor chîld] [$_{VP}$ is in bed with a 'flû].

Cinque argues that both the presuppositions in these two examples (the NP in (100a) and the VP in (100b)) as well as the focus constituents have "a detectable prominence" which, in the null theory, follows from the sentence grammar procedure that applies to all phrases blindly (i.e., independently of the discourse grammar rule). The approach I argue for here, however, achieves the same results *without* recourse to a sentence grammar stress rule. The f-structures and associated stress patterns (equivalent to the ones indicated by Cinque) of these sentences follow:

(101)   a. [Our$_{TOP\text{-}sub}$ [poor child]$_{FOC\text{-}sub}$]$_{TOP}$ [is in bed with a flu]$_{FOC}$
                          L*   H*   H*
                          2   3   1
         b. [[Our poor child]$_{FOC}$]$_{TOP}$ [is in bed with a flu]
              H*
              1   3   2

The stress assignment in (101a) follows without further ado from the application of the stress rule to the indicated f-structure. It is the subordinate f-structure on the subject which replaces the need for an additional structural stress rule. In (101b), however, the stress rule only applies to the focus constituent and the additional stresses on the presupposed part of the sentence are inherited from the stress assignment in the question (in a weakened form) as indicated in section 4.1.2. Note that, depending on context, (101b) is either restrictive, contrastive or an answer to an echo question, as predicted by the fact that no stage topic is available. It follows that a subordinate f-structure on the subject is required as indicated.

One of the foremost strengths of Cinque's proposal is its ability to predict the different stress assignments on right- and left-branching languages without any stipulation. Details aside, Cinque's rules will always assign main stress to the most deeply embedded constituent. In a right-branching language this constituent will be to the right and in a left-branching language, to the left, predicting the observed distinctions on purely structural grounds. (In contradistinction to Jacobs (1994), Cinque's approach is not sensitive to informational autonomy.)

My argument with Cinque is the relationship between the "syntactic" stress assignment rule and what he calls the discourse grammar procedure. My proposal has essentially been that f-structure determines prominences on constituents and that this stress is actualized by a rhythm rule. (See section 4.1.1.) This rule (which lowers initial and middle stresses) is syntactic in that it applies to syntactic constituents and could easily be made sensitive to whether a language is left or right branching, thus incorporating a version of Cinque's syntactic stress rule into the current framework. This would render a theory which is basically the reverse of Cinque's in that the syntactic stress rule would apply to the *output* of f-structure-determined stress assignment. An immediate advantage of this combination is that correct predictions can be made in cases in which, as Jacobs (1994: 130) points out, Cinque makes the wrong predictions (his (24c) and (37b)):

(102) a. . . . daß Karl [ein Buch mit Mühe   lesen] kann.
          that Karl a   book with difficulty read   can
       b. . . . Weil [$_{IP}$ Fritz [$_{VP}$ gút   kochen] kann]
          because Fritz   well cook   can
          "because Fritz can cook well . . ."

According to Cinque, the null theory predicts primary stress on the XP immediately to the left of the verb in German because this XP is the most deeply embedded constituent of the VP. Although this is the correct result in many cases, the stress derived in this fashion in (102a and b) can only be taken contrastively. The correct stress assignments (for VP focus) are:

(103) a. . . . daß Karl ein Buch mit Mühe lésen kann.
       b. . . . Weil Fritz gut kochen kann

I have not discussed modification of verbs here so far. In section 4.4.4 it was noted that stress on verbs depends not only on contextual factors but also on how "heavy" they are. If we view the modifier+verb as a unit, this would provide us with a heavy verb which would require focusing and stress overruling the simple application of the (new) rhythm rule.[25] Evidence for this proposal comes from English:

(104)   a. Karl reads a book with dífficulty.
         b. Fritz cóoks well.

In the English version, the PP modifier in (104a) cannot be integrated into the verb since integration obviously depends on adjacency. Hence the main stress occurs at the end of the VP constituent as required for English. In (104b), however, the modifier is adjacent to the verb, and if it is integrated, the main stress ends up on the verb. The issue of how light and heavy verbs interact with f-structure and stress assignment is too complex to enter any further here.

There is, however, one more point that Cinque makes, which is directly relevant to a comparison of the f-structure theoretical approach to stress assignment and the null theory. Consider the following contrast (Cinque's (38a, b)):

(105)   a. [$_{CP}$DerArzt [$_{C'}$ wird [$_{AgrP}$[$_{VP}$ einen Patiénten untersuchen]]]].
            the doctor will   a   patient   examine
            "The doctor will examine a patient."
         b. [$_{CP}$Der Arzt [$_{C'}$ wird [$_{AgrP}$ den Patienten$_i$ [$_{VP}$t$_i$ untersúchen]]]].
            the doctor will   the patient   examine
            "The doctor will examine the patient"

The null theory predicts stress in preverbal position as in (105a). In order to account for the stress on the verb when the object is definite, Cinque assumes that definite objects are scrambled out of the VP as the structure in (105b) indicates. It is possible that such a scrambling rule can be independently argued for as Cinque claims.[26] The stress contrast, however, follows without special stipulation from f-structure theory: when the object is definite it naturally functions as the topic in a subordinate f-structure taking the verb as its focus, rendering the correct stress assignment to the verb; when the object is indefinite such a subordinate f-structure does not make sense unless the indefinite itself is modified:

(106)   Der Artzt wird ein guten Freund von mir   untersúchen.
         the doctor will a   good friend of mine examine

Here the verb is stressed despite the indefinite object due to the fact that the object itself has a subordinate f-structure licensing it as topic. Cinque's approach would require scrambling to apply to some indefinite objects and not to others.

The points suggested here indicate that a fruitful line of research might be to investigate the shape a syntactic stress-actualization rule would take if it is applied to the output of the here suggested stress rule which applies to f-structure. Such a rule could be made sensitive to whether it applies to a right- or left-branching tree in the spirit of Cinque's null theory.

4.7.4 Steedman (1991, 1994)

I am in general sympathy with the discussion of intonation in Steedman. Steedman argues for theme/rheme annotation of constituents of surface structure. His approach is driven by his interest in providing evidence for Combinatory Categorial Grammar. Much work has been done on coordination within the framework of this theoretical approach, dealing with problems of constituency in Right Node Raising constructions. Steedman here shows that a sequence such as "Mary prefers" within "Mary prefers corduroy" is analyzed as a constituent within CCG allowing both the coordination phenomena as well as intonational phrasing of such "constituents." In Erteschik-Shir (1987) I propose an analysis of Right Node Raising involving parallel formatting which does not necessitate the assumption that "Mary prefers," etc. be a syntactic constituent. At the same time, my version of f-structure annotation applies to parallel formatted coordinate structures, allowing for the same predictions as the ones made by Steedman concerning the isomorphism between constraints on intonational phrasing and coordination.

Steedman (1994) assumes a simple database model which consists of a small set of facts, represented by first-order terms. His procedural account is not given in sufficient detail to decide what it has in common with the one proposed here. It is evident, however, that there are several similarities. First, Steedman's model requires both theme and rheme. Second, he notes following Halliday (1967) that pitch accent can occur within both the theme and the rheme in cases of contrast. He further offers an analysis of the intonation of sentences with *only* and *even* and again gives evidence for a "two-level" account of focus distinguishing between theme/rheme and accent/background. I have tried to account for similar data by using embedded f-structures. A careful comparison of the current approach to a more extensive sample of Steedman's work is therefore clearly called for.

In this chapter I have outlined the basic predictions made by the theory of f-structure with respect to intonation. My purpose has been to show that a simple stress rule applied to f-structures suffices to account for the distribution of pitch accent in sentences. In addition, I showed that f-structure provides much of the relevant annotation to account for the intonational contours described in P&H. It is my hope that future developments in the theory of f-structure, together with an examination of the intonation of sentences chosen according to the classification of f-structures suggested here, will render even more significant results. I did not intend this chapter to give a complete account of stress and intonation and limited myself to some of the major issues onto which f-structure can shed some light.

I have left three important topics involving nuclear stress assignment aside. The first is an account for out-of-the-blue sentences (with stage topics) in which only the subject is stressed as in:

(107)   The SUN is shining.

This intonation pattern for out-of-the-blue sentences is a lexical property of the predicate. Predicates which invoke this stress pattern include unaccusatives which can be shown to be "light" in the sense discussed above. I intend to develop this idea in Erteschik-Shir (in prep. a).

The second issue has to do with the f-structure and accompanying intonation of complex sentences with complement clauses. The third topic is the characterization of those syntactic positions that do not allow (main) focus assignment, for example the direct object position in datives:

(108)   John gave MARY the book.

The focus in (108) can only be taken to be contrastive. The latter two topics will be dealt with briefly in chapter 6.

5 *Scope and R-dependencies*

5.1   Scope and f-structure

A variety of results follow from the view that f-structure mediates between syntax and semantics. This chapter concentrates on issues related to scope and demonstrates that f-structures are scopally disambiguated. One important result is that the topic by definition takes scope over the rest of the sentence. Further, the existence of f-structures with implicit stage topics allows for unscoped interpretations.

I argue here that topics are quantificational in that they provide the domain for overt quantifiers. A topic provides a link to the preceding discourse in which it is introduced by a focus constituent which may or may not be restrictive. In the former case, its quantificational nature follows from the application of the semantic rule of predication which requires assessment for every single member of this restricted set. A simple definite topic such as *the man* can be viewed as quantificational, in that predication ranges over the "single" member of the topic-set. The link of the topic to the discourse also makes the contextual restriction of quantifiers fall out automatically. So, for example, the topic *everyone* must be interpreted as "everyone we are talking about," it is a context-specified set represented by a card with the heading *everyone*$_i$, i.e., it is referential.

To show how f-structure determines scope, I examine scope relations among two quantifiers, a quantifier and negation and scope in multiple *wh*-questions.

5.1.1   R-dependencies

I use the term R-dependence when reference is defined by f-structure update, as in the sentences in (1).

(1)   a. John talked to a boy.
          b. He criticized her.
          c. Two girls arrested three boys.
          d. Everyone talked to someone.

In (1a) the indefinite object in the focus triggers the construction of a new card. The content of this card is determined solely by the entry made by update. All we know about *a boy* is that he is someone John talked to. He does not have an "identity" independently of the utterance at hand. This is what I call R-dependence. If an R-dependency involves introducing a new card into the hearer's file, the card is assigned its reference merely in terms of the predication in which it occurs; it may be specific to the speaker, but not to the hearer. In this sense R-dependencies are speaker oriented and the only requirements on such dependencies are the ones applying to f-structure. R-dependencies thus encompass those dependencies that follow from the f-structure determined update rules. In chapter 2, I therefore referred to coreferential pronouns, which are interpreted by being entered on the cards with the relevant headings, as R-dependent pronouns.

In chapter 1, I argued for the Topic Constraint on f-structure repeated here:

(2)   Topic Constraint (first version):
       $*TOP_i [SUBJECT_{TOP-sub} [\ldots NP_i \ldots]_{FOC}]_{FOC}$

The Topic Constraint says that if both the subject and another argument qualify as topics, i.e., represent cards on top of the file, the *subject* must be picked as the topic of the main f-structure. The constraint is also intended to reflect the intuition that the unmarked f-structure is one in which the subject is the topic. This was not stated as part of the constraint in chapter 1. The Topic Constraint is amended accordingly (> = less marked):

(3)   Topic Constraint (second version):
       i. $*TOP_i [SUBJECT_{TOP-sub} [\ldots NP_i \ldots]_{FOC-sub}] _{FOC}$
       ii. $SUBJECT_{TOP} [\ldots NP_i \ldots]_{FOC} > TOP_i [SUBJECT [\ldots NP_i \ldots]]_{FOC}$

(4) is therefore the unmarked f-structure for the sentence (1b), for example:

(4) $TOP_{i-sub} [He_{TOP} [criticized her_{TOPi}]_{FOC}]_{FOC-sub}$

Both pronouns are referentially dependent on cards discoursally placed on top of the file and the main f-structure takes the subject as its topic. Note that the object pronoun is interpreted via coreference licensing (due to the subordinate f-structure). The reference of the pronoun is not determined sentence internally via the update on the main topic card. If the hearer does not have a card on top of the file for the pronoun before the utterance, the sentence will not be interpretable.

If both subject and object qualify as *potential* topics, i.e., they are definite and therefore represent existing cards, the subject will be chosen unless the discourse pushes heavily for the other f-structure. Although f-structures are available in which the object is interpreted as a topic, the unmarked interpretation is still the one in which the subject is taken to be the topic. This can be seen in the following interchange which fixes *John* as the topic:

(5)   Tell me about John:
       a.   He is in love with Mary.
       b.   ??Mary is in love with him.

How do f-structures with stage topics rate in relation to the f-structures with subject or object topics? In sentences with no potential NP topics, only the stage topic f-structure is available:

(6)   sTOP$_t$ [A girl talked to a boy]$_{FOC}$

This is the only f-structure possible for the sentence which answers a question such as "What happened next?" The following example illustrates a case in which the object is a potential topic and the subject is not rendering the following possible f-structures:

(7)   a.   TOP$_i$ [A girl talked to John$_i$]$_{FOC}$
             (Answers: Tell me about John)
       b.   sTOP$_t$ [A girl talked to John]$_{FOC}$
             (Answers: What happened next?)

(7a), in which the object is interpreted as the topic, is less natural than (7b) with the stage topic. This is to be expected because the sentence with the object topic could be rephrased with the topic in subject position.

It remains to compare stage and subject topics which are both less marked than sentences with object topics.

(8)   a.   John$_{TOP}$ [talked to a girl]$_{FOC}$
             (Answers: Tell me about John)
       b.   sTOP$_t$ [John talked to a girl]$_{FOC}$
             (Answers: What happened next?)

Here the sentence is equally natural in both contexts and I conclude that there is no marking distinction to be made between these two f-structures leaving us with the following final version of the Topic Constraint:

Topic Constraint (final version):
       i.   *TOP$_i$ [SUBJECT$_{TOP-sub}$ [... NP$_i$ ... $_{FOC-sub}$]$_{FOC}$
       ii. $\begin{Bmatrix} \text{SUBJECT}_{TOP} \text{ [...]}_{FOC} \\ \text{sTOP}_t \text{ [...]}_{FOC} \end{Bmatrix}$ > TOP$_i$ [SUBJECT [... NP$_i$ ...]]$_{FOC}$

The Topic Constraint, which applies to R-dependencies, provides an explanation for the well-known fact that certain scopal interpretations are much harder to get than others. (1c), for example, illustrates an example with two weak quantifiers. Weak quantifiers can be interpreted as topics only if they are interpreted partitively. Again the unmarked case will be the one in which the subject is taken as the topic, but if a set of boys is available in the context and a set of girls is not, the object and not the subject will function as the main topic. Since the topic has wide scope, context will be seen to determine scopal relations in sentences. Similarly for (1d).

R-dependencies are defined by f-structure update rules. Any NP in an R-dependency which receives a specific interpretation must therefore represent an existing card in the file. Importantly, sentences with R-dependencies are constrained only by f-structure and the Topic Constraint. Chapter 6 defines a different kind of dependency and provides an account in terms of focus structure for the distinction between the two types of dependency and the constraints on them.

5.2   Machinery

5.2.1   *Plural sums, plural sets*
In this section I present some machinery for the interpretation of plurals inspired mainly by Massey (1976) and Landman (1989a, 1989b and in prog.). This machinery enables me to show how plural topics function. What is more important, it will allow me to give an f-structure-theoretical account of scope phenomena.

How are sentences with plural topics assessed? Examine the following:

(9)   a. Tom, Dick, and Harry are intelligent.
       b. The students are intelligent.

Tom, Dick, and Harry can be conceived of as a set whose members are *Tom, Dick,* and *Harry,* or as a *sum* individual whose "person parts" are *Tom, Dick,* and *Harry.* Following Massey (1976), the set is represented as in (10) and the sum individual as in (11):

(10) $\{t,d,h\}_i$

(11) $+(t,d,h)_i$

The set reading is a distributive reading in which each of the members of the set figures as an independent entity. The sum individual reading renders a group or collective reading, i.e., the "person parts" are not accessible. Figuratively, the former reading follows from an interior perspective on the conjunction and the latter as an exterior perspective on it. Following common usage, I refer to these readings as "distributive" and "collective" respectively.[1]

Similarly, plural noun phrases such as *the students* may receive both a set and a sum reading. Let us now examine how these two interpretations of plurals make for two different modes of assessment when the plural is the topic. (9a) necessitates that the hearer, as well as the speaker, has on top of his file either the set (10) (i.e., a restrictive set card consisting of three individual cards) or an individual sum card (11). In the first case the sentence is assessed separately with respect to each of the individual cards in the set. This is how the distributive reading is derived for conjunctive and plural topics. Let us examine the collective reading for (9b) in which the *students*$_i$ is the topic. In this case the truth value of the sentence is determined without an examination of the individuals within the set, since there is no access to the "person parts" within the "fused" set.[2] The hearer will not be able to determine whether information s/he has about an individual student in the class is or is not relevant to assessment. If, for example, the hearer has the following entry on the relevant card

(12)   Mary$_j$ is in e$_i$

then, under the collective reading, the hearer will not be able to access the individuals contained in the group, hence will not be able to tell whether the information in (12) is relevant to the assessment. The collective interpretation of the subject does therefore not render a plausible reading for a sentence such as (9b). This is, of course even clearer from the speaker's perspective. In order for the speaker to say (9b), he must scan the individual members of the set of students, i.e., he has a set of cards (representing the individual students) which together receive the heading *students*$_i$. There are cases in which the collective reading is more easily derived:

(13)   Tom, Dick, and Harry weigh 270 lb.

Clearly, a truth value can be assigned to (13) without access to information concerning the weights if the three individuals. It would be sufficient to have seen the group get on a scale together, i.e., the sentence can be assessed with respect to the sum.

I have shown that plurals form sets which are either interpreted collectively or distributively when they are topics. The collective reading is attained by predicating of the singleton set formed by viewing the set as a sum. The distributive reading is derived by applying predication to each individual member of the topic set. It follows that a quantificational reading is available for plural topics.

5.2.2   Weak determiners
Let us now examine weakly quantified topics:

(14)   a. TWO students are inTELLigent.
        b. Two STUdents are inTELLigent.

(15)   a. SOME students are inTELLigent.
        b. Sm STUdents are inTELLigent.

A possible context for (14a) is one in which a set of students is supplied by the context:

(16)   [I have a class of six students.]
        TWO (students) are intelligent,
        THREE (students) are mediocre, and
        ONE (student) is a total idiot.

In (16) the set of students focally introduced in the bracketed sentence is fully partitioned. The subject of (14a) is therefore interpreted partitively if the necessary restrictive set has been introduced in the preceding discourse. The same analysis applies to (15a).[3] The intonation of (14a) and (15a) supports this analysis. In both cases a subordinate f-structure is indicated in which the unstressed noun "students" is the topic and the stressed quantifier is the focus:

(17)   [TWO$_{FOC\text{-sub}}$ students$_{TOP\text{-sub}}$]$_{TOP}$ · · ·

(14b) and (15b) are acceptable under a contrastive reading (see chapter 3) or else under a specific reading (see chapters 1 and 2). The focused (stressed) nouns enable the necessary subordinate f-structure. Weak determiners allow for either specific or partitive readings by means of subordinate f-structures. These readings have been referred to as "presuppositional" readings in Diesing (1992), and as "strong" readings (of weak determiners) by de Hoop (1992). I will use the latter term.

It is also possible to verify (as was done for the partitives) that assessment of these topics must be distributive. Distributive readings range over the sets defined by these strong NPs. A "weak" topic is a contradiction in terms involving quantifying over undefined sets.

5.2.3   Strong determiners

What it means for an NP to be strong or definite is that a card representing a discourse-restricted set (of students, here) is assumed to be available in the hearer's file. This set can be interpreted as a sum or as a set. Again, the set interpretation is necessary for the distributive assessment of the sentence. Examine the following examples:

(18)   a. Every student is intelligent.
         b. Every student in my class is intelligent.
         c. Everyone is intelligent.

To determine the truth value of (18a) each of the individual students in the set must be examined. This set is represented by a restrictive set of cards on top of the file which receives a unified heading. The individual cards which constitute this set must be examined in order for a truth value to be assigned. The restrictive set can be introduced by a subordinate f-structure as in (18b). I assume no partitioning of this set since *every* ranges over all the members of the set.

How the set is to be partitioned is a property of the particular quantifier in question. The evaluation process for *most* is more complex than the one suggested for universal quantifiers. In the following

(19)   Most students in my class are intelligent.

a topic set encompassing the students in my class is available and this set is partitioned by the quantifier. As before, the derived set provides the main topic for assessment. How do we achieve such a partitioning with *most*? Clearly there is no single set that *most students* could represent. As mentioned by an anonymous reviewer, when our model contains students a, b, c, d, then the sets {a,b,c}, {a,c,d}, {b,c,d} and {a,b,c,d} provide possible partitions for which the evaluation of the sentence comes out true. If *most* is interpreted roughly as "more than half," then the result is achieved if any partitioning of the set of students which results in more than half of them is licensed. The result of partitioning should therefore not be viewed as defining a necessarily unique new subset. For *most, many*, etc. it suffices that a subset of the appropriate size is definable. Note the interpretation of the pronoun in the following:

(20)   Most of the students came to the party. *They* had a good time.

The pronoun refers to whichever set of students (counting as *most* students) actually came to the party.

Whether the quantifier is strong or weak, if it quantifies a topic, it must receive a strong reading, i.e., there must be a card, or set of cards available on top of the hearer's file. I have shown that topic sets generate a quantificational reading when they consist of more than one member. This reading is obtained because the rule of predication must distribute over the individual members of this set. In

(21)   The boy is intelligent.

The set $\{boy_i\}$ (which happens to have only one member) is assessed in the same manner. The quantificational reading is therefore a direct outcome of the fact that topics may have set readings and that sets may have more than one member.

5.3   Quantifier scope

I will now argue that f-structures are scopally transparent and can be interpreted directly. LF processes such as Quantifier Raising (QR) are rendered superfluous. I will also argue that suggestions such as May's (1977) that focus constituents are raised by QR in LF are not only superfluous but give bad results.

For the moment, I limit the discussion to scope interactions in simple transitive sentences. At least the following three f-structures are available for sentences with quantifiers in subject and object position (Q_1 = subject, Q_2 = object):

(22)   a. $[Q_1]_{TOP}$ [V $Q_2]_{FOC}$
        b. TOP_2 [Q_1 V $Q_2]_{FOC}$
        c. $sTOP_1$ [Q_1 V $Q_2]_{FOC}$

Two important results follow from the interpretation of f-structures argued for in the previous chapters:

1.   Topic quantifiers take wide scope over any other quantifier.
2.   There are nonscoped f-structures.

I will start by discussing Topic scope: a topic has been defined as a card on top of the file. The existence of such a card presupposes the existence in the discourse of the referent of the card "heading." Predication takes the focus constituent and assesses its truth value with respect to the topic. It follows that the topic necessarily has wider scope than any constituent contained within the focus. Thus, in (22a) Q_1 is the topic, Q_2 is contained within the focus. Predication applies as follows: for each individual contained in Q_1, the truth of the focus constituent containing Q_2 is assessed, i.e., Q_1 has scope over Q_2. If we follow the same reasoning for (22b), we get the opposite scope relation. Two scoped readings thus follow without further ado from applying predication to these f-structures.

In (22c) the topic is a stage topic, hence neither of the quantified NPs is a topic and a nonscoped reading results. In the next section I show, following Landman (in prog.), that there are actually four nonscoped readings, all of which have the same focus structure. Under this view, for each case in which a quantified NP is analyzed as the topic, there are two readings to be derived.

5.3.1   Cardinal scope

In section 5.2.1 a distinction was made between a set reading (distributive) or a sum reading (collective) of plural NPs.[4] According to Landman a sentence such as (23) has the eight readings listed in (24) and (25). (24) represents four unscoped readings in which each of the cardinals enables a collective and a distributive reading. (25) represents the four scoped readings which Landman derives by a special scope rule. (C = collective, D = distributive, subscript s = subject, subscript o = object, scope = parenthesis):

(23)   Two girls arrested three boys.

(24)   a. C C $\{+(a,b)\} \rightarrow \{+(1,2,3)\}$
        b. C D $\{+(a,b)\} \rightarrow 1$
                           $\rightarrow 2$
                           $\rightarrow 3$
        c. D C $a \rightarrow \{+(1,2,3)\}$
                  $b \rightarrow$
        d. D D $a \rightarrow 1$
                  $b \rightarrow 2$
                    $\rightarrow 3$

(25)   a. D_s (C_o) $a \rightarrow [1,2,3]$
                           $b \rightarrow [4,5,6]$
        b. D_s (D_o) $a \rightarrow 1$ $b \rightarrow 4$
                            $\rightarrow 2$ $\rightarrow 5$
                            $\rightarrow 3$ $\rightarrow 6$
        c. D_o (C_s) $[a,b] \rightarrow 1$
                           $[c,d] \rightarrow 2$
                           $[e,f] \rightarrow 3$
        d. D_o (D_s) $a \rightarrow 1$ $c \rightarrow 2$ $e \rightarrow 3$
                           $b \rightarrow$ $d \rightarrow$ $f \rightarrow$

The f-structure of all the cases listed in (24) is (22c) which has a stage topic. For each plural NP, as we saw above, there are two possible interpretations: collective and distributive. (24a) gets collective readings for both NPs, i.e., the group "two girls" arrested the group "three boys." (24b) says that the group "two girls" arrested three individual boys. (24c) involves two individual girls who arrest a group of three boys. (24d) is the double distributive reading in which two individual girls arrest three individual boys, i.e., there is *some* pairing between the two girls and the three boys such that for each girl there is one or more boys (of the three) that she arrests, and no boy gets left unarrested. (Since the reading leaves the number of pairings unspecified with a minimum of three and a maximum of six, the number of "arrows" which indicates the number of "pairings" has been left open. This reading includes the "all-all" reading in which each of the two girls arrests each of the three boys. This reading, according to Landman, is the borderline case of (24d).

All of these are assessed with respect to the discourse here-and-now, i.e., only *one* event is involved for each reading (and only two girls and three boys are involved in each case). A distinction is thus made between the number of pairings, in this case the number of arrests (which ranges between one and three), and the number of events. Imagine, for example, the following spatio-temporal parameters: "today, between 6 and 7 pm, in Beer Sheva." These parameters define the stage upon which all the arrests take place. No individual stage for each separate pairing is made available. This is a requirement of the stage-topic reading evidenced by the presence of an overt stage topic:

(26)   a. Today, two girls arrested three boys.
        b. At 6 o'clock, two girls arrested three boys.
        c. On the corner, two girls arrested three boys.

The two scoped readings (25a) and (25b) are derived from the f-structure in (22a) by allowing the object to be either distributive or collective. Similarly, for (25c and d) which are derived from the f-structure (22b). These readings in which the object NP is interpreted as having wide scope are highly marked. According to the Topic Constraint, if both the subject and the object are candidates for topichood, i.e., both represent available cards on top of the file, then the subject will take precedence as the main topic. In the cases discussed here, both the subject and object are cardinal. Pending contextualization both are therefore equally likely candidates for topichood. Only a context that enhances the object-topic reading will make such a reading possible. This is the reason it takes brute force (i.e., ample contextualization) to convince speakers of the readings in which the object has scope over the subject.

In section 5.2.2, I showed that the intonation of partitive readings differed from that of specific readings of cardinal NPs. Partitioning is parasitic on an inside view of the set and can be associated with a distributive reading. A specific cardinal NP, on the other hand, refers to a group. The various readings in (24) and (25) should be intonationally distinguishable. I will give the intonation patterns predicted, although it is clear to me that the intuitions of speakers are not fine-tuned enough to associate these patterns with the relevant readings.[5]

(27)   a. Two GIRLS arrested three BOYS. (sTOP$_t$ C C)
        b. Two GIRLS arrested THREE boys. (sTOP$_t$ C D), (TOP$_o$ C)
        c. TWO girls arrested three BOYS. (sTOP$_t$ D C), (TOP$_s$ C)
        d. TWO girls arrested THREE boys. (sTOP$_t$ D D), (TOP$_s$ D), (TOP$_o$ D)

I predict that the most popular intonation pattern for sentences of this sort will be (27d) since three different readings are associated with it. It is therefore not surprising that speakers find it hard to supply the variety of readings available for each intonation pattern. (27a) is also not impossible to get, but the other two are not only tongue twisters, but also brain twisters.

The three f-structures in (22), together with Landman's analysis of plurals as either distributive or collective, renders the eight readings listed above. Landman's scope rule becomes superfluous if predication is read off f-structures, since this is what forces a distributive reading of topics. The unscoped readings are also a direct outcome of the view that f-structures allow for stage topics.

Since stage topics are ruled out for individual-level predicates, it is predicted that the four unscoped readings are not available for them. Only the readings (25) and none of the readings in (24) should be available for (28):

(28)   Two students know three languages.

Note, however, that the f-structure (22a), with an additional subordinate f-structure in the VP, in which the object quantifier is the topic, gives a symmetric interpretation mimicking (24d). The intonation involves stressing the verb to the exclusion of the NPs:

(29)   TOP$_i$ [Two Chinese girls]$_{TOP}$ [ADORE [three American boys]$_i$]$_{FOC}$

Such a reading is not excluded in the present system.

In chapter 1, section 1.6.3.2, we noted that certain (individual-level) predicates block a reading in which the object is interpreted as the topic. For such sentences only the readings predicted by the f-structure (22a) (in which the subject is the topic) are possible. This is the case in the following examples:

(30)   a. Two boxes contain three books.
         b. Two lakes are close to three houses.
         c. Two women have three husbands.
         d. Two dogs require three caretakers.

The only readings we get for the sentences in (30) are

(31)   a. D_s (C_o) a $\rightarrow$ [1,2,3]
                            b $\rightarrow$ [4,5,6]

         b. D_s (D_o) a $\rightarrow$ 1   b $\rightarrow$ 4
                            $\rightarrow$ 2 $\rightarrow$ 5
                            $\rightarrow$ 3 $\rightarrow$ 6

Neither of the other two scoped readings, nor the four unscoped readings are possible for these predicates.

I take this fact as strong evidence in favor of my position that f-structures are disambiguated with respect to scope. F-structure thus replaces LF in deriving structures which directly feed the semantic component. The LF rule of quantifier raising (cf. May 1977, 1985) will not be necessary. May (1989) argues that LF does not render structures disambiguated with respect to scope. The readings are rather semantically derived. F-structure, under my view, is disambiguated and feeds the semantic rule of predication to render the correct readings. These disambiguated f-structures interact with the semantics of the various quantifiers as will be argued presently.

In the next section I argue that all cases of quantifier scope boil down to f-structure predication. Under this view, there is no need for semantic scope rules since scope is read off f-structure. The theory of f-structure and predication also leaves obsolete any type of syntactic quantifier raising rules. If quantifier raising (QR) is rendered obsolete, LF loses at least some of its raison d'être.[6]

5.3.2   Some–every *scopes*

Let us test whether these predictions can be verified with other quantifiers:

(32)   a. Someone arrested everyone.
         b. Everyone arrested someone.

In chapter 1 it was noted that *someone* cannot be a main topic (unless it is contrastive). The two readings in which *someone* would be a topic are thus excluded from the sentences in (32). Further, *someone* is singular, therefore the distributive/collective distinction is irrelevant. That cuts another three readings and we are left with three readings for each sentence represented by the following f-structures:

(33) a. sTOP$_t$ [everyone$_D$ arrested someone]$_{FOC}$
      b. sTOP$_t$ [everyone$_C$ arrested someone]$_{FOC}$
      c. Everyone$_{TOP}$ [arrested someone]$_{FOC}$

(34) a. sTOP$_t$ [someone arrested everyone$_D$]$_{FOC}$
      b. sTOP$_t$ [someone arrested everyone$_C$]$_{FOC}$
      c. TOP$_i$ [someone arrested everyone$_i$]$_{FOC}$

(33a) involves one event in which one person gets arrested by each of the members of the set defined by *everyone*. (33b) differs only in *everyone* being viewed collectively, i.e., the arrest is performed as a group action. In (33c) *everyone* is the topic of the sentence. *Everyone* must therefore be a discourse-specified set represented by an indexed card on top of the file. Since predication involves assessment for each individual member of this set, a distributive reading is achieved. This reading takes an "undefined" *someone* for each of the members of the set and gives us the interpretation:

(35) $\forall x, \forall y$ (x arrested y)

The Topic Constraint picks (33c) as the least marked f-structure for the sentence. It follows that (35) is the most natural reading. The readings derived from the f-structures with stage topics are very highly marked. This is because strongly quantified NPs necessarily presuppose a contextually defined set, i.e., they represent an existing card. In principle, this card, as any other definite, need not be positioned on top of the file forcing a topic reading. However, for the pronominal form *everyone* (as opposed to *every teacher*, say), only a few contexts would allow unambiguous reference to such a card if it were not already to be found on top of the file. It follows that the most likely use of *everyone* is as a topic or at least as a subordinate topic. If a context with a stage topic is contextually forced, the following f-structure with a subordinate f-structure is therefore most plausible:

(36) sTOP$_t$ [everyone$_{TOP-sub}$ [arrested someone]$_{FOC-sub}$]$_{FOC}$

The subordinate f-structure again derives a "scoped" reading in which *everyone* has wide scope. The readings resulting from (33a and b) in which a "single" *someone* is arrested, are therefore almost impossible to get, unless of course an *overtly* triggered subordinate f-structure on *someone* is provided as in:

(37) Everyone arrested someone, namely his best friend.

The story is the same for the f-structures in (34a and b) except that the "arresting" is reversed. Here again, properties of the strong quantifier force a subordinate f-structure as follows:

(38)   sTOP$_t$ [TOP$_{i\text{-sub}}$ [someone arrested everyone$_i$]$_{FOC\text{-sub}}$]$_{FOC}$

The f-structure (34c) is almost impossible to contextualize at least with the predicate "arrest." Destressing *everyone* together with an appropriate context generally works. Note that, according to the Topic Constraint, since *everyone* is a strong quantifier and *someone* is not (unless it is used partitively), the odds are already skewed in favor of *everyone* being the topic.[7]

Each only allows a distributive reading in which the individual members of a set are scanned, i.e., no collective reading is available independently of whether *each* quantifies a topic or not. This is the reason *each* always seems to take wide scope. Vendler (1967) argues this point by noting the following differences between *each* and *every*:

(39)   a.   each of them vs. *every of them
          b.   ??each one of them vs. every one of them

(39b), according to Vendler, is redundant for *each* since it already implies *one*. *All*, on the other hand, can get a collective reading, even when it functions as a topic:[8]

(40)   a. All *the items in the store* cost $500.
          b. Every item in the store costs $500.

(40a) allows a collective reading in which the total value of the items in the store is $500. This reading is excluded in (40b). Note that the italicized NP necessitates a referential card. *All* may be used similarly to *any* to emphasize that no item is excluded, i.e., the NP is viewed as a plural individual and *all* is used as an emphatic marker, rather than as an operator in this case.

My purpose here is not to list the properties of each individual quantifier, but rather to argue that the full range of interpretations of sentences with (two) quantifiers is predicted by the three f-structures in (22). For strong quantifiers in subject position, the topic constraint predicts that unscoped readings will be very highly marked. For strong quantifiers in object position, a subordinate topic reading is the most natural, making unscoped readings for strong quantifiers very highly marked in general. If the quantifiers involved each allow both distributive and collective readings, a total of eight readings are available. The specific properties of individual quantifiers interact with the three f-structures to either limit (as in the case of *each*) or extend (*all*) the actual number of readings.

5.3.3   *Scoped stages*
In the preceding sections I showed that topics provide a restrictive set over which quantifiers range. Stage topics are no different in this respect. They too

function as the restriction on quantifiers. Relevant quantifiers are *sometimes*, *everywhere*, *always* etc. These quantifiers cannot be used as stage topics with individual-level predicates, neither can they be used with stage-level predicates unless they are assigned a f-structure with a stage topic.[9] Examine (41) and its f-structure (42):

(41)   Sometimes a boy meets a girl.

(42)   sometimes$_{sTOPt}$ [a boy meets a girl]$_{FOC}$

Here, a set of times $\{t_i, \ldots t_n\}$ are derived exactly as *some students* was derived in section 5.2.2. The focused sentence is then assessed with respect to each of these times. (The stage topic also includes a location with respect to which the sentence is assessed. Again this aspect of the stage topic is supplied by the context.)

What I have argued so far is that any individual NP topic will have wide scope with respect to any quantifier in the focus constituent. This follows from the predication rule, in which the focus is predicated of the topic. I have also argued for a class of unscoped readings. These are the cases in which the whole sentence is predicated of a stage topic. It follows that if the stage topic is overt, any quantifier phrase included in it will also take wide scope:

(43)   a. In every city, John loves someone.
        b. In every city, someone loves you.
        c. In some city, John loves everyone.
        d. In some city, everyone loves you.

None of these are ambiguous as predicted.

As noted by one of the anonymous reviewers the following example *is* ambiguous:

(44)   In every city that he visited John met someone he went to high school with.

The ambiguity here results from two subordinate f-structures that can be assigned to the main object:

(45)   a. someone$_{FOC}$ [he went to high school with]$_{TOP}$
        b. someone$_{TOP}$ [he went to high school with]$_{FOC}$

The f-structure in (45a) renders the reading in which the stage topic has wide scope as expected and for each city in the topic set a different "*someone*" is derived. The f-structure in (45b), in which *someone* is a subordinate topic, is also possible. In this case reference is made to an existing card, i.e., a particular "someone" and no scopal interaction transpires, rendering the seeming wide-scope reading of the object. It is therefore important, in making scopal predictions according to f-structure, to examine not only the main f-structures but also the potential subordinate ones.

5.4   Scope of negation and quantified subjects

The following well-known example, discussed in the previous chapter, is ambiguous and each meaning is associated with a different intonation contour (cf. Jackendoff 1972: 352).

(46)   ALL the men didn't go.
       a. not all the men went (B-accent: fall–rise)
       b. none of the men went (A-accent: fall)

According to Horn (1989) interpretation (a) results from predicate denial. In view of the fall–rise intonation (a) must be uttered in a metalinguistic context as shown in chapter 4. Interpretation (b) results from term negation of the verb, i.e., negation is incorporated in the verb, deriving the focus "not-go."

I intend to show how these facts follow from the f-structures assigned. In addition, I will explain why replacing *all* and *every* in examples such as (46) with *some* removes the ambiguity (another well-known fact). This explanation relies on observations made by Labov (1972).

Let me start by assigning an f-structure to the positive version of (46).

(47)   [ALL$_{FOC}$ the men$_{TOP}$]$_{TOP}$ [went]$_{FOC}$

The topic includes a subordinate f-structure (the stress on *all* makes this overt) in which *the men* is the topic and the quantifier forces a distributive reading. Each individual inside the topic set of *men* must be assessed separately. Assume that the result of the assessment comes out as follows: "some of the men went and some of them didn't go." In this case (47) comes out FALSE. If the predicate is negated, the truth value is reversed: Those cases in which the positive predication would be assessed as FALSE, the negative version comes out TRUE. (46) therefore comes out TRUE if some of the men went and some didn't, i.e., we get the interpretation in (46a).

What is the f-structure of the interpretation in (46b)? According to Horn this is a case of term negation, i.e., the f-structure would be:

(48)   [All the men]$_{TOP}$ [not-go]$_{FOC}$

This would give the interpretation we are after without requiring a metalinguistic context. This reading is, however, hard to get for most speakers. Only a few speakers (or dialects) allow term negation, it seems.[10] As we saw in chapter 4, however, this reading can be derived with sufficient meta-linguistic clues as well.

Horn and others note that the ambiguity disappears when quantifiers such as *all* and *every* are replaced by *some*. I will now proceed to explain the interpretation rendered in the cases with *some*, and will then show that the distinction between weak and strong quantifiers is not the one we are after. Examine the two f-structures responsible for the ambiguity using *some*:

(49)   [SOME$_{FOC}$ of the men$_{TOP}$]$_{TOP}$ didn't [go]$_{FOC}$

(50)   [some of the men]$_{TOP}$ [not-go]$_{FOC}$

Let us examine the interpretation of the nonnegative version of (49). What the subordinate update does in this case is define a partition of the set of people and a new card with the heading

(51)   {men$_j$} $\in$ {men$_i$}

An important feature of *some,* in its strong use, is that the new set (derived by partitioning) does not allow for a distributive reading.[11] The predicate *go* is therefore assessed with respect to the collective set {men$_j$} and not with respect to the individuals within it. If the predicate does not hold of this set the nonnegative version comes out false and (49) comes out true. The interpretation therefore is that it is false that the set of men, {men$_j$}, went.

Interpreting the f-structure (50) gives us essentially the same result. My claim is that the unambiguity with *some* follows from the fact that *some* does not distribute, not from a difference in f-structure.

Since there are weak quantifiers that distribute, the ambiguity is maintained for them:

(52)   FIVE students didn't go.
         a. Not five students went, (only four did.)
         b. None of the five students went.

Cardinals can be interpreted distributively, hence (52) is ambiguous.

Note that the same sentence quantified with *each* is strange no matter which interpretation is sought:

(53)   *Each of the boys didn't go.

According to Vendler (1967: 78) *each* necessitates taking the individuals in the set one by one. It is strange to say:

(54)   Each deputy rose at that moment.

But *each* is preferred to *every* in

(55)   Each deputy rose as his name was called.

What this seems to indicate is that *each* forces a reading in which for each of the individuals in the set a separate assessment occurs. Whereas, *all* and *every* in topic position must distribute as well, the interpretation also involves generalizing to the set as a whole. If no generalizing occurs, predicate denial cannot occur, since negation in this case functions to negate the predicate with respect to the generalized topic. If we attempt the stage-topic f-structure, we also fail since *each* forces assessment for a series of separate events and the stage topic fixes the event as a single definite event.

   In this section I have analyzed the two f-structures relevant to the interpretation of quantified subjects in negative sentences. I have shown that plugging a variety of different quantifiers into these f-structures gives different results depending on the semantics of the particular quantifier selected.

5.5   Scope in multiple (in situ) *wh*-questions[12]

In this section, I show that an account of scope in multiple *wh*-questions follows from the f-structure-theoretical approach as well. The following classic example illustrates a (scopally) ambiguous multiple *wh*-question:

(56)   Who remembers where we bought which book?
   a. John (remembers where we bought which book)
   b. John remembers where we bought *Aspects* and Peter remembers where we bought *Syntactic Structures*.

The answer in (56a) answers the narrow-scope reading of the phrase *which book* in the question, and the paired-list reading in (56b) answers the wide-scope reading. I suggest that the two readings, with their associated intonations, are distinguished in the following two f-structures:

(57)   a. TOP$_i$ [WHO REMEMBERS [where we bought which book]$_i$]$_{FOC}$
   b. [WHO]$_{TOP}$ [remembers where we bought [WHICH$_{FOC}$ book$_{TOP}$]]$_{FOC}$

In (57a) the topic is the whole embedded question. That this is a likely analysis, i.e., that a card could exist with the whole embedded question as its heading, follows from the possibility of the following very natural sequence:

(58)   Where did we buy which book? Who remembers this?

The second question in this sequence has the exact same f-structure as (57a), but here the topic is marked by means of the demonstrative pronoun. Once the embedded question has been defined as the topic, we are left with a single *wh*-question in the focus, hence the simple answer.

It should now be obvious how the paired-list reading is obtained for (57b). If *who* is analyzed as the topic of the sentence, we necessarily have available a contextually defined restrictive set. For each individual within this set, a new *wh*-question is asked. This is how we get a list question. The answer will therefore consist of a list of answers, one for each individual within the topic set. Scope in multiple *wh*-questions is therefore transparent from f-structure as well.

5.6   Scope and f-structure: other views

The "tendency" for topics to take wide scope has been noted before (see, for example, Ioup (1975), Kuno (1982), Reinhart (1983), and others). The opposite view has, however, also been prevalent, namely, that focused constituents are the ones to take wide scope. May (1977) proposes that the rule of quantifier raising apply to focused constituents in order to raise them and give them wide scope. This view is also to be found in Williams (1988: 143) who claims that heavily stressed objects get wide scope as in Williams' (26):

(59)   Someone loves EVERYONE.

It seems to me that this is factually wrong. I have shown above (section 5.3.3) that contrastively focused constituents get a wide scope interpretation and that this follows from the fact that these constituents form a subordinate f-structure in which the contrast set provides the topic, and the overt stressed constituent, the (contrastive) focus. Noncontrastive focused constituents necessarily take narrow scope, however.

It has also often been noted that it is easier to get the reading in which the subject has scope over the object, the unmarked case under the current view. Reinhart (1979) offers a syntactic view of this situation. She argues that the c-commanding quantifier in surface structure necessarily has wide scope. Exceptions to this generalization involve f-structures with stage topics or cases in which the subject is not a candidate for topichood: Chierchia and McConnel-Ginet (1990: 117) mention the following exceptions to the c-command constraint:

(60)   a. There was a name tag *near every plate.*
        b. A flag was hanging *in front of every window.*
        c. A student guide took every visitor to two museums.

The subjects are not possible candidates for topichood. I have italicized the unmarked topics in (60a and b) in which the topics are stages. In (60c) either the object or the PP can be interpreted as the topic and take scope over the subject as well as the remaining quantifier constituent. What looks like a structural constraint is in effect a consequence of the structural relationship between subjects and objects and the fact that subjects are unmarked topics, i.e., the Topic Constraint.

A recent analysis of scope in German and its interaction with focus is offered in Krifka (1994). Krifka discusses scope inversion under a rise–fall pattern as in the following illustrations (his (4a, 12a (rise is marked by "/" and fall by "\")):

(61)   a. ($\forall \exists$ only)
           [$_{CP}$fast jeder   Junge$_i$ [$_C$HAT [t$_i$ [mindestens einen   Roman
           nearly every NOM boy has   at least   one ACC novel
           [gelesen]]]]]
           read
        b. ($\exists\forall$, $\forall\exists$)
           Fast /JEDer Junge hat mindestens \EINen Roman gelesen.

Whereas the subject necessarily has wide scope in (61a), (61b), with the rise–fall intonation, allows object wide scope as well. Krifka's explanation involves details of German syntax and focus assignment that would take us too far afield. An explanation within the current framework is however also available. In German, topics are fronted and word order therefore largely determines f-structure. (61a) must therefore be interpreted with the subject as topic fixing the scope as indicated. According to Krifka, the rise–fall intonation in (61b) indicates multiple foci, as in the context of a multiple *wh*-question. If this is the case, we can conclude that the two focal stresses in the rise–fall cases signal subordinate f-structures since this is the only way, in the currect framework, that more than one focus can be generated. Krifka also suggests that the stressed quantifiers determine the alternatives to the expression in focus (p. 144). Although such topic sets can be made contextually available for both the NPs, the word order should still allow only the subject to be interpreted as the main topic. The fact that a $\exists\forall$ reading is also availabe can be explained, however, if we assume a subordinate metalinguistic f-structure on the object. The following context could work. Assume that an ordered list of novels were assigned as summer reading to a set of boys and that they were supposed to read as many novels as possible starting from the top. In this context a contrast is formed between (at least) "one" novel and "no" novels, and the interpretation is derived in which one particular novel, namely the one figuring on top of the list, was read by all the boys. This type of reading can be made contextually available without interfering with the main f-structure which is syntactically determined in German.

The current framework may also afford an explanation for the fact that scope inversion is blocked or very hard to get with stage topics (Krifka's (49a)):

(62)   ($\exists \forall$, ??$\forall \exists$)
         Heute hat mindestens /EIN Junge fast   \JEDen Roman gelesen.
         Today has at least   one boy   almost every novel   read

This sentence must be interpreted with a stage topic which leaves only an unscoped reading, i.e., only (at least) *one* boy is involved. I assume that the presence of a stage topic makes a context which triggers scope reversal extremely hard to conjure up. Unfortunately, Krifka does not indicate the necessary context for scope reversal.

Krifka's explanation necessitates focus marking in d-structure. According to Krifka discontinuous foci occur in s-structure in German requiring focus marking in d-structure independently. Although it seems that scope inversion receives a natural explanation in f-structure theory, the other case presented by Krifka to argue for his position must be examined here as well (p. 145 (43)):

(63)   Peter gab   das Verbrechen sofort \ZU.
         Peter admitted the crime   immediately AFFIX

Krifka proposes the following derivation:

(64)   D-structure: $[_{CP}e [_{C}e [_{IP}$Peter [das Verbrechen [sofort [zu [gab]]]]]]]
         Focus Assignment: $[_{CP}e [_{C}e [_{IP}$Peter [das Verbrechen [sofort [zu [gab]]$_F$]]]]]
         C^0 movement: $[_{CP}e [_{C'}$gab$_i [_{IP}$Peter [das Verbrechen [sofort [zu [t$_i$]]$_F$]]]]]
         Spec-CP movement: $[_{CP}$Peter$_j [_{C'}$gab$_i [_{IP}$t$_j$ [das Verbrechen [sofort [zu [t$_i$]]$_F$]]]]]

The verb has moved out of the surface focus constituent leaving a trace. If focus is marked on s-structure, the rules that interpret f-structure will involve reconstruction to trace position. Stress assignment will also correctly derive stress on the affix left in the focus constituent. I therefore see no reason why the focus should not be marked on s-structure in these cases as well.

It was the purpose of this chapter to show that scope can be read off f-structure. It was argued that the topic takes wide scope because predication involves assessment for truth value of each individual member of a restrictive topic set.

6   I-dependencies in focus structure

6.1   I-dependencies

In this chapter I define I-dependencies as distinct from R-dependencies discussed in previous chapters. I-dependencies are illustrated in the sentences in (1):

(1)   a. John talked to himself. (anaphora)
          b. Everyone loves his mother. (bound anaphora)
          c. Who read what? (multiple *wh*-questions)
          d. Who did everyone talk to? (quantifier *wh*-interactions)
          e. Who did you talk to t? (*wh*-trace dependency)
          f. John didn't eat anything. (negation and focus of negation)
          g. John is the teacher. (copular sentences)

Whereas R-dependencies are constrained by the Topic Constraint, I-dependencies are constrained by the Subject Constraint. It is my purpose to illustrate how this f-structure-theoretical account provides an explanation for the distribution of I-dependencies.

The dependent in an I-dependency characteristically does not trigger the construction of a new card, instead its "identity" is fixed by the dependency. In the examples in (1) the objects are dependent for their identity (or reference) either on their subjects or on an operator ((1e) and (1f)). Just as the reflexive in (1a) is coindexed with its antecedent subject and therefore I-dependent on the subject, the objects in the other sentences in (1) are similarly I-dependent. The example of bound anaphora in (1b) is another example in which an I-dependency holds. Each of the *mother*s introduced I-depends on the member of the set defined by *everyone* which is examined. (1c) requires a "list" answer in which the "answer" to each *what* depends on the particular member of the set of *who*s that provides the subject of that member of the list in the answers:

(2)   John read the *New York Times*, Peter read the *Boston Globe*, ...

(1d) illustrates an I-dependency in which the *wh*-phrase is dependent on the members of the set represented by the quantifier. In (1e) the trace is identified by the fronted *wh*-phrase. (1f) illustrates an I-dependency triggered by a partitioning operator. A new subset is "identified" by partitioning operations making this set a dependent in an I-dependency. Finally, in copular sentences such as (1g), the subject and object are referentially identified.

Pronouns (including anaphors) and *wh*-words can be I-dependent, i.e., they can, but need not, receive their interpretation via an I-dependency. Note that I-dependent pronouns and *wh*-words are classified together contra Binding Theory. The distinction between I-dependence and R-dependence is similar to Reinhart's (1983, 1986) distinction between bound anaphora and coreference as noted in chapter 2. Cases of bound anaphora are I-dependent, coreference, as Reinhart herself argues, is a discourse matter.

The main claim of the chapter is that I-dependencies are constrained by the Subject Constraint which imposes a syntactic constraint on them. Thus, the lack of ambiguity in (3a and b), as compared to the ambiguous (1b and d), is accounted for by the same constraint that rules out (3c).

(3)   a. Who talked to everyone?
       b. His mother loves everyone.
       c. *Himself talked to John.

The Subject Constraint also accounts for the restriction on f-structures for negated sentences (discussed in chapters 3 and 5) as well as the licensing of negative polarity items. Finally, the Subject Constraint restricts reconstruction in cases of *wh*-movement accounting for constraints on *wh*-movement (island constraints), Crossover, multiple *wh*-questions, and *wh*-quantifier interactions. The Subject Constraint therefore plays a central role in the grammar of English rendering a new view of the division of labor among the syntactic modules.[1]

6.1.1   The Subject Constraint
The structural constraint on I-dependencies, the Subject Constraint, is roughly that an I-dependency can only occur in a *canonical* f-structure, i.e., an f-structure in which, on the one hand, the topic and subject are identified and, on the other, the focus predicate and the VP are identified. In the cases in which the antecedent of the dependency is not an operator, the Subject Constraint restricts the I-dependency to hold between a *subject* main topic and a NP in its focus, the latter depending on the former. The following is a first approximation of the Subject Constraint:

(4)   **Subject Constraint** (first version):[2]
I-dependencies are licensed in the following f-structure:
SUBJECT$_{TOP}$ [. . . NP. . .]$_{FOC}$

<I-dependency

The arrow indicates the direction of the dependency. I refer to the participants in the I-dependency as *antecedent* and *dependent*. This constraint restricts I-dependencies to f-structures in which the subject is the topic and the dependent is contained in the focus. The difference between the Topic Constraint and the Subject Constraint is that the former imposes the f-structure in (4) as the unmarked (main) f-structure for R-dependencies. The latter enforces the same f-structure as an absolute restriction on I-dependencies.

It follows that I-dependencies can always occur between a subject and its object, but not vice versa. The account of reflexives resulting from the application of the Subject Constraint is not innovative in view of the fact that subjects always c-command any NP in the predicate.[3] The idea that the other cases of I-dependencies illustrated in (1) are constrained in the same way is what I intend to argue here. In languages in which the basic constituent structure differs, or in which there is free word order, the consequences of the Subject Constraint will also be different. I will briefly return to this issue in the concluding chapter.

I suggest the following reason why I-dependencies, but not R-dependencies are syntactically constrained in this way. The Subject Constraint can be viewed as a way of reducing the processing burden of the hearer when an I-dependency is involved. The weaker Topic Constraint is all that is needed for an R-dependency. What I am proposing here is that if an R-dependency involves introducing a new card into the hearer's file, the card is assigned its reference merely in terms of the predication in which it occurs. Hence, the only requirements on such dependencies are the ones applying to f-structure. I-dependencies impose a greater processing burden on the hearer. In these cases the hearer must be able to single out the new card in some way, i.e., this card must be specific to the hearer in some sense. In the case of reflexives, for example, the card is identified with an existing card in the hearer's file.

The following sections give detailed analyses of the various types of I-dependencies and their distributions.

6.2   Multiple *wh*-questions

In chapter 5 I discussed scope in multiple (in situ) *wh*-questions and showed that the paired-list reading is obtained by interpreting one of the *wh*-phrases as ranging over the topic set. In this way, for each member of the topic set a new question is generated, resulting in the list reading. In this section I will examine several properties of multiple *wh*-questions which show that an I-dependency is involved.

First, in the case of an answer to a multiple *wh*-question, each separate answer in the list can be viewed as involving an I-dependency. The complete answer, i.e., the paired list as a whole, is, however, R-dependent.

(5)   John read the *Boston Globe*, Peter read the *New York Times*, . . .

It follows that a new card is constructed for the set of newspapers in this case, but that the members of this set which form I-dependencies do not have independent cards associated with them as is characteristic of an I-dependency. Evidence for this claim is the possible continuations for list answers such as (5):

(6)   a. *It is a good paper.
        b. They are good papers.[4]

Second, following Erteschik-Shir (1986a) and Pesetsky (1987), observe that multiple *wh*-questions such as the following can only be asked if a set of *who*s is contextually supplied:[5]

(7)   a. Who read what?
        b. Who went where?

An asymmetry appears here: in principle, in order to generate the paired-list reading it should be sufficient that any one of the *wh*-phrases be interpreted as the topic, but it turns out that it is impossible to contextually force an interpretation in which the object is the *only* topic. Take, for example, (7a). Imagine that students could choose among three assigned books to read. For each book, the question asks who read it. Unless the set of students is restricted, the answer potentially involves an infinite list of readers for each book and the question turns out not to be acceptable. According to the Topic Constraint, subjects are chosen over objects as main topics when both are equally available, and the odds can be shifted contextually. Here, the *wh*-phrases are equal in the hierarchy of topic availability and only context can determine whether a topic set is available, yet only the subject ends up as a candidate for topichood. One other variable in the topic game is whether the NP is human or not. Humans win over inanimates in the competition. Let me therefore make both human, or even better, stack the odds in favor of the object by making the subject inanimate and the object human:

(8)   What was eaten by who?

Again, the only available interpretation is one in which the subject *wh*-phrases are taken to range over a restrictive set, i.e., the subject must be the main topic. If *John*, *Peter*, and *Mary* each ate something different, and I have no clue what the available set of foods was, I cannot ask (8). The f-structure in (9), therefore must be blocked:[6]

(9)   *TOP$_i$ [wh V wh$_i$]$_{FOC}$

If it is assumed that an I-dependency holds between the two *wh*-phrases, the Subject Constraint will apply to rule out the f-structure in question.

6.2.1   Which N *vs.* who *and* what

Pesetsky (1987) characterizes D-linking as follows: "When a speaker asks a question like *Which book did you read?*, the range of felicitous answers is limited by a set of books both speaker and hearer have in mind. If the hearer is ignorant of the context assumed by the speaker, a *which*-question sounds odd. Similarly, in a multiple *which*-question like *Which man read which book?* the speaker and hearer have a set of men and a set of books in mind. The members of ordered man–book pairs in a felicitous answer will be drawn from the sets established in the discourse. No such requirement is imposed on *wh*-phrases like *who*, *what*, or *how many books*. These phrases may be *non-D-linked*" (p. 108).

In chapter 3, section 3.2, I claimed that *wh*-phrases such as *which student(s)* form a subordinate (partitive) f-structure in which a context-specified set of students is the topic and the rule of predication triggers a scanning of this set. The question is then asked for each member of the set selected. D-linking therefore boils down to a topic set being available. I also showed that such *wh*-forms are interpretable as the topic of the question. The question arises how d-linking interacts with the I-dependency. Compare the following example to (7a):

(10)   a. Which student read which book?
       b. TOP$_{i\text{-sub}}$ [[[which]$_{FOC}$ [student]$_{TOP}$]$_{TOP}$
              [read [[which]$_{FOC}$ [book]$_{TOP}$]$_i$]$_{FOC}$]$_{FOC\text{-sub}}$

Details aside, the f-structure in (10b) is identical to one in which both subject and object are pronouns. Partitive *wh*-phrases have in common with pronouns that they access cards from the top of the file. The topic of the subordinate f-structure in partitive *wh*-phrases is defined by the noun. Although its range is topic bound, the *wh*-phrase itself (or rather its answer) is identified for each element of the topic set selected. Accordingly, the object *wh*-phrase defines each answer as I-dependent on the member of the topic set selected. It follows that the I-dependency does not differ from that in (7).

Nonetheless, *which*-phrases differ from plain *wh*-phrases such as *who* and *what*. The former must necessarily be linked to a card on top of the file, the latter type will only be so if contextually forced to. This distinction parallels that of strong and weak quantifiers discussed in chapter 5. *Which*-phrases must receive a strong reading, *who* and *what*, etc. are weak and can therefore receive both strong and weak readings.[7]

6.2.2 Superiority

Pesetsky (1987) argues that D-linked *wh*-phrases are not quantifiers and therefore do not move at LF. This explains the fact that superiority facts show up only with non-D-linked *wh*-phrases:

(11) a. Who ate what?
b. *What did who eat?
c. Which boy took which of the books?
d. Which of the books did which boy read?

What rules out (11b), according to Pesetsky, is the Nested Dependency Condition which applies at LF. The details of this condition are not important here. What is important is the purely structural nature of the account. Even more interesting is the way Pesetsky accounts for the fact that superiority effects evaporate when the *wh*-phrases are D-linked: since D-linked *wh*-phrases are not quantifiers, they do not move at LF and thus escape the Nested Dependency Condition. I agree with Pesetsky that the distinction between D-linked and non-D-linked *wh*-phrases is at stake here and I will show below how this follows from the focus structure of sentences with multiple *wh*-phrases. Pesetsky admits that D-linking is not limited to phrases such as *which boy, which of the books*, etc. Pesetsky gives the following example (his (35b)):

(12) I know that we need to install transistor A, transistor B, and transistor C, and I know that these three holes are for transistors, but I'll be damned if I can figure out from the instructions *where what* goes!

Here only the context and not the form of the *wh*-phrases renders a D-linked interpretation. In order to make the correct distinctions, Pesetsky would have to allow LF-movement to be contextually triggered.

As argued in section 6.2, the Subject Constraint applies to multiple *wh*-questions constraining the f-structure to one in which the subject is the topic. The Subject Constraint applies in the same way to the examples in which *wh*-movement has occurred.[8] This imposes the following f-structure on the examples in (11b–d):

(13)   What did who_TOP [eat t]_FOC

In the good cases, (11c and d), the partitive *wh*-phrases in subject position are necessarily interpreted as topics, licensing the structures. (11b) is ruled out because no such topic set is contextually available. (12) is again acceptable because the context specifies a set of transistors (a set of *whats*).

I could leave the discussion of superiority effects here, but that would leave the following puzzle. As Pesetsky clearly indicates there is a quantum difference between (14a) on the one hand and (14b and c), on the other:

(14)   a.   *What did who see?
        b.   Which boy did which girl see?
        c.   Which of the boys did which of the girls see?

The *wh*-phrases in the subject position of (14b and c), *Which boy* and *which of the boys*, are strong and therefore automatically qualify as topics. I argued before that strong readings can be supplied by context for simple *wh*-phrases such as *who* and *what* when no movement is involved. Why is this reading so hard to get in cases of movement? Even (12) is not that good. Note first that the same phenomenon occurs when we replace the *wh*-subject with an indefinite or a weak quantifier:

(15)   a.   What did two boys find?
               (*One found a dime and the other a penny.)
        b.   *What did a boy find?
        c.   Which book did two boys find?
        d.   ?Which book did a boy find?

In (15a) the distributive reading, which would result from a strong reading of "two boys," is not available. Although weak quantifiers can get strong readings, this reading is blocked in the case of extraction. (15b) again shows that *wh*-movement requires that the subject be interpreted as a topic leaving only a generic or contrastive reading for the indefinite subject. In chapter 3, I showed that *wh*-questions can be interpreted in two ways, either by interpreting the fronted *wh*-phrase itself as a topic or through reconstruction to trace position. Here it is argued that an I-dependency holds between a *wh*-phrase and its trace in cases of reconstruction.[9] The fronted *wh*-phrases in (15a and b) do not qualify as topics, hence reconstruction *must* take place. It follows from the Subject Constraint that the subjects of these sentences must function as the main topics in the f-structure, explaining the ungrammaticality of (15b).

Topic *wh*-phrases are illustrated in (15c and d). In (15c) the quantifier phrase is contained in the focus constituent, hence no distributive reading is expected. (15d) only violates the Topic Constraint. It is therefore much better than (15b) which violates the Subject Constraint.

It is therefore possible to account for the data in (15) except for the fact that no strong reading is available for the weak quantifier in (15a). Again, I assume that such a reading could be forced with the help of detailed context. In the context of (12) one could probably say:

(16)   I couldn't figure out where two transistors go.

Note that the context here does not just supply a set of three transistors, but actually introduces each one separately. What is left to explain is therefore why the requirement for interpreting a weak quantifier as a topic in the extracted cases necessitates that each member of the topic set be available, whereas only the set as a whole is contextually required in the unextracted case. I offer the following explanation: the stronger requirement results from an f-structure such as the following:[10]

(17)   [Which picture]$_{TOP}$ [[did who$_{TOP}$ [see e]$_{FOC}$]$_{FOC}$

                  └────────────┘

                      I-dependency

If the fronted *wh*-phrase is interpretable as a topic, it forms a main f-structure in which the rest of the sentence is predicated of it. This blocks the analysis of the subject *wh*-phrase as the main topic (required due to the I-dependency). It can only be interpreted as a subordinate topic by brute force, i.e., if the context makes its interpretation as a focus impossible.

If, on the other hand, the fronted *wh*-phrase is not interpretable as a topic as in (14a), two separate I-dependencies are formed with the trace position as the dependent. One is the I-dependency between the two *wh*-phrases discussed above. The other is the one required by reconstruction of a fronted *wh*-phrase to trace position. (The latter case will be discussed in detail in section 6.6.)

(18)   What did who see t

         │   └────┘

         └──────────┘

Why is this structure ruled out? I-dependencies enable the interpretation of the dependent element. Therefore a constituent cannot be interpreted if it is a dependent in more than one I-dependency. This is the f-structure-theoretical equivalent of the bijection principle. I formulate this principle as Principle I:

> **Principle I**: A constituent cannot be a dependent in more than one
> I-dependency.

I assume that I-dependencies are marked on f-structure. In view of the fact that
a doubly identified constituent will result in an uninterpretable f-structure, it
is not necessary to stipulate this principle. I will continue to refer to it below
as a separate principle for the sake of clarity. It follows that (18) in which the
trace is doubly identified is ruled out.

The Subject Constraint also correctly predicts the ungrammaticality of the
following questions:

(19)   a. *About who(m) did Anne talk to who(m)?
           *Who(m) did Anne talk to who(m) about?
        b. About who(m) did Anne_TOP [talk to who(m) t]_FOC
            |_____|__|

(20)   a. *Who(m) did Anne talk to about who(m)?
        b. Who(m) did Anne_TOP [talk to t about who(m)]_FOC
            |_____|___|

(19), like (18), is a case of double identification. (20) is different: the trace
here could be analyzed as the dependent in the I-dependency between the
fronted *wh*-phrase and its trace (which is licensed) and at the same time, it
could be the antecedent in the I-dependency between the two *wh*-phrases. It
is this second I-dependency which violates the Subject Constraint because the
trace (antecedent) is not in a subject position. Note that the ungrammaticality of this question would not be predicted if the superiority constraint were
formulated in terms of crossover. Note further the acceptability of a multiple
wh-question in a dative:

(21)   What did Anne give to who(m)?

Here the direct object in the dative is taken to be a subject following Larson
(1988) and Hale and Keyser (1993). It follows that the *wh*-trace is in a subject
position and the Subject Constraint is not violated.

The Superiority Constraint therefore boils down to the Subject Constraint
on I-dependencies.

The fact, pointed out by Kayne (1984), that an *extra wh*-phrase improves
superiority violations illustrated in (22a) and (23a), receives a natural explanation in the current framework:

(22)   a. What did who hide where?
        b. What did [who]_TOP [hide t where]_FOC
           |_____|____|__|

(23) a. Who knows what who saw?
      b. Who knows what who$_{TOP}$ [saw t]$_{FOC}$

The f-structures in (22b) and (23b) allow the definition of two separate I-dependencies to be defined with no violation of the principle which rules out double identification. These examples are, however, grammatically degraded, due to the fact that two I-dependencies are processed simultaneously.

6.2.3 *Multiple* wh-*questions with stage topics*
The following examples illustrate multiple wh-questions in which one of the wh-phrases is a potential stage topic.

(24) a. When did you see what?
      b. What did you see when?

(25) a. Where did you buy what?
      b. What did you buy where?

In (24a) and (25a) the fronted temporal and locational wh-phrases provide stage topics. They are *not* D-linked phrases and the interpretation in which the question asks for a pairing of "times" or "places" and whats is licensed by a context in which such a set of times or places is provided. An I-dependency is thus defined in these examples which have the following f-structure:

(26) a. When$_{sTOPt}$ [did you see what]$_{FOC}$
      b. Where$_{sTOPt}$ [did you buy what]$_{FOC}$

These examples provide evidence that an f-structure with a stage topic also licenses an I-dependency. It is therefore necessary to revise the Subject Constraint accordingly:

(27) **Subject Constraint** (second version):
      SUBJECT$_{TOP}$ [. . . X . . .]$_{FOC}$
      sTOP$_1$
      <I-dependency

This formalization of the constraint says that an I-dependency can occur in a structure in which the dependent is contained in the focus constituent and the main topic is either the subject or a stage topic. The constraint is thus extended to include what was viewed in chapter 5 as another canonical f-structure. This extension of the constraint is therefore a natural one. The Subject Constraint constrains I-dependencies to unmarked f-structures and blocks them from occurring in an f-structure in which the object is a topic. The Subject Constraint might be rephrasable as follows:

(28)   * TOP$_i$ [. . . V NP$_i$ . . .]$_{FOC}$

         <I-dependency

This version of the constraint simply states that an I-dependency is blocked in an f-structure in which the object functions as the topic. Such an f-structure was defined as highly marked in the discussion of the Topic Constraint. We therefore maintain our view that the Subject Constraint is an absolute constraint on I-dependencies, whereas the Topic Constraint is a weak constraint on R-dependencies. In the latter case the f-structure in which the object is picked as the topic is highly marked but not impossible to invoke contextually.

The following examples illustrate that superiority effects do not evaporate when the fronted *wh*-phrase defines a stage.

(29)   a. In which countries do which of these climatic conditions occur?
         b. Which of these climatic conditions occur in which countries? (from Kuno 1982)

(30)   a. ??Where do what climatic conditions occur?
         b.   What climatic conditions occur where?

(30a) demonstrates the superiority effect and improves only if the range for the subject *wh*-phrase is contextually specified. Compare the sentences in (31) to the good cases in (26) in which the I-dependency holds between the stage topic and an object:

(31)   a. *When did who see Peter?
         b. *Where did who buy a present?

In view of the revised version of the Subject Constraint, this distinction must now be reexamined. The following two f-structures represent the f-structures required to license the I-dependencies in (31b) and (25a) respectively:

(32)   Where$_{sTOPt}$ [did who$_{TOP-sub}$ [buy a present e]$_{FOC-sub}$]$_{FOC}$

(33)   Where$_{sTOPt}$ [did you$_{TOP-sub}$ [buy what e]$_{FOC-sub}$]$_{FOC}$

In (32) the I-dependency is not licensed because the subordinate f-structure indicated is illicit (exactly in the same way it was in (17)). The subject wh-phrase cannot function as a subordinate topic unless contextual brute force is applied as before. The subordinate f-structure in (33), however, is licit and nothing prevents the I-dependency here. Note that the I-dependency is marked between two elements contained in a focus constituent. In the cases examined so far we required that the dependent be contained in the focus, but the antecedent was not. Here the antecedent is in fact the (stage) topic of the main f-structure. It will be shown below that I-dependencies in fact occur in f-structures in which the antecedent (as well as the dependent) is contained in the focus constituent and does not function as a main or subordinate topic.

The examination of multiple wh-questions showed that the Subject Constraint on I-dependencies, together with a careful analysis of the data in terms of f-structure, provides a complete account of the superiority effect.

6.3   Quantifier: *wh*-interactions

The following well-known data (used to illustrate I-dependencies in the Introduction to the book) follows in a straightforward manner from the Subject Constraint:

(34)   a. Who did everyone talk to? (ambiguous)
        b. Who talked to everyone? (not ambiguous)

(34a) is ambiguous allowing both a single question and family-of-questions reading. In the family-of-questions reading, the wh-phrase is I-dependent on the quantifier subject. The I-dependency takes the same form as the one involved in multiple wh-questions. It follows that in the f-structure of (34a), the subject must be the topic for the family-of-questions reading to be available. This f-structure is given in (35a). The f-structure for the single-answer reading in which no I-dependency holds is given in (35b):

(35)   a. Who did everyone$_{\text{TOP}}$ [talk to t]$_{\text{FOC}}$
        b. Who$_{\text{TOP}}$ [did everyone talk to t]$_{\text{FOC}}$

The f-structure in (35a) licenses an I-dependency: a different "answer" is identified for each member of the set defined by the subject topic *everyone*. This is what gives the list answer to the question. (35b) does not allow this reading since *who* cannot be I-dependent due to the Subject Constraint. This f-structure therefore renders only the single-answer reply to the question. Compare now the f-structures assigned to (34b):

(36)   a. Who$_{\text{TOP}}$ [talked to everyone]$_{\text{FOC}}$
        b. TOP$_i$ [who talked to everyone$_i$]$_{\text{FOC}}$

In (36a) no I-dependency can hold between the dependent *wh*-phrase and the quantifier upon which it depends, since this f-structure violates the Subject Constraint. The Subject Constraint allows for the quantifier to depend on the *wh*-phrase, but quantifiers are not possible dependents. (Only pronouns and *wh*-phrases have so far been identified as such.) This is because quantifiers are R-expressions which have independent reference and do not allow for I-referentiality. In (36b) *everyone*, which we have seen can trigger a dependency, is the topic, but the Subject Constraint is violated, blocking the I-dependent reading. This is why only a single-answer response is possible for this question.

I offer two pieces of evidence that the f-structure in (35a) is indeed correct for the family-of-questions reading. Note first that if the discourse forces a topic reading of the quantifier as in the following interaction, only the list response is possible:

(37)   Speaker: Tell me about everyone.
        Hearer:
        a. *Everyone went to the beach.
        b.   John went to the beach, Susan . . . .

It follows that the list answer is identified with a topic reading of the quantifier (as demonstrated in chapter 5). The second piece of evidence comes from stressing the quantifier. This blocks its reading as a topic and also blocks the family-of-questions reading.

(38)   Who did EVERYONE talk to? (not ambiguous)

The stressed quantifier receives a contrastive interpretation here. The topic is therefore the set which includes the members "everyone" and "not everyone." The latter option is then eliminated by the subordinate (metalinguistic) f-structure argued to hold in cases of contrast (see chapter 3).[11]

The Subject Constraint on I-dependencies has so far been shown to hold in two cases: first, multiple *wh*-questions, in which a *wh*-phrase is I-dependent on another *wh*-phrase, and second, when a *wh*-phrase is I-dependent on a quantifier.

6.4   Bound anaphora

Bound anaphora instantiates the basic idea behind the notion of an I-dependency, namely that the bound NP is identified for the hearer by means of the NP upon which it is dependent: in the case of anaphora, the antecedent identifies the anaphor. It follows that the Subject Constraint applies to all cases of bound anaphora. Reinhart (1976) argued that the structural relation of c-command constrains bound anaphora.[12] Since the Subject Constraint blocks I-dependent subjects, dependent on their objects, i.e., exactly those cases in which c-command does not hold, it is left for me to show that there are no cases in which bound variable anaphora occurs, c-command holds, but the Subject Constraint is violated. Two types of cases of this sort present themselves. The first type consists of examples with double objects:

(39)   a.   Rosa put *each of the books* in *its* box.
        b.   *Rosa kisses *each of the kids* in *his* picture. (Reinhart 1983: 125)

In the double-object case, (39a), c-command holds and the anaphoric relation is licensed. In Erteschik-Shir (in prep. a) and Erteschik-Shir and Rapoport (in progress), we introduce a version of Hale and Keyser's (1993) proposals concerning the lexical structure of double-object constructions (based on Larson's (1988) proposal for their syntactic structure). In this framework the direct object would be a subject. Hence, the correct prediction can also be made by the Subject Constraint. Riad (1988: 31) argues for an optional pre-dication structure between the direct and indirect object in parallel Swedish examples. Swedish has a reflexive possessive, *sin*, which complies with the constraints on bound anaphora. The following examples from Riad (1988) show that the direct object in a double-object construction can felicitously be the antecedent for a reflexive possessive in indirect object position:

(40)   Chefen$_i$ gav Olle$_j$ sin$_{i/j}$ lön
        The-boss gave Olle REFLposs pay

I assume with Riad that the direct object can be the subject of predication, or in my terminology the topic of an f-structure. If the direct object is taken as the main topic, the reflexive possessive will be coindexed with it. If, however, the main subject is taken as the topic, the possessive will be co-indexed with the subject. In either case the Subject Constraint licenses the I-dependency. (39b) is correctly excluded by the Subject Constraint as well as by c-command.

The following cases, also from Reinhart (1983: 129), show that the problem is more complex:[13]

(41)   a.   You should give *nobody* matches near *his* child's crib.
        b.   *Near *his* child's crib, you should give *nobody* matches.
        c.   Near *his* child's crib, *nobody* would keep matches.

(41a) is licensed by the Subject Constraint if *nobody* is taken as a subject and a topic.[14] The f-structure of the pertinent part of the sentence therefore complies with the Subject Constraint:

(42)   You should give [*nobody*$_{TOP}$ [matches near *his* child's crib]$_{FOC}$]

In (41b) the fronted PP forms a stage topic:

(43)   [Near *his* child's crib]$_{sTOP_i}$ [you should give *nobody* matches]$_{FOC}$

(43) is in clear violation of the Subject Constraint correctly ruling out the anaphora. How can this analysis be reconciled with the acceptability of (41c)? Examine the following f-structure:

(44)   [Near *his* child's crib]sTOP$_{t\text{-}sub}$
         [*nobody*$_{TOP}$ [would keep matches t]$_{FOC}$]$_{FOC\text{-}sub}$

Here, in the main f-structure the Subject Constraint is obeyed. Why can't a similar f-structure be assigned to (41b), as follows?

(45)   [Near *his* child's crib]sTOP$_{t\text{-}sub}$
         [you should give *nobody*$_{TOP}$ [matches] $_{FOC}$] $_{FOC\text{-}sub}$

Since the PP stage topic here is not selected by the verb as it is in (41c), no trace is available, hence the dependent pronoun is not reconstructible to a position within the focus in violation of the Subject Constraint. A double-object example, in which the PP *is* selected, is again possible in accordance with the Subject Constraint:

(46)   ?Near his child's crib Peter placed nobody.

This f-structure in which the object is selected as a main topic in spite of the availability of a subject, is, however, marked by the Topic Constraint, rendering the sentence less than perfect.[15]

    The following case might seem even more problematic since it conforms to the canonical f-structure required by the Subject Constraint.

(47)   *People from *each of the small western cities* hate *it*. (Reinhart 1983: 124)

Note, however, that according to the constraint, the I-dependency is licensed between the dependent pronoun and its antecedent subject topic. Here the subject is the topic, but it is not a possible antecedent for the pronoun. An antecedent contained in a subject topic is not licensed by the Subject Constraint. This solution to the problem presented by (47) generates a new problem, however. The following type of example was presented in Higginbotham (1980) as counterevidence to Reinhart's c-command restriction:

(48)   *Every boy's* mother thinks *he* is a genius.

Again the antecedent for the pronoun is contained in the subject topic but anaphora is licensed. Reinhart (1983: 178) provides an *ad hoc* (according to her) modification of c-command which allows the determiner of possessive NPs to c-command whatever the NP as a whole c-commands. This solution is problematic since acceptance of sentences such as (48) are both language specific and dialectical. It would be surprising if constraints based on structural relations such as c-command relations could differ according to dialect. Let us therefore examine the f-structure of (48) more carefully and compare it to that of the unacceptable (47). Both involve subordinate f-structures as follows:

(49)   [*Every boy's*$_{TOP-sub}$ mother$_{FOC-sub}$]$_{TOP}$ [thinks *he* is a genius]$_{FOC}$

(50)   [People$_{TOP-sub}$ [from *each of the small western cities*]$_{FOC-sub}$]$_{TOP}$ [hate *it*]$_{FOC}$

The subject in each f-structure contains a subordinate f-structure. In (49), in which anaphora *is* licensed, the antecedent is the topic of the subordinate f-structure. It follows that a card representing a particular set of boys must be available on top of the file (and that the subordinate update generates a set of cards consisting of a mother for every one of the boys contained in the set). It is the availability of the set of boys as a topic card which licenses the I-dependency, at least in those dialects in which it is possible. In (48), the subordinate f-structure is reversed. I therefore maintain the Subject Constraint but in light of (49) allow for a subordinate topic within the subject main topic to license an I-dependency. Allowing a subordinate topic as an antecedent as well as a main topic, can naturally be assumed to be subject to dialectical variation. These data therefore provide a weak argument in favor of the Subject Constraint.

I-dependencies between pronouns and antecedents contained in a stage topic are also licensed.

(51)   a. On *every chair* sat *its* owner.[16]
        b. Near *every picture* Rosa puts *its* duplicate.
        c. In *every country* John visited *its* most beautiful sights.

These cases conform to a canonical f-structure with a stage topic and the I-dependency is therefore licensed by the Subject Constraint.

In this section I have argued for an account of bound anaphora in terms of the Subject Constraint. I have left out a clear counterexample (pointed out by a reviewer) which shows that the antecedent of the bound anaphor is not restricted to subjects:

(52)   The teacher talked to every girl about her grades.

I will return to this example in the next section after providing an account of Reflexivity in terms of the Subject Constraint.

6.4.1   Reflexivity

The Subject Constraint will also correctly exclude reflexives in cases in which c-command does not hold. The domain of the dependency in the case of reflexives is known to be further constrained. The binding conditions constrain anaphors to be bound in their governing category. Reinhart and Reuland (1993) (In the following = RR) limit the domain to that of the argument structure of a given predicate.[17] I propose instead that the relevant local domain is the minimal predication structure. In this I follow Riad (1988) whose notion of predication, however, is syntactic rather than f-structure theoretical.[18] Riad (1988: 17) proposes the following General Reflexivization Principle:

(53)   GRP: A reflexive element has its predication subject as antecedent.

Riad limits the domain of reflexives to the smallest predication. Since the Subject Constraint in my framework identifies the antecedent of a reflexive not only as the topic of the predication but also as the syntactic subject, the two approaches will make the same predictions rendering an account for reflexivity in the Scandinavian languages in which one kind of reflexive requires a subject antecedent. In Danish, I-dependent reflexives are distinguished morphologically from non-I-dependent ones. The former are naturally accounted for by the Subject Constraint, the latter are categorized as pronouns. Once an account has been offered for reflexivity in Danish, I return to English showing that English reflexives unite the two functions which are morphologically distinguished in Danish. In the following analysis I follow Vikner's (1985) basic insights, but for clarity translate directly into f-structure terminology.

The inventory of third-person pronouns in Danish follows:

(54)	pronoun	pronoun + selv	possessive
a.	sig	sig selv	sin
b.	ham/hende	ham selv/hende selv	hans/hendes
	"him"/"her"		

I now show that the pronouns in (54a) must be interpreted through an I-dependency, but the ones in (54b) must not. In addition the "selv" morpheme imposes further locality restrictions.[19]

Examine the following data from Vikner (1985):

(55)   Anne$_i$ hørte Susan$_k$ snakke med Tina$_m$ om sig$_i$
                                                   sig selv$_k$
                                                   hende$_{i/o}$
                                                   hende selv$_m$
       Anne heard Susan talk   to   Tina about her(self)

Note first that the antecedent of "sig" must be a subject. In the case of "sig" the antecedent is the subject of the upper clause, in the case of "sig selv" it is the subject of the lower clause. Importantly, the antecedent cannot be "Tina" who does not occupy a subject position. The relation between "sig" and its antecedent is therefore accounted for by viewing it as an I-dependency which conforms to the Subject Constraint. The difference between "sig" and "sig selv" must be due to properties of "selv." If "selv" is viewed as locally bound, in some sense of locality yet to be defined, the difference between "sig" and "sig selv" should follow.[20] I propose that the local domain in which "selv" must be bound is the *minimal predication* in which it occurs.[21] I define the minimal predication as the smallest canonical f-structure. The f-structure of (55) illustrates this point:

(56)   Anne$_{TOP}$ [hørte [Susan$_{TOP\text{-}sub}$ [snakke med Tina om sig selv]$_{FOC\text{-}sub}$]$_{FOC}$

The minimal predication containing "sig selv" is the small clause with "Susan" as its topic-subject correctly licensing the I-dependency. I view the locality constraint on "selv" as ambiguity reducing. "Selv" requires an antecedent within the minimal predication; a pronoun not marked by "selv" cannot occur within that domain:

(57)   **Minimal Predication** (definition):
       An f-structure: SUBJECT$_{TOP}$ [. . . X. . . NP . . . Y . . .]$_{FOC}$ is minimal iff no X, Y = TOP or FOC.

(58)   **Locality Constraint**:
       (i) [$_{NP}$ sig/pron [$_{N'}$selv]] must be coindexed within its minimal predication.
       (ii) [$_{NP}$ sig [$_{N'}$ . . . e . . .]] / [$_{NP}$ pron [$_{N'}$ X]] must be independent within its minimal predication.[22]

The Locality Constraint is agnostic as to whether coindexing occurs through an I-dependency or not. The constraint simply reflects the function of "selv" as a locality marker and applies both to I-dependent pronouns ("sig") and to coreferent pronouns.[23] The basic distinction between "sig" and pronominals is independent of "self" marking: the former are limited to I-dependencies, the latter are not. In Danish ambiguity is minimized in that (almost) separate domains are defined for each pronoun type: "sig" signals an I-dependency and "selv" identifies the domain of the antecedent as the minimal predication.

I now turn to the two remaining cases in (55). The pronoun "hende," as any pronominal, is interpreted via coreference according to the principles discussed in chapter 2. When self-marked ("hende selv") the pronoun must find its antecedent within the minimal predication due to the presence of the locality marker. The two potential antecedents are the local subject ("Susan") and "Tina." In fact, only the interpretation in which "Tina" is taken as the antecedent is acceptable. It follows that the "coreferent" pronoun and the I-dependent one are in complementary distribution. The I-dependent one must take a subject antecedent according to the Subject Constraint. The coreferent one is blocked from taking such an antecedent and can only select a nonsubject as a possible antecedent.

The nonself-marked pronoun "hende" must find its antecedent outside its minimal predication, leaving the subject of the main clause and any other available referent as potential coreference licensers. But we have just concluded that coreferent Danish pronouns cannot take subject antecedents, yet "Anne" *is* a possible antecedent for "hende" here. In section 6.4.2 below I discuss emphatic logophors. It seems to me that the antecedent "Anne" is only licensed when emphatic stress is added. If this is indeed correct, the coreferent pronoun is not entering an I-dependency here leaving the domains for I-dependent pronouns and coreferent ones distinct. It is important to note that Danish only has separate I-dependent pronoun forms for objects in third person. In all other cases Danish behaves like English.

Without examining the intricacies of anaphora in Danish, I have demonstrated that the basic f-structure theoretical notions, minimal predication and I-dependency, play a role in defining the different types of pronouns as well as the locality constraints involved. In English, however, the functions of "sig," "sig selv," "ham" and "ham selv" are divided between only two forms, "he" and "himself" leading to a different division of the domain between reflexives and pronominals which I will discuss only briefly here by examining the English version of (55):

(59)   Anne$_i$ heard Susan$_k$ talk to Tina$_m$ about her$_i/_o$
                                              herself$_k/_m$

Here the reflexive can be both I-dependent and coreferent. As in Danish, English "self" can be viewed as a locality marker requiring an antecedent in the minimal predication. I therefore claim that "self" is a locality marker in English as well and must conform to the locality condition defined for

Danish. English reflexives, however, incorporate the functions of both Danish reflexive types. They can either participate in an I-dependency (= "sig selv") or corefer (= "ham selv"). English (nonreflexive) pronominals can also be interpreted either via an I-dependency or by coreference. They are distinct from reflexives in that they cannot be local.

That pronouns may form I-dependencies is evident from the discussion in section 6.4 as well as from the following data:

(60)   a.   John$_i$ thinks that he$_i$ likes Mary.
       b.   *He$_i$ thinks that John$_i$ likes Mary.

If an account of the ungrammaticality of (60b) were to be derived from constraints on coreference, one would have to prevent an f-structure in which *John* in the subordinate clause is the main topic. Since the subordinate clause in this case *can* form the main f-structure of the sentence, this line of investigation should not be pursued further. The ungrammaticality of (60b) follows from the Subject Constraint if we assume an I-dependency. But we must still block an interpretation of the pronoun via coreference in (60b). I propose enforcing interpretation via an I-dependency if possible, i.e., if two potentially I-dependent elements are in a canonical configuration, then they must be interpreted as I-dependent. I formulate this principle as a second principle of interpretation:

> **Principle P**: A potentially I-dependent element is obligatorily interpreted via an I-dependency if one is available.

Both Principle I and Principle P are regarded as constraints on the interpretation of f-structure. Principle P applies vacuously to NPs for which no antecedent can be found in the proper configuration and allows for non-coreference since pronouns cannot be I-dependent on a non-coreferent antecedent, even if the correct f-structure can be assigned. Pronouns can in principle either be interpreted via an I-dependency or via coreference. Principle P forces an I-dependency interpretation when both potential readings are available. This principle is therefore similar to Reinhart's (1983 and later work) non-coreference Rule in spirit.

The following f-structure of (60b) will now be ruled out:

(61)   He$_{\text{TOP-}i}$ [thinks that John$_i$ likes Mary]$_{\text{FOC}}$

According to Principle P, the coindexed pronoun and NP in (61) necessarily form an I-dependency. According to the Subject Constraint, however, the I-dependency is ruled out. Principle P, together with the locality constraints

under discussion, limit the available options for the interpretation of pronouns. Other f-structures that can be assigned to (60b) follow:

(62)   a. TOP$_i$ [he$_{TOP-sub}$ [thinks John$_i$ likes Mary]$_{FOC-sub}$]$_{FOC}$
         b. He thinks [[John$_{TOP}$ likes Mary]$_{FOC}$]
         c. He thinks [TOP$_i$ [John likes Mary$_i$]$_{FOC}$]

(62a) takes *John* as the main topic. However, in order to interpret the pronoun
via coreference, the pronoun must be a topic too, hence the subordinate
f-structure. The subordinate f-structure is identical to (61), however, ruling
out the construction as before. In (62b and c) the matrix is not part of what
is predicated of the topic and is therefore not part of the entry proper on the
topic card. It follows that coreference will not be licensed ruling out the
coindexing for all possible f-structures within the subordinate clause.

An immediate problem presents itself for the f-structure analysis of anaphora
since reflexives occur in out-of-the-blue sentences with indefinite subjects as
follows:

(63)   A: What happened?
         B: A man killed himself!
            sTOP$_i$ [a man killed himself]$_{FOC}$

The second version of the Subject Constraint introduced in section 6.2.3 is
repeated here for convenience:

> **Subject Constraint** (second version):
> SUBJECT$_{TOP}$ [... X ...]$_{FOC}$
> sTOP$_i$
> ↑_____|
>   <I-dependency

The Subject Constraint as it is currently formulated rules out the I-dependency since the antecedent subject is not a topic. A slight modification of the
Subject Constraint renders the correct result without interfering with the predictions made so far:

(64)   **Subject Constraint** (final version):
         SUBJECT$_{TOP}$ [... X ...]$_{FOC}$
         sTOP$_i$
                      |
            <I-dependency

The difference between this version and the previous ones is that the antecedent of the dependency is not identified with the topic. This requirement holds

in multiple *wh*-questions and in quantifier *wh*-constructions because the list readings can only be triggered by the topic. The requirement is therefore not a general requirement on I-dependencies but follows from specific properties of a subset of them. We have already seen one case in which the antecedent of the dependency is not a topic. This was the *wh*-trace dependency which will be discussed in detail below. Negation is also regarded as an operator which triggers an I-dependency. Here too no topic antecedent is to be found. The Subject Constraint as it now stands imposes a canonical f-structure on I-dependencies and requires that the dependent be contained in the focus.

The final version of the Subject Constraint does not block the I-dependency in (63), but it no longer follows that the antecedent of an I-dependent reflexive must be a subject as required.[24] I propose the following principle to account for those I-dependencies which have a nonoperator antecedent:

> **Principle A** (first version):
> The antecedent in an I-dependency is a SUBJECT TOPIC if it *can* be, otherwise it is a SUBJECT.

This is another principle of interpretation which applies to f-structure, and it, like the previous two (Principle I and Principle P), functions as a means to limit ambiguity.[25]

Principle A, together with the Subject Constraint, now renders the correct distribution of I-dependent pronouns both in English and in Danish.

A version of Principle A is also relevant to explain the bound anaphora counterexample mentioned at the end of the previous section repeated here:

(65)   The teacher talked to *every girl* about *her* grades.

Here the italicized antecedent is not a subject (and does not c-command the anaphor), but the I-dependency holds. Again, a canonical f-structure can be assigned to the sentence, with the dependent in focus, licensing the I-dependency. But Principle A, as it is currently defined, is violated.[26] Before making the required revision to the principle, it is fruitful to examine potentially ambiguous bound anaphora cases of this kind:

(66)   Every teacher talked to every student about his grades.

(67)   Every student talked to every teacher about his grades.

The natural interpretation for both cases is one in which the antecedent is "the student" whether this constituent is in subject position or not. The rule of interpretation must therefore allow the "natural" antecedent to take precedence over a subject topic. Principle A is reformulated as follows to take these facts into account:

Principle A (final version):
The antecedent in an I-dependency is a SUBJECT TOPIC if it *can* be, otherwise it is a SUBJECT or an OBJECT TOPIC.

Principle A can only apply if an I-dependency is licensed in the first place, i.e., if a canonical f-structure can be assigned to the sentence and the dependency is contained in the focus. The principle then allows the antecedent to be selected according to which antecedent makes most sense. Principle A does not license an object topic as the antecedent for a reflexive in subject position, however:

(68)   * TOP$_i$ [Himself saw John$_i$]$_{FOC}$

In this f-structure the antecedent is an object topic, but the f-structure is not canonical and the Subject Constraint blocks the I-dependency.

In the next three sections, I support my view that the domain of locality for local anaphors is the minimal predication by examining anaphoric relations in ECM structures, double-object constructions and prepositional phrases.

6.4.1.1   Minimal predications on stages
RR present the following data from Dutch (their (107)–(108)) exemplifying complements of perception verbs:[27]

(69)   a. *Henk$_i$ hoorde hem$_i$.
            Henk heard him
         b. *Henk$_i$ hoorde zich$_i$.
            Henk heard SE
         c. Henk$_i$ hoorde zichzelf$_i$.
            Henk heard himself.

(70)   a. *Henk$_i$ hoorde [hem$_i$ zingen].
            Henk heard [him sing]
         b. Henk$_i$ hoorde [zich$_i$ zingen].
            Henk heard [SE sing]
         c. Henk$_i$ hoorde [zichzelf$_i$ zingen].
            Henk heard [himself sing]

I assume the following f-structures for the two sentence types ("a" stands for any pronoun or anaphor):

(71)   a. [Henk$_i$]$_{TOP}$ [hoorde sTOP$_i$ [a$_i$]$_{FOC}$]$_{FOC}$
         b. Henk$_i$ hoorde sTOP$_i$[[a$_i$]$_{TOP}$ [zingen]$_{FOC}$]$_{FOC}$
         c. [Henk$_i$]$_{TOP}$ [hoorde sTOP$_i$[a$_i$]$_{FOC}$ zingen]$_{FOC}$

Following the discussion of objects introduced on stage in chapter 2, sections 2.1.1 and 2.1.3, I assume that both f-structures of perception verbs involve a subordinate f-structure with a stage topic. In (71a), a_1's existence on the "stage" heard by Henk is asserted. In (71b) the event of a_1's singing on the stage is asserted to take place. The two f-structures differ, however, in what counts as a minimal predication for the anaphor. The subordinate f-structure in (71a) has the NP predicated of a stage. This kind of predication does not itself count as a minimal predication since the stage topic is not overt. Therefore, the minimal predication in which a_1 can potentially seek an antecedent is the sentence itself. The locality constraint therefore only licenses a "self" anaphor. In (71b), however, the subordinate f-structure consisting of the topic, a_1, and the focus "zingen" is a minimal predication. The locality constraint therefore does not prevent a non "self"-marked pronoun from occurring here. Since the pronoun forms an I-dependency with the matrix subject, only I-dependent "zich" (and not the pronoun "hem") is licensed.

Evidence for this analysis was brought to my attention by Fred Landman (pers. com.). He noted that (69b) is acceptable (without "self"-marking) if a locative PP such as "on the tape" is added. This would make for an overt stage topic, the minimal predication would count, and the nonself-marked pronoun is therefore licensed.

A slightly different f-structure, is, however, also available for (70) given in (71c). This f-structure is interesting in that it also allows an I-dependency to be defined between focused a_1 and the matrix subject in the same way as in (71a) licensing the reflexive "zichzelf." The difference between the f-structure in (71b and c) is that in the former a_1 is the topic of a subordinate f-structure and in the latter it is the focus of a stage topic leaving the predicate undefined with respect to its topic. Verbs of perception select stage topics and the focus of this stage topic is either the whole complement or just the NP as in (71c). The latter option is available only because of the lexical properties of perception verbs which optionally select just this NP. The "stage" perceived in this case has a_1 on it. The "singing" is not part of the stage in this f-structure. Note that "zingen" is *not* part of the subordinate f-structure (with the stage topic). It is, however, part of the focus in the main f-structure. It is therefore natural to assume that V-raising in Dutch is licensed in exactly this f-structure. RR argue that V-raising (either in s-structure or LF) generates the correct reflexive argument structure. They must assume V-raising in LF in English to account for the reflexives in languages in which overt V-raising does not occur. Here I argue that V-raising is licensed by the same f-structure that licenses the reflexive. My account therefore does not require V-raising in LF.

The same account applies to intensional predicates such as *believe*. Predicates of this type are similar to the perception verbs just discussed in that they select stage complements. The difference between the two types of predicates is that with intensional predicates the selected stage complement is unindexed, i.e., it is the "imaginary" stage discussed in chapter 3, section 3.1.3. The distribution of pronouns in such predicates cannot be examined in Dutch and Danish which do not have this type of ECM predicate. In English the ECM subject must be reflexive. This follows if an f-structure such as (71c) is assumed. But the f-structure in (71b) cannot be ruled out in view of the following data:

(72)   a.   John believed Peter₁ to have criticized himself₁.
       b.   *John₂ believed Peter₁ to have criticized himself₂.

(73)   a.   John₁ believed himself₁ to have criticized himself₁.
       b.   [John₁]_TOP [believed sTOP [himself₁]_FOC to have criticized himself₁]_FOC

(72a) is licensed and (72b) ruled out exactly because of the f-structure (71b) in which the reflexive forms an I-dependency with the subject of the matrix. (73a) follows from the f-structure type in (71c), shown in (73b): both reflexives are in the main focus and form an I-dependency with the main subject–Topic. Neither is contained in an (overt) minimal predication. It follows that neither the Subject Constraint nor the locality constraint are violated. Both reflexives are therefore licensed.[28]

In this section I have identified ECM type phenomena with predicates that select stage topics. I leave for future research the idea that case marking in these cases can be derived from f-structure-theoretical properties as well. I have also shown how such stage topics do not interfere with minimal predications.

6.4.1.2 Double-object constructions

In section 6.3, I referred to Riad (1988) and data from Swedish indicating that an *optional* f-structure can be assigned to the two objects in a double-object construction. The following f-structures are therefore possible:

(74)   a. John showed [[the book]_TOP to Mary_FOC]
       b. John showed [Mary_TOP [the book]_FOC]
       c. John_TOP [showed the book to Mary]_FOC

I assume further that the topics in (74a and b) are subjects in the small clause in which they occur. The following distribution of pronouns follows from these assumptions and the Subject Constraint:

(75)   a. John showed Mary$_1$ to herself/*her$_1$.
        b. John showed *herself/*her$_1$ to Mary$_1$.
        c. John showed Mary$_1$ herself/*her$_1$.
        d. John showed *herself/*her$_1$ Mary$_1$.
        e. John$_1$ showed himself/*him$_1$ to Mary.
        f. John$_1$ showed Mary to himself/*him$_1$.

(75f) is only licensed if it is assumed that the small clause f-structure is optional. Otherwise the reflexive would violate the locality constraint on "self" anaphors. Note that in order to rule out the nonself-marked pronoun in (75e), we have to assume that optional subordinate f-structures are assigned only if needed, i.e., if an I-dependency must be defined within it.

6.4.1.3 Locational f-structures

Vikner (1985: 55) assumes an analysis in terms of an optional predication structure for the following example as well:

(76)   Anne$_i$ fandt Susan$_j$ i sin$_{i/j}$ seng.
                        hendes$_{i/j}$
     Anne found Susan in her$_{i/j}$ bed

The I-dependent possessive "sin" (as indicated in (54a)) forms an I-dependency with its antecedent. The pronominal possessive must be independent in its minimal predication according to the locality constraint (58) if the constraint is revised to take into account the two kinds of possessives as well. The fact that the pronominal possessive can receive both the index of the small clause subject and the main clause subject could be accounted for if the small clause subject did not count as a subject in the latter case. Vikner's account, however, does not explain the lessened ambiguity when the sentence is used to answer the question "Where did Anne find Susan?" In (77), I indicate the possible interpretations as well as the f-structure for the sentence in this context:

(77)   Anne$_{\text{TOP}i}$ fandt Susan$_j$ [i sin$_{i/*j}$ seng] $_{\text{FOC}}$
                     hendes$_{*i/j}$

In this f-structure only the locational PP is focused. The PP is predicated of the main clause subject forcing coindexing of the I-dependent "sin." Since "Susan" is not part of the focus, this NP can provide an antecedent for "hendes."[29]

I would like to pursue a line of investigation which follows from f-structure theoretical considerations for relevant data provided in RR. RR argue that in locative and directional PPs, P forms its own predicate (their (15) and (16)):

(78)   a. *Max$_1$ speaks with him$_1$.
        b. *Max$_1$ relies on him$_1$.

(79)   a. Max$_1$ saw a gun near him$_1$.
        b. Max$_1$ put the gun near/under/on him$_1$.
        c. Max$_1$ sat Lucie next to him$_1$.

According to RR, in (79a) the pronoun is contained in an adjunct and in (79b and c) the whole PP, not just the NP pronoun, is selected by the verb. Therefore, in contrast to the pronouns in (78), these pronouns are not viewed as arguments of the verb in either of the cases in (79). According to RR, since the pronoun and its antecedent are not coarguments of the same predicate, the coindexed pronoun not does not violate their condition on reflexivity. In the current framework an alternative explanation presents itself. Locative and directional PPs (whether selected by the predicate or not) allow an f-structure in which they play the role of stage topics:

(80)   sTOP$_1$ [Max$_1$ put the gun [near him$_1$]$_1$]$_{FOC}$

An I-dependency is not licensed since the dependent pronoun functions as a topic. The rules of coreference can therefore apply, correctly licensing the pronoun as was shown in chapter 2. The fact that these PPs occur overtly in topic position indicates that this is a possible f-structure:

(81)   a. Near him$_1$, Max$_1$ saw a gun.
        b. Near him$_1$, Max$_1$ put the gun.
        c. Next to him$_1$, Max$_1$ sat Lucie.

RR then show that a small clause analysis of the following cases (their (63) and (65)) can be made to work:

(82)   a. Max$_1$ rolled [the carpet$_2$ over him$_1$]
        b. *Max$_1$ rolled [the carpet$_2$ over it$_2$]
        c. Max$_1$ rolled [the carpet$_2$ over himself$_1$]

(83)   Max$_1$ examined the carpet$_2$ underneath it$_2$.

RR distinguish the cases in (82) from (83) as follows. In (82a), for example, *over* is a relation holding between the carpet and Max. For (83), they adopt a suggestion by Hoekstra that an abstract EVENT argument is involved as follows: the relation *underneath* holds between the carpet and the event of Max's examining the carpet. In this fashion they achieve the same result as they would if they assumed a stage topic for the latter but not for the former. (83) is interpreted according to an f-structure such as the one given in (80) licensing the pronoun.[30] This f-structure is not available for the sentences in (82), however, as shown by the topicalization test:

(84) a. ? Over him$_1$, Max$_1$ rolled the carpet.
      b. ??Over it$_2$, Max rolled the carpet$_2$.

(84a) receives the following interpretation: the place where Max's rolling of the carpet took place is "over Max," i.e., an interpretation in which the carpet is tiny and Max reaches up over him rolling it there is derived. The interpretation for (82a), in which the carpet ends up rolled over Max, is however not available here. Similarly, what is wrong with (84b) is that the event of Max rolling the carpet must take place over the carpet. Since the carpet cannot be in two places at once, the sentence is ruled out pragmatically.

If a small-clause analysis is maintained for the sentences in (82), (82b) will be ruled out by the locality constraint since the pronoun is in an I-dependency in its minimal predication. (82c), is, however, also ruled out, since the I-dependency extends beyond the minimal predication. In order to account for this, one could either assume that the subordinate f-structure is optional as in the double-object case, or take the reflexive in (82c) to be logophoric. Following Kuno (1987), I take the latter tack as shown in the next section.

6.4.2   Logophors

A test for logophoric anaphora, according to RR among others, is that it violates c-command and locality constraints on anaphora.[31] According to Kuno (1987) a logophoric anaphor expresses the point of view of the speaker or the hearer. I would like to demonstrate here that an account of the special function of logophors follows in the current framework if logophors *are* assumed to adhere to the *same* constraints as do regular pronouns. The minimal predication defined for logophoric reflexives is, however, of a different sort. Let me illustrate:

(85)   sTOP$_1$ [A picture of myself is hanging on the wall]$_{FOC}$

This focus structure does not contain a minimal predication in which an I-dependency is formed with the reflexive. Remember, however, a point made already in chapter 1, section 1.3: among the permanently available cards on top of the file are the cards representing the speaker and the hearer. Let us assume that their respective indices are *1* and *2*. Let us further assume that a special feature of these cards is that *subordinate* foci contained in sentences can be entered on these cards. This allows for the following entry:

1

(is) a picture of myself₁

Allowing this entry gives us two separate results: 1. an account of the interpretation of the reflexive as having a topic antecedent; 2. an interpretation for
this f-structure which incorporates the point of view of the speaker. The
special discourse function of logophors can thus be made to follow from the
discourse theory if we allow the relevant focus to be entered in this way.
(This entry is additional to the entries following from the regular processing
of the sentence.) The condition on the reflexive in the "logophoric" entry
differs only in a minor way from the condition on local pronouns in general.
As any other pronoun, the logophoric pronoun must be interpreted on an
available topic card. In the case of logophors, however, this topic is not
syntactically present in the sentence. The locality marker "self" indicates that
the logophoric pronoun forms a minimal predication with *its* topic.

Let us now examine how this approach to logophors accounts for other
cases which have been categorized as such. Note, however, that if an overt
subject is present in the picture NP, or if the picture NP is definite, the
logophor is excluded or at least marked.[32]

(86)   a.   *John's picture of myself is hanging on the wall.
        b.   ??Your picture of myself is hanging on the wall.
        c.   ?The picture of myself is hanging on the wall.

In these examples the logophoric entries contain the following subordinate
f-structures:

(87)   a.   [John's]$_{TOP}$ [picture of myself]$_{FOC}$
        b.   [Your]$_{TOP}$ [picture of myself]$_{FOC}$
        c.   [The picture]$_{TOP}$ [(be) of myself]$_{FOC}$

According to the locality constraint, the antecedent of a self-marked pronoun
must be inside the minimal predication in which it is contained. The subordinate f-structures in (87) define minimal predications which block the
analysis given for the indefinite picture NP in (85). Since the indefinite
NP cannot be a topic, the subordinate f-structure is blocked, licensing the

logophoric (non-I-dependent) reading for the reflexive. The subordinate f-structure is the unmarked f-structure for the definite in (87c) (according to the topic constraint), but the logophoric entry on card 1 is also possible. This explains why the logophor with the definite is not totally ruled out. A plausible explanation for (86b) is that the subject pronoun is interpreted logophorically as well, allowing the naked picture NP (without its subject) to be entered on card 1. What is wrong with the sentence, under this analysis, is that it represents two points of view simultaneously.

So far, I have only allowed for an account of first- and second-person logophors. Third-person logophors are excluded if no antecedent is present in the sentence:

(88)   a. *A picture of himself is hanging on the wall.
       b. He said that a picture of himself was hanging on the wall.

Kuno shows that third-person logophors represent the point of view of the speaker or hearer of the "quoted" assertion. These cards, although not permanently available on top of the file, are positioned there by the discourse in the cases which allow third-person logophors, licensing the logophoric anaphors in exactly the same way as the first- and second-person ones.

Kuno (1987: 153, his 1.1,1.2) makes the following observations concerning logophoric anaphors in PPs:

(89)   a. John$_i$ pulled the blanket over him$_i$.
       b. John$_i$ pulled the blanket over himself$_i$.

(90)   a. John$_i$ hid the book behind him$_i$.
       b. John$_i$ hid the book behind himself$_i$.

According to Kuno, (89b) implies that John tried to cover himself up with the blanket to hide under, and (90b) implies that John held the book in his hand and put it behind his back. The (a) sentences do not carry these implications. I assume that these interpretations are derived from the logophoric entry of the reflexive PPs on the card for "John." For (89b) this means that the event reported in the sentence takes place over John from John's perspective and for (90b) that the event takes place behind John, from John's perspective. The rest of Kuno's interpretations should follow from this basic account of the interpretation of logophoric anaphors.

RR discuss another type of logophor, the emphatic or focus logophor.[33] Let me now show how an f-structure approach fares with them.

(91)   a. This letter was addressed only to myself.
        b. Max boasted that the queen invited Lucie and himself for a drink.
        c. There were five tourists in the room apart from myself.
        d. Max would like very much for himself to win.

For point of view (or perspective) logophors I argued for an extra subordinate f-structure on an available topic card. In the sentences in (91) an extra subordinate f-structure is also required in view of the analysis proposed for *only* in chapter 3: I argued for the following subordinate f-structure for *only*, for example:

(92)   This letter was addressed ONLY to $\left[\left[\left\{ \begin{matrix} [\text{myself}]_{\text{FOC}} \\ \text{everyone else} \end{matrix} \right\} \right]_{\text{TOP}} \right]$

Note first that the subordinate f-structure prevents an I-dependency between the reflexive and a potential antecedent since it interferes with an analysis of the sentence in terms of canonical f-structure. Second, the subordinate f-structure upon which *only* operates is a discourse-specified topic set including the speaker. This subordinate f-structure therefore allows the reflexive to find its antecedent among the members of the topic set and is therefore interpreted contrastively as argued in chapter 3. All cases of contrast therefore allow so-called emphatic logophors.[34] Giving a detailed analysis of each of the cases in (91) would take us too far afield. (91d), however, warrants a comment. RR argue that this anaphor is a focus anaphor. This is indeed the interpretation one gets if the reflexive is stressed. Unstressed, however, an informant allowed for the following point-of-view type implication: compared to the "objective" pronounless version, (91d) is more personal and implies a personal desire.

The properties of logophoric anaphora follow straightforwardly in the current framework, if logophoric pronouns are viewed as regular local pronouns with a special logophoric application of the discourse rules which accounts for the distinctive interpretation of the logophor.[35]

I have treated logophoric anaphors as local, but not I-dependent, pronouns. If an I-dependency were involved, the Subject Constraint, which requires that the antecedent of the dependency be a bona fide syntactic subject, would rule them out. I argued above that English reflexives unite the functions of both I-dependent and non-I-dependent pronouns which have different morphological actualizations in Danish. It is therefore predicted that the I-dependent "sig" will not occur as a logophoric pronoun in Danish. This is indeed the case:

(93)   Han sagde at   der   hang et billede af hamselv på vægen.
                                              *sigselv
        he   said   that there hung a picture of himself on the wall
        "He said that a picture of himself hung on the wall."

Since logophors are viewed here as local coreferent pronouns, their discussion does not belong in a chapter about I-dependencies. I chose to discuss these pronouns here since they are generally discussed in the context of reflexivity.

6.4.3   Crossover

The literature on crossover effects is massive. Here I will relate only to two recent contributions which I use to argue for my f-structure theoretical approach: Lasnik and Stowell (1991) and Postal (1993).

Strong Crossover (SCO) is illustrated in the following examples from Postal (1993: 542, his (11)):

(94)   a. *Who$_1$ did they inform him$_1$ that Joan would call t$_1$?
        b. *[Whose$_1$ sister]$_2$ did they inform him$_1$ that Joan would call t$_2$?

Postal distinguishes the primary SCO effect in (94a) from the secondary SCO effect in (94b). The latter he groups with Weak Crossover effects such as:

(95)   *Who$_1$ did his$_1$ sister call t$_1$ a moron?
        (Postal 1993: 540, his (3a))

The primary SCO effect follows from the Subject Constraint which is violated in (94a), as is demonstrated in (96):

(96)   Who$_{TOP1}$ [did they inform him$_1$ that Joan would call t$_1$]$_{FOC}$
        |_____|
                * I-dependency

In order for the pronoun to be dependent on the topic set over which a *wh*-phrase ranges, the latter (according to Principle A) has to be a topic *and* a subject. Although *wh*-phrases can be interpreted as topics, only a subject *wh*-phrase in a canonical f-structure licenses the dependency:

(97)   Who$_{TOP1}$ [said that Joan had called him$_1$]$_{FOC}$

A *wh*-phrase can only be nonreflexively I-dependent, i.e., its index may be dependent on an antecedent as argued above, but it is not coindexed with it. The Subject Constraint thus predicts Primary Strong Crossover effects.

The difference between WCO effects and Secondary SCO effects, on the one hand, and Primary SCO effects on the other is that in the former two cases the coindexed pronoun is itself not involved in an I-dependency. The I-dependency is instead formed on a constituent containing it. In principle then, a nonreflexive dependency could be formed with the *wh*-phrase as the dependent and the phrase containing the (coindexed) pronoun as the antecedent. I predict that the constraints on these two types of crossover will be the same. Postal (1993) shows that this prediction is correct. I will therefore refer to these two types of crossover as Weak Crossover, no longer distinguishing them.

In WCO as well as SCO the Subject Constraint is violated if the *wh*-phrase is viewed as the antecedent of the I-dependency. This is the only option for SCO as just demonstrated. For WCO, the reverse dependency must be examined as well. WCO effects have been recognized to be less pronounced than SCO effects. In particular it has been claimed that WCO effects are less apparent in restrictive relatives than in questions.[36] Note that a D-linked *wh*-phrase also lessens the effect:

(98)   a.   *Who$_1$ does his$_1$ mother love t$_1$?
       b.   ?the man$_1$ who$_1$ his$_1$ mother loves t$_1$
       c.   ??Which man$_1$ does his$_1$ mother love t$_1$?

The head of a relative clause is most easily interpreted as the topic of the predication formed by the relative clause. Similarly, the D-linked *wh*-phrase, as argued in section 6.2.2, is interpreted as a topic. The data in (98) is therefore totally parallel to the Superiority effects examined above. The analysis of WCO effects will therefore follow from the same considerations discussed there. I review these considerations now:

(99)   Who$_1$ does [his$_1$ mother]$_{TOP}$ [love t$_1$]$_{FOC}$

(100)   Which man$_{TOP1}$ does [his$_1$ mother]$_{TOP}$ [love t$_1$]$_{FOC}$

In (99) an I-dependency is licensed between the trace position of the *wh*-phrase and the antecedent subject. The fronted *wh*-phrase must be reconstructed forming another I-dependency as illustrated. According to Principle I, a dependent cannot be interpreted by more than one I-dependency. The structure in (99) is therefore blocked. The WCO effect is predicted to be weaker than the SCO effect in view of the fact that WCO sentences allow for a reversal of the I-dependency. The I-dependency in (100) does not violate the Subject Constraint. If the fronted *wh*-phrase is interpretable as a main topic, reconstruction to trace position is not required. This f-structure is, however, highly marked, due to the need to interpret both the fronted *wh*-phrase and the subject as main topics, explaining the fact that a crossover effect is present.

Crossover is also blocked in this framework in cases in which the "crossed over" pronoun is not in subject position:

(101)   *Who$_i$ did you tell his$_i$ mother that Susan wanted to visit t$_i$

In this case no I-dependency is licensed between the trace position and the antecedent "his mother" because the latter, although a potential topic, is not a subject. This case will therefore be ruled out directly by the Subject Constraint. I therefore predict that the sentence cannot be improved by enabling the *wh*-phrase to be interpreted as a topic:

(102)   *Which boyfriend$_i$ did you tell his$_i$ mother that Susan wanted to visit t$_i$

I have shown that SCO effects are a direct outcome of the Subject Constraint and that WCO effects are predicted by the same f-structure theoretical considerations which account for Superiority effects.

Further support for this analysis of crossover effects comes from the main observation in Lasnik and Stowell (1991), namely that the WCO effects are totally absent when no "true" quantifier is involved in the binding of the pronoun. The cases they cite belonging to this class are Topicalization, nonrestrictive relatives clauses, *tough*-movement and parasitic gaps. An analysis of the latter two cases in terms of f-structure is beyond the scope of the current enterprise. I assume, however, that the same factors that explain the two cases to be discussed here account for the remaining cases as well.[37] The absence of WCO effects in these sentence types follows from the fact that no I-dependency is involved (examples from Lasnik and Stowell (1991, their (33), (36)):

(103)   a. John$_1$, I believe his$_1$ mother loves e$_1$.
         b. This book$_1$, I would never ask its$_1$ author to read e$_1$.

(104)   a. Gerald$_1$, who$_1$ his$_1$ mother loves t$_1$, is a nice guy.
         b. This book$_1$, which$_1$ its$_1$ author wrote t$_1$ last week, is a hit.

In (103), the fronted NPs are topics and reconstruction to focus position is not required for their interpretation. Principle P does not force an I-dependency between the subject and the trace since the two are not coindexed. It follows that the pronouns get interpreted via coreference. The entry of the predicate sentence on the topic card licenses coindexing as argued in chapter 2, section 2.3.3. I therefore submit that Lasnik and Stowell's distinction between true and untrue quantifiers is an f-structure distinction between phrases that are topics and do not impose an I-dependency, and those that are not. The same account applies to nonrestrictive relative clauses. The clause gets interpreted by being entered on the topic card defined by the head. Appositives differ from restrictive relative clauses in forming a separate nonsubordinate f-structure to the one triggered by the main f-structure of the sentence. The interpretation of the pronoun is again via coreference.

Note that SCO effects are not absolved in this way since an I-dependency is forced (by principle P) between the coindexed pronoun and the trace. This I-dependency, however, violates the Subject Constraint. All the cases that escape Crossover Effects turn out to have an analysis which does not violate the Subject Constraint.

Lasnik and Stowell quote Chomsky (1976) who noted that focusing can generate WCO effects:

(105)   a.   His$_i$ mother SHOT John$_i$
        b.   ??His$_i$ mother shot JOHN$_i$
        c.   His$_i$ mother bought a PICTURE of John$_i$.

What is wrong with (105b) is simply that coreference licensing is violated since the stress on the antecedent blocks its interpretation as a topic. These data do not pose a problem for my account.

Postal (1993) introduces two thornier problems. The first, illustrated in (106) (Postal's (25)), is that the nature of the NP containing the pronoun can provoke a WCO effect with topicalization. The second, illustrated in (107) (Postal's (31)), is that if *only* or *even* modify the phrase containing the pronoun extraction fails to yield WCO effects:

(106)   a.   Sidney$_1$, I am sure his$_1$ job is important to t_1.[38]
        b.   *Sidney$_1$, I am sure your opinion of him$_1$ is important to t_1.

(107)   a.   *Which lawyer$_1$ did his$_1$ clients hate t_1?
        b.   Which lawyer$_1$ did only his$_1$ older clients hate t_1?

Postal associates the distinction in (106) with the fact that NPs such as "your opinion of X" form a scope island, whereas the possessive NPs do not. Another way to put this is that the position of the pronoun in the former case is not a possible topic position. (Chapter 5 shows that topics receive wide-scope interpretations.) The subordinate f-structures of the two NP types follow:

(108)   a.   his$_{TOP}$ job$_{FOC}$
         b.   your$_{TOP}$ [opinion of him]$_{FOC}$
         c.   *TOP$_i$ [your opinion of him$_i$]$_{FOC}$

The fact that (108c) is not possible means that the pronoun cannot get its interpretation from its entry on the card for "Sidney$_1$." The subordinate interpretation (108b) forces it to be entered on the card for "you" and coreference will be blocked.[39]

The second set of problematic data receives a straightforward analysis if the pronoun is analyzed as a logophor analogous to the emphatic reflexive logophors discussed in section 6.4.2. The pronoun is interpreted via the subordinate f-structure triggered by *only*.

Crossover effects have been shown to be a direct consequence of the Subject Constraint and f-structure constraints on coreference. These phenomena therefore provide further strong support for the f-structure-theoretical account presented here.

6.5   Other I-dependencies

I have argued that pronouns, including both pronominals and anaphors, as well as *wh*-phrases, can, but need not receive their interpretation via an I-dependency. In Scandinavian languages I-dependent pronouns are distinct from pronouns interpreted via coreference, but if marked with the "selv" morpheme both kinds must find their antecedent within the local domain. In English, however, only one pronominal form is available and the distinction which is overt in the Scandinavian languages is masked. This is why an analysis of English might produce a theory in which pronominals are distinguished from anaphors by a locality constraint as in Binding Theory. Binding Theory also associates *wh*-traces with R-expressions. I have shown here that one class of *wh*-phrases (and their traces) are I-dependent classifying them with I-dependent pronouns. Pronouns, reflexives and *wh*-phrases are also interpretable via coreference. (In the case of *wh*-phrases the antecedent of the coreference relation defines a restrictive set over which the question ranges.) The three categories which were distinguished in Binding Theory are here considered to be one. I therefore accept the traditional view that all three categories belong to the general category of pronoun to be distinguished from R-expressions. The following chart clarifies the point (pronouns have the feature +P):

(109)

		I-dependent	Coreferent
+P	pronoun	+	+
	reflexives	+	+
	wh-phrases	+	+
	R-expressions	−	−

R-expressions can be the antecedents in an I-dependency if they are strong, i.e., if they can fulfill the function of topic.

Even though I have argued for a structural constraint on f-structure, the Subject Constraint, I have also shown that a purely structural account (involving c-command, conditions on chain formation, etc.), divorced from f-structure, does not suffice, since only the Subject Constraint distinguishes topic antecedents which are required for crossover, etc. This would have to be stated as a separate requirement otherwise. Neither could interactions with other aspects of f-structure be brought in naturally.

I now turn to two other types of I-dependencies: those involving negation and those involving *wh*-movement.

6.5.1   *I-dependencies formed by partitioning*
First I show that, as a consequence of their function as partitioners, negation and *only* trigger the formation of I-dependencies. It follows that the Subject Constraint restricts the possible f-structures of sentences with these operators. I further show that the operation of partitioning is what gives content to the notion "affective" operator explaining why such operators license negative polarity items such as *any*. Yes/no questions "ask" for partitioning of the restrictive set upon which negation operates qualifying them as negative polarity licensers. Since topic *wh*-phrases are interpreted as "asking" a set of yes/no questions, one for each member of the topic set they define, they too license *any*.[40]

6.5.2   *Negation*
Remember that negation operates on a restrictive set of alternatives, eliminating one member of the set. Take, for example, the following illustration from chapter 3:

(110)   Joan$_{TOP}$ didn't [eat $\left[\begin{array}{l} [\text{the PIZZA}]_{FOC} \\ \left\{ \begin{array}{l} \text{delicacy}_1 \\ \text{delicacy}_2 \end{array} \right\}_{TOP} \end{array} \right]$]$_{FOC}$

Negation *identifies* by a process of elimination. It would, however, be an exaggeration to say that by eliminating "pizza" from consideration, the speaker fully identifies to the hearer what Joan ate. However, by using negation, the speaker manipulates an I-referential set on the hearer's card and that is sufficient to require an I-dependency between the negation operator and the focused constituent. Once an I-dependency takes effect, the Subject Constraint is invoked forcing a canonical f-structure on the sentence in which the dependent is focused, automatically accounting for association with focus. The final formulation of the Subject Constraint in section 6.4.1 is repeated here for convenience:

Subject Constraint (final version):
SUBJECT$_{TOP}$ [. . . X . . .]$_{FOC}$
sTOP$_1$

|
<I-dependency

In view of the fact that this verion of the constraint does not specify the position of the antecedent of the dependency, no further changes in its formulation are necessary and a partitioning operator (in I(nfl)) can trigger an I-dependency as well. This type of I-dependency also differs from the ones examined above in that negation operates on a variety of constituents, not just NPs.

This version of the Subject Constraint applies correctly to cases with overt stage topics. The following examples illustrate overt negative stage topics:

(111)   a. At (*in) no time did anyone do anything.
        b. Nowhere did she see any lights.

It is a well-known fact that fronted negative time and place phrases (which define stages) trigger inversion resulting in a structure isomorphic to a subject–predicate structure with the stage topic playing the role of the subject.

(112)   sTOP$_1$ [. . . X . . .]$_{FOC}$

The Subject Constraint identifies such a structure as canonical allowing any X in focus to be identified by negation predicting the correct polarity facts.

In chapter 3, section 3.1.3, it was pointed out that the f-structure of negative sentences is restricted further as indicated by the following examples:

(113)   a. *A man doesn't like Mary.
        b. *A man didn't read the book.
        c. *A man hadn't arrived.
        d. *A man wasn't available.

In view of the fact that negative sentences cannot be uttered out-of-the-blue (see chapter 3), the fact that (nongeneric, noncontrastive) indefinite subjects are blocked in negative sentences indicates that the subject, in these cases, must be assigned the topic role and that this role is not available for the object. This now follows without further ado from the Subject Constraint.

6.5.3   *Only*

That *only* forms an I-dependency is even more obvious than it is with negation since the power of elimination of this operator is such that it leaves a single member of the restrictive set for the rule of predication to apply to. I therefore predict that the same f-structure constraints, imposed by the Subject Constraint, apply here. This was precisely the conclusion reached in chapter 3. It was also noted there that no such constraints are imposed on *even*. This follows from the fact that *even* is not a partitioner.

It follows from the analysis of negation as forming an I-dependency, together with the Subject Constraint, that the scope of negation is defined by the main focus. Negative Polarity Items are therefore constrained to occur in this domain. This accounts for the structural restrictions on the occurrence of *any* in sentences with negation. It also follows that yes/no questions, which "ask" for the partitioning of a set, allow negative polarity items. Negative polarity items are also licensed in the context of *only*, but their distribution is severely limited:

(114)   a. Only Peter ate any/some porridge.
　　　　b. Peter only ate *any/some porridge.
　　　　c. Only in the desert does anything grow.

The generalization to be made here is that *any* is licensed only by a partitioning topic which is either a subject or a stage. The f-structures for (114a and b) follow:

(115)   a. [ONLY $\begin{bmatrix} \left\{ \begin{matrix} [\text{Peter}]_{\text{FOC}} \\ \text{everyone else} \end{matrix} \right\} \end{bmatrix}_{\text{TOP}}$]$_{\text{TOP}}$ [ate any porridge]$_{\text{FOC}}$

　　　　b. Peter$_{\text{TOP}}$ [ONLY ate $\begin{bmatrix} \left\{ \begin{matrix} [\text{any porridge}]_{\text{FOC}} \\ \text{everything else} \end{matrix} \right\} \end{bmatrix}_{\text{TOP}}$]$_{\text{FOC}}$

In chapter 3 I showed, following Kadmon and Landman (1993), that the function of the negative polarity item *any* is to eliminate the "other" member of the restrictive set available in negative sentences, where the other member of the set is defined according to some contextual dimension. This cannot be done in (115b) since *only* itself functions to eliminate the complement set totally, revealing why *any* cannot be interpreted there. In (115a), however, *only* operates on a topic set and *any* operates on a focus-internal set causing no interference as in the previous case. Note that if no contextual set is defined in the focus domain, *any* is not required.

In this section I argued that the restriction on f-structures found with negation and *only* follows from viewing these operators as triggering I-dependencies.

6.5.4 *The* wh-*trace dependency*

In chapter 3, I offered two different interpretations for *wh*-questions, one in which the fronted *wh*-phrase functions as the topic of the main f-structure and another in which the *wh*-phrase is interpreted in trace position by reconstruction. I will argue here that interpretation in trace position forms an I-dependency between the fronted *wh*-phrase and its trace. Constraints on *wh*-movement therefore take two forms. Either the fronted *wh*-phrase has to be interpretable as a topic necessitating a set derivable from context, or else the Subject Constraint on I-dependencies takes effect. The following two f-structures illustrate the two cases:

(116) $[wh\text{-}X]_{\text{TOP}} [\ldots t \ldots]_{\text{FOC}}$

(117) $[wh\text{-}X] \text{ SUBJECT}_{\text{TOP}} [\ldots t \ldots]_{\text{FOC}}$

The f-structure in (116) is restricted by the Topic Constraint on f-structure. A further restriction is that the *wh*-phrase function as the main topic. The empty position (the trace) can only be interpreted if the focus is entered on the main topic card as illustrated in chapter 3. The trace must therefore be a constituent of the main focus.

The f-structure in (117) requires reconstruction to trace position since the *wh*-phrase will otherwise remain uninterpreted. Reconstruction identifies the *wh*-phrase with a certain syntactic position, thus allowing for its interpretation via predication and update. It is this aspect of the relation between the fronted *wh*-phrase and the trace position which generates the I-dependency. Note further that this type of I-dependency has the characteristic property associated with I-dependencies: the dependent does not have an existence of its own, i.e., it does not license the construction of a separate card.

If reconstruction to trace position is viewed as forming an I-dependency between the *wh*-phrase and its trace, the Subject Constraint will apply.[41] The Subject Constraint restricts *wh*-trace positions to positions contained in the main focus of the sentence. The f-structure is canonical allowing either a subject topic or a stage topic. The position of the antecedent of the I-dependency is not marked, except for the fact that it must not be focus internal.[42] The Subject Constraint therefore says nothing else about possible landing sights for the moved constituent. The antecedent for the various types of dependencies must be defined by properties of the dependency itself. The dependencies discussed in sections 6.2–4 all involve dependencies between NPs. In these cases the main topic (subject or stage), or a topic constituent contained therein, provides the antecedent of the dependency. In the cases discussed in this section (negation, *only* and *wh*-movement) the antecedents are all operators which trigger an I-dependency. The structural positions of these operators are syntactically defined. The dependents of both types of I-dependency are, however, subject to the same constraint.

A possible line of investigation to structurally unify the antecedents of the different kinds of I-dependencies is to view them all as specifiers: subjects are SPEC,IP; stage topics and topicalized NPs are SPEC,TopP; and *wh*-movement is to SPEC,CP. Negation according to Rizzi (1990) is in SPEC,AgrP as well as in Subject and Topic positions. It follows that the antecedents of all I-dependencies are limited to Specifier position.[43] I believe this idea should be further examined within the current framework but will limit the discussion here to issues more central to f-structure theory.

Picture noun phrases provide a straightforward illustration of the need for a unified account of binding, negative polarity and extraction:

(118)   a.   John saw pictures of himself.
         b.   ?John saw the picture of himself.[44]
         c.   *John saw Susan's picture of himself.

(119)   a.   John didn't see pictures of anyone.
         b.   *John didn't see the picture of anyone.
         c.   *John didn't see Susan's pictures of anyone.

(120)   a.   Who did John see pictures of?
         b.   *Who did John see the picture of?[45]
         c.   *Who did John see Susan's picture of?[46]

The following f-structures distinguish the examples in (a) from those in (b) and (c):

(121)   John$_{TOP}$ [saw sTOP$_{t\text{-sub}}$ [pictures of X]$_{FOC\text{-sub}}$]$_{FOC}$

(122)   a.   John$_{TOP}$ [saw [the picture]$_{TOP\text{-sub}}$ [of X]$_{FOC\text{-sub}}$]$_{FOC}$
         b.   John$_{TOP}$ [saw Susan's$_{TOP\text{-sub}}$ [picture of X]$_{FOC\text{-sub}}$]$_{FOC}$

It can be argued that the predicates which allow I-dependencies with picture noun phrases are predicates which select stages.[47] (For the sake of simplicity, I have left out the subordinate f-structure with the stage topic in (122).) The f-structure in (121) is similar to the ones discussed above in section 6.4.1.1 in the context of reflexivity. There I argued that a subordinate stage topic does not interfere with the processing of the main f-structure. An I-dependency is therefore licensed taking X as the dependent. In the f-structures in (122), however, the definite subjects of the picture noun phrases provide topics. The dependent, X, can therefore form an I-dependency within this (subordinate) f-structure which conforms to the requirements of the Subject Constraint. The following illustrate such I-dependencies:

(123)   a. John saw Susan's picture of herself.
         b. John saw nobody's picture of anyone.

It follows from Principle P that since X is a dependent in the subordinate f-structure in both f-structures represented in (122), it cannot form an I-dependency in the main f-structure.

6.6   Islands

In this section I show that extraction islands can now be explained without adding any further machinery. Since Erteschik-Shir (1973), I have argued that islands are environments which cannot provide the main focus of the sentence.[48] Here, I show that this follows from the Subject Constraint which applies to an array of phenomena which I unify as belonging to the class of I-dependencies.

A Subject Constraint violation causes a strong grammaticality infraction usually associated with ECP effects. Since the Subject Constraint covers many of the subject–object asymmetries considered to be the province of the ECP, this is not surprising.

The idea that the nature of the extraction matters has also been around for a while. Ross (1971) suggests a hierarchy of extraction rules. In this hierarchy, topicalization is a "stronger" rule than question formation. In Erteschik-Shir (1973: 60) I demonstrate that *wh*-questions which presuppose a "list" license extraction where it would otherwise be blocked. More recently Cinque (1989, 1990) argues that D-linked or referential *wh*-phrases can enter a binding relation with their trace explaining their insensitivity to what he refers to as weak islands (negative and *wh*-islands). He adds that the relative *wh*-phrase is more easily interpreted as referential than the interrogative one. Although I believe referentiality is the wrong notion, Cinque's basic intuition prompted my understanding that these distinctions follow directly from the theory of f-structure, i.e., that the fronted constituent must be interpretable as the main topic in order for extraction out of weak islands to occur felicitously. A *wh*-moved constituent is interpretable as a topic in a number of different circumstances. First, if it is topicalized, it functions as the main topic of the sentence. Second, an NP modified by a relative clause is necessarily specific, as argued in chapter 1, qualifying it for topic status. Third, in D-linked *wh*-questions the fronted *wh*-phrase ranges over a topic set. Finally, metalinguistic focusing (as in clefting) again forms an f-structure in which the fronted constituent is the topic.

In order for the fronted constituent to be interpretable as the main topic, it does not suffice for this constituent to qualify as a proper topic. It is also necessary that the rest of the sentence qualify as a predicate for this topic. Whether this is possible or not depends on context, the focus properties of the lexical items chosen, as well as the structure involved. It follows that when extraction is licensed in this way in sentences, they will vary in acceptability: the "better" the topic extracted, the more natural the predicate, the better the result. This renders the effect of a weak constraint. All purely f-structure-theoretical constraints are similarly weak. The Topic Constraint is weak in this way too. It follows that f-structure constraints may be weak, and that structural constraints are necessarily strong, explaining how squishes of grammaticality can arise.

It is impossible to survey even a reasonable amount of the available data here. Instead I will demonstrate how the theory applies to a number of classical examples.

6.6.1   Sentential subjects
Sentential subjects are islands because extraction out of a sentential subject violates the Subject Constraint:

(124)   *Who is [that John likes t]$_{TOP}$ [interesting]$_{FOC}$

Reconstruction to trace position is not possible since the trace is not contained in the focus.[49] If the fronted *wh*-phrase is interpreted as a topic and no reconstruction is necessary an uninterpretable f-structure results:

(125)   *[Which girl]$_{TOP}$ [is [that John likes e]$_{TOP'}$ [interesting]$_{FOC'}$]$_{FOC}$

This is because the f-structure in (125) contains a subordinate topic, TOP', which has a gap in it. There is no way to interpret a gap in the heading of a topic card.

6.6.2   Relative clauses
Similarly relative clauses are islands. In chapter 1, section 1.6.2.2, I discussed the f-structure of relative clauses and showed that the relative clause functions

to position a card for the head of the clause on the top of the file, rendering an indefinite head of a relative clause specific.[50]

(126)   [[a student$_i$]$_{FOC-SUB}$ [who$_i$ I know]]

Since the relative clause does not serve as a focus, the Subject Constraint blocks reconstruction to trace position in the same way it did with Sentential Subjects. Interpreting the moved constituent as a topic again renders an ill-formed f-structure in which the main focus is undefined.

The fact that extraction out of relative clauses in Danish is possible in certain well-defined cases provided strong motivation for viewing extraction as determined by f-structure in Erteschik-Shir (1973: 37):

(127)   a. Det er der mange der har gjort.
            that are there many who have done e
            "There are many (people) who have done that"

         b. Det kender jeg mange der har gjort.
            that know I   many who have done e
            "I know many (people) who have done that"

         c. Det har jeg set mange der har gjort.
            that have I   seen many who have done e
            "I have seen many (people) who have done that"

In Erteschik-Shir (1982) I claimed that the property that distinguishes these relative clause constructions from the ones that do not allow extraction is that the matrix must serve merely to introduce the head of the relative clause into the discourse. An existential matrix does so by introducing an NP onto a stage. The other predicates which license extraction are predicates which can be used to select real or imaginary stages. The following f-structure is therefore available here:

(128)   Jeg har set sTOP$_1$ [mange der har gjort det]$_{FOC}$

This f-structure is similar to the ones discussed above in section 6.4.1.1 in the context of reflexivity (and the analysis is the same as the one offered for picture NPs which license I-dependencies in section 6.5.4). There I argued that a subordinate stage topic does not interfere with the processing of the main f-structure. Here, more significantly, the stage topic takes the relative clause as its focus making it the main focus of the sentence. Extraction is therefore possible since the following f-structure is well-formed:

(129)   Det har jeg set sTOP$_1$ [mange der har gjort e]$_{FOC}$

Importantly, the Subject Constraint cannot be violated in Danish. The following examples show that only a "topic" can be extracted:

(130)   a. *Hvad er der mange der kan li t?
           What have you seen many that have done t
        b. Hvad slags is er der mange der kan li t?
           What kind of ice cream are there many who like t

Reconstruction to trace position must therefore be blocked by the Subject Constraint as before.[51]

The requirement that the head of the relative clause be indefinite in order for extraction to be possible receives the same explanation as was offered for extraction in picture noun phrases above.

6.6.3   Negation and wh-islands

As argued above (section 6.5.2) negation forms an I-dependency with a dependent focus. Further, reconstruction to trace position forms an I-dependency as well. The following schematized f-structure, with I-dependencies marked, illustrates extraction across negation.

(131)   wh-phrase [subject NEG . . . t . . .]

Neither of the I-dependencies violates the Subject Constraint. Principle I is, however, violated: the trace position is uninterpretable since it is the dependent in two different I-dependencies. It follows that reconstruction to trace position across negation will be blocked. As suggested in chapter 3, extraction will therefore only be licensed for constituents interpretable as topics explaining the following data from chapter 3:

(132)   a. What didn't you see on your trip?
        b. Which sights didn't you see on your trip?
        c. Which of the famous sights you were told to see didn't you see on your trip?

Much discussion has been addressed to the extraction of adjuncts.[52] My theory predicts that time and place adjuncts which form stage topics can be extracted (as long as a contextual topic set is provided), but that other adjuncts cannot be interpreted as the topics of the sentences in which they occur. I assume with Rizzi (1990: 46) that causal adverbials are adjoined to the clauses they modify and that their wh-version can be directly generated in COMP. The following set of facts follows:

(133)   a. ??When/On which evening didn't you see a movie?
        b. ? Where/At which beach don't you swim?
        c. * How/*In which manner didn't you prepare the pancakes?
        d. * How/?With which tool didn't you fix the car?
        e.   Why didn't you go?
        f. ??How many fish didn't you catch?

(133a and b) are good to the extent a context is provided with a set of times and a set of places, respectively. Contexts providing a set of times are harder to imagine explaining why (133a) is harder to contextualize. Manner and reason adverbs are not interpretable as topics of the sentence they modify. No context can therefore improve (133c). *Why* in (133e) is interpreted in situ as argued above. Instrumental arguments can be interpreted as topics. The Topic Constraint, however, marks (133c) even when an appropriate context is provided.[53] The double question-mark on (133f) expresses the fact that it is hard to contextualize the fronted phrase as ranging over a topic set. Imagine five fish in an aquarium that needs to be cleaned out. I manage to catch a few of them and then ask for help. My helper can ask (133f) if he wants to know how many fish I had trouble catching. Negation partitions the topic set into caught and not-caught fish. The question requests the size of the not-caught subset.

Similarly, embedded questions form I-dependencies as do all questions. An embedded *whether*-question forms an I-dependency of the same sort as negation (see chapter 3). Other embedded *wh*-questions are formed by *wh*-movement again forming a double I-dependency:

(134)   *wh*-phrase [subject V [*wh*-phrase [subject . . . t . . .]

I argued in the beginning of the chapter that an I-dependency holds between two *wh*-phrases in a sentence. This is the subordinate I-dependency marked in (134). The other I-dependency is the one required for reconstruction to trace position. (A third I-dependency holds between the *wh*-phrase in the lower COMP and its trace. This I-dependency does not violate any constraints and is therefore not marked.) Principle I blocks (134) as before. The same data is therefore predicted for extraction out of embedded questions. There is one difference, however. The causal adjunct modifies the sentence with which it adjoins. Hence, it can only be interpreted as modifying the matrix. Its interpretation inside the subordinate question violates Principle I. Since adjuncts which are not possible stages cannot function as topics, such a sentence will have no possible derivation:

(135)   Why/For what reason did you ask who went?

Here the only interpretation is the one in which the reason for asking is requested, not the reason for going.[54]

It is pertinent here to consider the approach to weak islands in Szabolcsi and Zwarts (S&Z) (1993). S&Z argue that although D-linking may play a role in accounting for the type of *wh*-phrase which is immune to the weak island effect, the overriding factor is that they range over individuals. A strong argument for their view is that "how many" extraction is possible in Romanian on an individual, but non-D-linked reading. Since D-linking is marked by clitic doubling in Romanian, the data is clear. I cannot address this argument without a detailed study of clitic doubling in Romanian, Romanian f-structure properties, and in particular an understanding of what the canonical f-structure is in Romanian. This type of question must be answered in order to test f-structure theory in any language. It is, however, possible that D-linking (which is responsible for clitic doubling in Romanian) and the notion of restrictive topic sets are not equivalent notions. In particular, I believe that restrictive sets necessarily range over individuals and therefore the two approaches may be reconcilable.[55]

Extraction out of negation and *wh* islands is therefore governed by f-structure. The fronted phrase must be interpretable as a topic. Reconstruction in both cases violates Principle I.

6.6.3.1 *That*-clauses

That-complements introduced by so-called bridge verbs allow the following three f-structures, depending on context and stress.[56]

(136)   a. I_{TOP} [believe (that) Mary saw Susan]$_{FOC}$
         b. I believe (that) Mary$_{TOP}$ [saw Susan]$_{FOC}$
         c. TOP$_i$ [I believe [(that) Mary saw Susan]$_i$]$_{FOC}$

The matrix subject functions as the main topic in (136a) and the whole VP including the complement clause is focused. In (136b) the complement clause forms the main f-structure and the matrix is backgrounded. Only a few predicates occur in this f-structure. (136c) requires a context in which the content of the complement is presupposed qualifying the complement as a main or subordinate topic.

Extraction from the complement clause is licensed by the Subject Constraint only in (136a) which has a canonical f-structure.[57] Reconstruction is therefore possible to either subject or object position in the complement clause. The f-structure (136b) fixes the main f-structure as the subordinate clause. Reconstruction is not possible since the Subject Constraint requires that the matrix subject be a topic forming a canonical f-structure. In (136c) reconstruction is blocked since the complement clause is not focused.

If the fronted phrase is interpretable as a topic and no reconstruction is necessary, extraction is again blocked in (136b and c). The resulting f-structures will be ill-formed in both cases. In (136b) the whole sentence cannot be predicated of the fronted topic and in (136c) the resulting predicate is ill-formed.

The only f-structure for *that*-clauses with factives for which the complement is presupposed (by hearer as well as speaker) is (136c). It follows that extraction out of the complements of factives will be blocked. Many factive predicates, however, allow for an interpretation of their complements in which only the speaker presupposes the truth of the complement. In such a case the complement will not be interpreted as a topic, since no card is available to the hearer with the complement as its heading. It follows that the f-structure in (136a) is appropriate and extraction is possible. Examples of factive predicates of this sort are *know, be clear, forget*, and others. The f-structure, of course, depends on a number of factors other than the factivity of the predicate, tense among them.

There are, however, factives which allow extraction, but only if the fronted constituent is interpretable as a topic. The following examples modified from Cinque (1990: 29) illustrate this point:

(137) a. Which politician do you regret that you spoke to?
       b. *How do you regret that you behaved.

Only factive predicates which can function as partitioners allow this type of extraction.[58] This type of predicate forms an I-dependency with a constituent in the complement (or the whole complement) with which it associates in the same way as negation. The explanation for extraction here is therefore no different from the one proposed for negation. Support for this view comes from the fact that negation in the matrix has the same effect:

(138) a. Which politician don't you believe that you spoke to?
       b. *How don't you believe that you behaved?

Manner-of-speaking verbs are another class of non-bridge verbs as discussed in Erteschik-Shir (1973):

(139) a. ??Who/??Which girl did you mumble that you'd seen?
       b. * Who/ *Which girl did you lisp that you'd seen?

Here it does not help to d-link the *wh*-phrase. In Erteschik-Shir (1973) I argued that the predicates themselves are necessarily focused forcing the complement to be backgrounded (i.e., not part of the main f-structure):

(140)   Peter$_{TOP}$ lisped$_{FOC}$ [that you'd seen Mary]

Since the complement clause is not part of the main focus extraction from within it will violate the Subject Constraint. A fronted topic will not be possible since the complement clause will not be entered on the relevant topic card blocking the interpretation of the gap inside it.[59]

Speakers vary as to which manner-of-speaking verbs require an f-structure such as (140). For some speakers and some of these predicates and in certain contexts, the f-structure in (136a) is also available.

6.6.3.2   Topic islands

A few predicates which select a *that*-clause allow topicalization within it:

(141)   a. I said that this book Mary gave to Peter.
         b. I believe that on this shelf Peter put the radio.

Topicalization is generally possible only in main clauses. I assume that topicalization in a *that*-complement forces an interpretation in which the complement forms the main f-structure as in (136b). This automatically limits the phenomenon to those predicates that allow the matrix to be backgrounded. If this is the correct f-structure extraction will be blocked as required:

(142)   a. *This is the person who I said that this book Mary gave to.
         b. *This is the radio that I said that on this shelf Peter put.

This account leaves unexplained the following data from Culicover (1993) who shows that sentential adverbials in general do not give rise to such topic islands:

(143)   a. This is the tree that I said that just yesterday had resisted my shovel.
         b. This is the tree that I said that just yesterday I had tried to dig up with my shovel.

Note that leaving out *just* reduces acceptability. Without *just*, the reading in which the sentential adverbials must be interpreted as stage topics is prominent. I therefore assume that the sentential adverbials which do not cause topic islands do not function as topics in their f-structures.

6.6.4   *Metalinguistic extraction*

In chapter 3, I showed that contrast (negative or positive) is a metalinguistic phenomenon:

(144)   a. Bill didn't catch TWO fish.
         b. Bill caught TWO fish.

Here, I would like to add only that regular *wh*-questioning and relativization cannot apply in these cases supporting the view expressed in chapter 3 that metalinguistic phenomena belong to a special metalinguistic component of f-structure. According to Horn (1989) echo-questions are metalinguistic and so are clefts. Echo-questioning and Clefting with the proper metalinguistic tune should be possible in both examples in (144).

(145)   a. HOW many fish didn't you catch?
         b. HOW many fish did you catch?

(146)   a. It was not TWO fish that Bill caught, but THREE.
         b. It was TWO fish that Bill caught, not THREE.

6.7   Modularity revisited

It was not my intention in this chapter to bring new data, nor to cover all the old data relevant to I-dependencies as I have defined them here. What I have tried to accomplish is to show the potential power of the framework proposed here. First of all, I have included a large array of phenomena which have been defined as I-dependencies. Second, I have argued that the Subject Constraint, defined in terms of f-structure, applies to all types of I-dependencies. Third, principles I, P and A were introduced to regulate the interpretation of I-dependencies. Finally, I showed that *wh*-moved constituents which themselves provide the main topic (or range over a topic set) can be interpreted without recourse to reconstruction, hence no I-dependency is formed and the only requirement is that the f-structure be well-formed.

The Subject Constraint on I-dependencies accounts for certain subject–object asymmetries traditionally accounted for by the Empty Category Principle. Both constraints control the identification of categories. The violation of both constraints leads to strong ungrammaticality. Adopting the Subject Constraint leaves little work for the ECP. The *that*-trace effect, for example, was one of the initial phenomena motivating this constraint. Neither f-structure nor the Subject Constraint can contribute to an account of this phenomenon without further ado. Culicover (1993) provides data which casts doubt on the correctness of using the ECP to account for the *that*-t effect. One piece of evidence from Culicover (his (6)) exemplifies a violation of the ECP which is nonetheless grammatical:

(147)   Leslie is the person who I said that under no circumstances would t run for president.

In this example a fronted negative stage topic which triggers inversion supplies a canonical f-structure in the complement. A possible line of investigation might therefore be that extracting a subject renders a noncanonical f-structure in the complement. Since this is no problem when the complementizer is deleted, one would have to show that the presence of the complementizer restricts f-structure in some way. This may have some truth to it, at least historically, since the complementizer *that* is optional only in the complement of a bridge verb. I will, however, not pursue this line of investigation further here, and will assume that the *that*-trace effect requires a separate account.

A class of phenomena of a very different sort also belong to the class of I-dependencies. These are copular sentences, both identificational ones and predicational ones. Since the raison d'être of copular sentences is to identify, this is not an outrageous idea. I illustrate briefly with examples modified from Fiengo and May (1993) who provide interesting discussion of these and related cases:[60]

(148)   a. Griswold is the best cook in town.
         b. The best cook in town is Griswold.

(149)   a. Griswold is a cook.
         b. *A cook is Griswold.

If both types of copular sentences are viewed as forming I-dependencies, then this data is accounted for. In both f-structures in (148) the topic can be the subject in conformity with the Subject Constraint. The Subject Constraint, is, however, violated in (149b). Interestingly, as pointed out to me by Tova Rapoport, replacing the subject with a specific indefinite does not improve (149b):

(150)   *A certain cook is Griswold.

The subject of (150) is *speaker* specific, not *hearer* specific as required in an I-dependency. The I-dependency is therefore blocked, explaining the unacceptability of the sentence.

In this chapter, I have defined a module of grammar which I refer to as I-dependency Theory. This theory applies to semantically defined dependencies. I-dependency Theory syntactically constrains these dependencies by means of the Subject Constraint defined on f-structure. I-dependency Theory does the work of Binding Theory and Movement Theory. It also accounts for properties of negation and other partitioning operators. I-dependency Theory therefore prompts a different allocation of grammatical functions to modules.

Conclusion

The purpose of this book was to show that f-structure is a basic component of the language faculty which interacts essentially with phonology, syntax and semantics as well as pragmatics. F-structure marks the organization of sentences into focus and topic constituents. In Erteschik-Shir and Lappin (1987) we argue that all modes of perception are organized into foreground and background constituents. Focusing is viewed as a single task-specific mechanism which identifies the foregrounded constituent in representations of all modular systems. Focusing is therefore a nonmodular process which provides the interface between the modular system and the central cognitive mechanisms.[1] It follows that although focusing plays a central role in grammar, it is not unique to the language faculty. The identification of a topic is, however, characteristic of linguistic structure. In vision, for example, foregrounding is necessary for the formation of a visual report, but this report is not "about" anything, i.e., it does not have a topic.[2] Whereas the capacity to identify a topic is a distinctive property of the human brain and of the language faculty in particular, focusing is a basic property of all cognitive systems.

The linguistic level of f-structure in which both topic and focus are identified is therefore a fundamental part of Universal Grammar (UG) which determines the class of possible languages. I have argued in this book that the rule of predication takes f-structures as its input producing a well-formed discourse representation. F-structure can therefore be viewed as an interface level between the grammar and the conceptual–intentional system replacing LF. F-structure also mediates grammar and PF (Phonetic Form), itself an interface level with the articulatory–perceptual system. This is necessary for the derivation of intonation. That the interpretive level should feed PF is strongly argued in Brody (1995) although for reasons that have nothing to do with focus. Brody's work is just one illustration of the fact that the issues discussed here are coming nearer to the center of debate.[3]

I have shown that certain conditions on SDs (structural descriptions) can be defined at f-structure. In Erteschik-Shir and Rapoport (to appear, in progress) we show that certain f-structure properties are derivable directly from properties of verbal projections. It might therefore be feasible to hold that UG principles of the various modules of grammar all apply at f-structure. This would present a different perspective on the execution of the Minimalist Program (Chomsky 1995).[4] Applying the basic tenets of this program to the f-structure-theoretical model of grammar proposed here would clearly have very different results.

Replacing LF with f-structure, as I suggest, is a natural consequence of its function as an interface to conceptual–intentional structure since focusing is an innate reflex, essentially involved in perception as a whole, and topic identification is an innate and essential part of conceptual–intentional structure itself.

If grammar is f-structure driven it is important to explore how principles of f-structure are parameterized across languages, an issue I have not taken up in this work. A potentially interesting question to address is the parameters of canonical f-structure. In English canonical f-structure takes the syntactic subject or alternatively a stage as its topic. Presumably languages may differ as to what their canonical f-structure is. A language such as Hungarian which has fixed positions for the focus, a language such as Chinese which is Topic prominent or a language such as Japanese, which has morphological markers to do the job may present a variety of canonical f-structures different from the one in English. It is even conceivable that certain languages have no canonical f-structure at all. In such languages, I-dependencies would be predicted to be totally unrestricted. The connection between basic word order and the position of the focus in languages with fixed focus positions has been addressed by Kidwai (1996) among others. The f-structure-theoretical approach outlined here prompts a different perspective on this issue: here what is at issue is the relation between basic word-order typology and complete canonical f-structure.

Another parameter to investigate would be Topic-drop and Topic-prominent languages in general. In many languages speaker and hearer (first and second person) and here-and-now stage topics may be freely dropped. Other languages allow all topics to be implicit.

The discussion of these questions must await detailed analyses of a variety of languages within the framework advocated here. One contribution of the f-structure-theoretical perspective proposed here is the questions it defines for its cross-linguistic application:

1. Are the focus types defined in this work universal? The classification of types of focus would be more meaningful if it took into account focus-preposing languages such as Hungarian in which (according to Szabolcsi and

Zwarts 1993 and Szabolcsi 1995) the preposed focus is confined to the type referred to as the "exhaustive listing" type. One of the problems which arises in connection with this question is indeed whether this type of focus, much discussed in the literature on Hungarian, is exactly parallel to what I refer to as a restrictive focus or if the two notions only partially coincide. This issue has been taken up recently by É. Kiss (1996). She argues that the focus type to be found in preverbal focus position in Hungarian (her focus operator) is akin to the English cleft position.[5] She defines the focus operator as "a constituent exhaustively identifying a subset of a set of relevant individuals," i.e., a definition essentially identical to a restrictive focus. (The information focus (i.e., a nonrestrictive focus) occurs postverbally in Hungarian and does not play a role with respect to scope. What is missing in studies of focus in Hungarian is a full analysis in terms of f-structure including both topic and focus marking. This is essential if indeed the preverbal position is reserved for a restrictive foci which incorporates properties of both focus (the focused subset) and topic (the contextually given set of individuals). In Hungarian *wh*-phrases must also occur preverbally. Interestingly this is the case for all *wh*-phrases whether they are restrictive or not. The relation between fixed focus positions and *wh*-positions is clearly not a simple one. One possible avenue of speculation is that the preverbal position in Hungarian is a particular kind of topic position (remember that restrictive foci are topic). If this were the case then the explanation for the locus of *wh*-phrases in Hungarian and English would merge since the latter are naturally viewed as fronted to English topic position.

2. Are the constraints proposed in the work universal? Szabolcsi and Zwarts (1993) suggest that weak island effects occur in Hungarian exactly as in English and Dutch. Others have claimed universality for island constraints, pointing out that the constraints apply in LF rather than in the syntax for languages such as Chinese which lack overt *wh*-movement. This suggests the universality of the proposed constraints. It is not difficult to rephrase the Subject Constraint to apply to restrict interpretation rather than reconstruction. Hence, there is no need to assume LF movement for a language in which *wh*-phrases occur in situ.

At this point I must, however, leave a serious account of other relevant languages and language types to future research. Work on f-structure depends heavily on very fine native intuitions and is even more treacherous in this respect than other linguistic research. The implementation of f-structure theory cross-linguistically must therefore await careful analysis of the f-structure properties of a variety of languages.

Notes

1 The interpretation of f-structure

1 F-structures are annotated s-structures in the tradition of Jackendoff (1972). Culicover and Rochemont (1983) propose that s-structure is annotated for its focus constituents, and introduce the term f-structure to refer to the representation that mediates between s-structure and semantics. F-structure in the current framework marks *topics* as well as foci on s-structure. F-structure is therefore similar in this respect to Jacobs (1991) who introduces focus-background structure (FBS) which annotates syntactic structures with a focus feature and assigns Topic to a dedicated syntactic position (adjoined to C). Jacobs also introduces rules that pair semantic FBSs with syntactic FBSs.

2 The idea that the common ground is structured in this way is adapted from Reinhart (1981).

3 Stalnaker (1978) uses the term *context set* for a given discourse as the set of circumstances or worlds compatible with the true propositions in the common ground.

4 A few references not otherwise mentioned in the text follow: Daneš (1974) is a collection of papers giving the Prague School (functional) perspective on Topic and Comment (= Theme and Rheme). Halliday (1967) offers a different perspective on similar issues. Gundel (1974) and more recently Gundel (1994) (and the references cited therein) provide discussions of Topic and Focus, respectively. Prince (1981) and Chafe (1974, 1975) are valuable for comparing the notions Topic and Comment with given and new, respectively.

5 Reinhart allows sentences without topics. In this case φ alone is selected. In the framework to be developed here *all* sentences have topics.

6 In early work I used the term "Dominance" in place of Focus because I disagreed with the then accepted view that the presupposition of a sentence is the complement of the focus constituent.

7 I use "sentence" loosely here to include utterances which are not strictly syntactic sentences as well as complex sentences.

8 An initial version of this section is to be found in Erteschik-Shir (1992a).

9 I use the terms "evaluate" and "assess" as abbreviations for "determine the truth value of."

10 The lie-test, introduced in the previous section, effects an application of the predication rule, i.e., what is denied in B's response in (13a) is that the VP is true of the subject.

11 Foci are always overt. Topics, for example stage topics which represent the here-and-now, are not. The requirement that a topic must form a syntactic constituent obviously makes sense only for overt topics. As pointed out above, this restriction does not apply to contrastive foci.

12 The idea that the common ground is structured in this way is adapted from Reinhart (1981).

13 The state of the top of the file before the utterance of a sentence is closely related to the backward-looking center in P. C. Gordon, et al. (to appear). Their forward-looking center includes those NPs that are focused in the sentence (and therefore positioned on top of the file) as well as the current topic, i.e., the state of the top of the file *after* the utterance. (The backward- and forward-looking centers replace the attentional focus of Grosz and Sidner 1986). In the current framework the NPs on top of the file at a particular point in a discourse define the potential topics of the next sentence.

Ariel (1990) defines accessibility in terms of sentence topics. Her most accessible entity is parallel to the entities represented by cards on top of the file in the current framework.

14 When the hearer does not have information to the contrary the sentence will yield a positive truth value.

15 Indefinites in focus do not necessarily introduce new indexed cards. "Do you have a dog?" is not a question about a particular dog. I postpone the discussion of the interaction of negation and questions with the update system to chapter 3.

16 It follows that if there is more than one pronoun in a sentence, each one of them must be a topic in the f-structure of the sentence. We shall see below that subordinate f-structures make this possible.

17 Uniqueness will be discussed in detail in chapter 2. I also offer an analysis of donkey sentences which follows from the f-structure perspective on uniqueness developed here.

18 In this section I limit the discussion to bare plural generics.

19 We shall see below that new generic cards can also be derived. The point here is that a stock of generic cards is always available.

20 Note that the ambiguity disappears when "cigars" is not in focus, hence not stressed:

  (i)   John SMOKES cigars.

The Focus rule cannot apply, blocking the interpretation generated by the construction of a new card. (See Krifka (1995).)

21 See Lasersohn (1993) for a recent discussion of a semantics which assigns truth values to sentences relative to information states. In discussing the "King of France" cases, I assume that B knows there is no referent and ignore the case in which B doesn't know whether there is one or not.

22 For the idea that scene-setting expressions that specify the temporal or spatial background for the sentence also function as a topic see Gundel (1974) and Reinhart (1981). According to Sgall et al. (1986: 202), an initial locative is necessarily interpreted as a topic in (i), whereas an initial temporal is not (as in (ii)):

  (i)   In a hotel some people can't sleep QUIETLY.
  (ii) During summer big fires occurred in several TOWNS.

23 See also Horn (1989: 488).
24 Reinhart and Reuland (1989) show that logophoric anaphors find their reference in such a center. The availability of these three card types on top of the file suggests that logophoricity can receive a natural explanation in f-structural terms. (Such an account is offered in chapter 6, section 6.4.2.)

If-clauses and other similar constructions which form the restriction in Heimian tripartite structures will also be analyzed as topics. These topics have internal structure involving a separate application of the predication rule. (See chapter 2.)
25 It would be more precise to have two indices on stage topics, one for time and one for place. I will generally use the index *t* for both. When I wish to stress the locative property of the stage, I use the index *l*.
26 In chapter 2, I make a distinction between Absolute Uniqueness (pertaining only to individuals introduced onto a stage) and Discourse Uniqueness.
27 So-called locative subjects in Bantu languages agree, like normal subjects, with the verb or predicate complement. Locative subjects occur only when the other NPs are indefinite (and therefore do not qualify as topics) and they always function as topics. (See Bresnan and Kanerva 1989: 39 and Bresnan and Mchombo 1995: 199.)

The distinction between sentences with stage topics and sentences with individual topics is equivalent to the thetic-categorical distinction made in Kuroda (1972: 154). Kuroda uses this distinction to explain the distributions of -wa and -ga in Japanese subjects. In categorical judgments, subjects are marked with -wa, in thetic judgments, they are marked with -ga. Translated into f-structure framework, Japanese subjects which are topics are marked with -wa, the ones that are in focus are marked with -ga. Guéron (1980) uses a similar distinction and constrains PP extraposition to sentences with a stage topic (*presentation* sentences).
28 See chapter 2, section 2.4.3.2 for the analysis of assymetries within the current framework.
29 See chapter 6, section 6.6.2, for the properties of relative clauses that can constitute foci and those that cannot.
30 See also Büring (1994) for an analysis of scope in terms of topics.
31 The Prague school rheme is generally taken to be the complement of the theme, hence, the predicate in our view. For the discussion in this section the distinction between focus and predicate is disregarded.

See also section 1.8 in this chapter for further discussion of the relevance of tripartite structures to f-structure.
32 Partee (1994) argues that so-called deaccented foci provide a challenge to the type of approach I argue for here. See chapter 4, section 4.1.2 for a discussion of this issue.
33 For an analysis in terms of event-induced measures of quantification see Krifka (1990b) who is the source of the example. For further discussion of this approach see Eckardt (1994). In chapter 2, section 2.4.1, I discuss similar examples in more detail.
34 For many of the original observations see Milsark (1974).
35 A generic stage topic can be viewed as playing the role of a possible world, whereas an indexed stage topic identifies an event.

36 Kratzer herself argues that "stage level properties are properties of stages, and individual level properties are properties of individuals" (p. 2). Diesing (1988) in a footnote (p. 21) mentions that VP-internal subjects are focused, hence stressed and adds that this correlates with the theme/rheme distinction. Von Fintel (1989) raises the question of how focus projection interacts with the Diesing/Kratzer framework. Some of the topics I discuss below are given a Heimian analysis in Diesing (1992).

37 The notion: "subordinate f-structure" will be introduced to explain the occurrence of weak NPs as subjects of individual-level predicates, i.e., as topics.

38 See chapter 3 for the discussion of contrast.

39 In chapter 4, section 4.4.1, I show that a low-pitch accent is assigned to such subordinate foci.

40 I do not consider much discussed examples such as the following:

   (i)   Dodos are extinct.

   In view of the fact that *extinct* is a "kind-level" predicate it can only be entered on the generic card. Such an entry is disallowed on the card for the singular which selects an instance of the kind:

   (ii)   *A dodo is extinct.

41 According to Katalin É. Kiss (pers. com.) Hungarian indefinites, such as *a student*, can be topicalized with the interpretation "one of the aforementioned students." This is excluded in English with the indefinite *a*, but allowed with the numeral *one*. F-structure theory derives this interpretation by subordinate predication selecting *one* student from the restrictive discourse specified set as shown in the next section.

42 For a discussion of when the subject of the sentence rather than the speaker is the one who "has the reference" of the specific NP, see Kennedy (1990).

43 For the intonational effect of subordinate f-structures, see chapter 4.

44 Transitive individual-level predicates of this sort are awkward with the f-structures (53a) and particularly (53b). This issue will be futher developed in chapter 2.

45 It is inaccurate to say that the derived subject of *any* passive must be its topic. Passives may also have stage topics when the predicate is stage level. The *by*-phrase is, however, never a possible topic.

   Note that there is a "symmetrical" version of the sentence:

   (i)   John and Mary LOVE each other.

   which answers:

   (ii)   What is the relationship between John and Mary?

   (56) would not be an appropriate answer to (ii). The relevant card for assessment in this case would be a card with the conjoined heading.

46 In chapter 4 I derive this intonation from the f-structure indicated. The same intonation also allows for a contrastive context. This does not change the points made here.

47 See chapter 5 for further discussion of this constraint.

48 An object *can* be the topic of *be close to* if the subject does not require a fixed location (such as *a swamp*):

(i)   A car is close to the gas station.

As von Fintel's examples, cited in section 1.6, make clear, predicates cannot be lexically classified as either individual or stage level without regard to context and world knowledge. Similarly, the predicates discussed here are individual level only when predicated of locationally fixed objects.

49 According to Kratzer, the variable "l" may be bound by quantifiers. I show how this is done in f-structure-theoretical terms in chapter 5.

50 For discussions of this issue, see, in addition to Reinhart (1981) and the references she cites, also von Stechow (1991) and Prince (1988).

51 See also Vallduví and Zacharsky (1994).

52 Lambrecht offers an excellent overview of different approaches to the basic notions he uses.

53 Some informants find the continuation acceptable. Others note that the continuation is improved if uttered by another speaker. This could be related to the "marble" sentence type:

A: I lost ten marbles and found only nine of them.
B: It is probably under the sofa.

B's reference to the missing marble is thus akin to the reference to the unfocused car in the continuation here. In both cases the relevant card has not been introduced by the focus rule.

54 In chapter 5 I argue that quantifier scope is derivable from f-structure and that it follows from the rule of predication that topics must have wide scope.

2 Reference and coreference

1 See Chierchia (1992a) for this distinction.

2 The section on Uniqueness has been inspired mainly by the following: Bolinger (1980), Carlson (1977), Chastain (1975), DeCarrico (1985), Diesing (1992), Donnellan (1966, 1978) Enç (1990), Heim (1987), Higginbotham (1987), and Vendler (1967) and additional references cited in these. For clarity of presentation I refrain from indicating points of agreement and disagreement. The largest debt undoubtedly goes to Carlson (1977) who distinguishes between the readings of NPs introduced via stage-level and individual-level predications.

3 Note that I use the term *discourse uniqueness* for what is usually termed *specificity*. (See, for example, Enç 1990 for discussion.)

4 Carlson (1977), among others, makes this point.

5 See Carlson (1977) for the relevance of tense to the choice of a stage- or individual-level interpretation.

6 For Kadmon Uniqueness includes *both* absolute uniqueness and specificity (what I refer to as discourse uniqueness), i.e., she does not differentiate between distinguishing properties such as "the glass that was expensive" or "the glass that affected my mood" and the property of having been broken on a particular stage. This distinction turns out to be important as will be shown in the following.

244 Notes to pages 63–69

I differ further from Kadmon in positing that the effect is an anaphoric definite NP, such as *it* in (6).

7 I disregard the f-structure in which the object is the main topic. This f-structure would take the bare plural "sheep" generically (see chapter 1), and would mean that it is a property of sheep in general that Oscar owns them. This makes little sense in our world.

8 The (focused) VP which contains a verb and an indefinite NP object has been analyzed as a unit in which the object is lexically incorporated into the verb rendering the interpretation that Oscar is a "sheep-owner." Incorporation is only possible for nonspecific NPs. (see Rapoport 1991)

9 Donnellan (1978) uses the term "speaker reference" for specificity.

10 As noted by one of the anonymous reviewers, the following intonation is acceptable and yields a generic reading for "a dog":

(i)   Hans ADORES a dog.

This intonation follows from an f-structure in which both subject and object function as topics, rendering the correct interpretation.

11 Whether the speaker or the subject of the sentence take responsibility for the subordinate predication is a much discussed issue which I will not engage in here.

12 Note that (i) is no better than (ii):

(i)   ??John adores a lawyer.
(ii)   ??John adores a man.

In Erteschik-Shir (in prep. a) I discuss the relation between the lexical structure of predicates and their f-structures and explore the idea that transitive individual-level predicates, due to their lexical structure, require that both their arguments be topics. This will be made to follow from a structure in which one of the arguments must be interpreted as an "individual stage" as suggested in chapter 1, section 1.6.

13 Partitives are also discourse unique. The subordinate predication induces the partitioning of a topic set. Since this set (e.g., "the students" in "two of the students") is an individual and not a stage, their specificity follows by definition. Interestingly, the new part, "two students" is not specific in the sense that some particular property can be assigned to them since nothing identifies the individuals selected by partitioning from the others in the set.

14 This analysis is very much along the lines of a proposal by Carlson (1977: 192) who treats these verbs "as making an existential claim about stages of the direct object, yet at the same time creating an intensional context in which this existential claim is being made."

15 See Karttunen (1974) and Carlson (1977) for detailed analyses of this issue. Wilkinson (1993) shows that specific readings for bare plurals are excluded in any context.

16 Feasibly the specific reading results from a combination of the two f-structures, the specific one overlaid on one involving the stage. The subordinate stage predication depends on the existence of a card in the file for "Smith's murderer" explaining the use of the definite description.

17 For a discussion of some of these ideas see Erteschik-Shir (1988). In that paper I also recognize my debt to the Prague school theory of Functional Sentence Perspective.

18 Two different factors play a role in disambiguation. The first is the fact that the subject is the unmarked topic here. The second is pragmatic. Invasions are aggressive acts leaving the U.S. as the most likely candidate for the reference of *it*.

19 For similar strategies see Roberts (1987) and Kadmon (1987, 1990). For a discussion of the lifespan of discourse referents see Karttunen (1974). Note that the pronoun in the continuation of (30) is interpretable. The continuation, however, does not have the aura of a cohesive piece of discourse. I assume that the uncohesiveness is a result of the hearer accessing the "attached" card.

20 I analyze the universal quantifier *every* as ranging over a set of donkeys. The individual donkeys can be accessed by singular pronouns whenever the set over which the quantifier ranges is taken as the main topic of the f-structure. This will be shown below and in chapter 5.

21 See Heim (1982: chapter 3), in particular her notion of "prominent NPs". See also Webber (1988) and the references she cites for a list of the possible inference types at play here. An anonymous referee pointed out that the following example seems fine: "Since we are talking about dams, what about the beaver?" "The beaver" clearly does not form a subset of "dams." It is, however, only for speakers for whom beavers are somehow associated with dams that the sentence is good. "Beavers" are thus a subset of an associative or inferred set called into consciousness by the reference to dams. The notion of subset must therefore be taken in this broad sense.

22 Fiengo and May (1994) propose that the individuals in a split plural antecedent are "fused." This explains the missing plural antecedent in the following example:

(i)   John told Mary that *they* should leave.

Whatever the f-structure of (i), the cards for both *John* and *Mary* will be on top of the file by the time the subordinate clause is entered. I impose a condition on fusion, namely that fusion applies to cards on top of the file. In chapter 5, I show that coordinate NPs can behave as "fused" collective plurals as well.

23 Unless, of course, *him* refers to a topic supplied by the previous discourse. In that case a different focus structure would be assigned, one in which *Dan* is not the main topic.

24 Note that if one could argue for a subordinate f-structure for the prepositional phrase, as we could for the *when*-phrase above, then, and only then, subordinate update would license the pronoun.

25 The following illustrates a pronoun in object position (in the case of a preposed verb phrasal PP):

(i)   For Ben's car, I am willing to give him two grand.

Coreference is licensed since the object must not necessarily be taken as the topic. The entry is therefore not made on this card. According to Reinhart, (i) follows from the fact that the object is not in the domain of the PP.

26 Topic sets can also be derived in cases such as the following:

(i)   In John's newly renovated apartment on 5th Avenue, he smoked pot.

This sentence should be possible if the apartment is contrasted to other apartments of John's or if it is understood to indicate that it is unusual to smoke pot in an apartment of the sort indicated by the modifiers. In either case a "set of apartments" is contextually derived.

27 These cases were at the time analyzed as weak crossover cases. The following two sentences (from Lappin 1982) were viewed as violating the same constraint:

   (i)   *Who did the woman *he* loves betray t?
   (ii)   *The woman *he* loves betrayed *someone*.

   I distinguish cases in which the dependency is between a wh-phrase and a pronoun as in (i) from those in which the dependency is between a quantifier and a pronoun. The latter case involves an R-dependency and is discussed here, the former case forms an I-dependency and is to be discussed in chapter 6.

28 In chapter 4 I demonstrate that the indicated intonation is the intonation of all-focus sentences, i.e., sentences with stage topics. An anonymous reviewer reminded me of the famous: *Dogs must be carried* ambiguity with the following two intonation patterns:

   (i)   DOGS must be CARRIED.
   (ii)   DOGS must be carried.

   Under the intonation in (i) (which is the intonation for the sentences under discussion) the analysis below applies. The intonation in (ii) is presentational and implies that "entry" is only allowed if you carry a dog. The discussion here is limited to the sentence type with the intonation indicated in (i).

29 Akatsuka (1986) argues contra Haiman (1978) that the antecedents of conditionals are not simple topics, since they are not given, but rather contrastive. If a contrastive topic is understood as a topic which defines a set, and assessment ranges over the individuals within this set, then the approach I argue for does not conflict with Akatsuka's. Also see Rooth (1985) for a similar view of conditionals.

30 The stage topic in (70) is generic due to the future tense combined with the generic subject. (The reader may verify that other tenses and/or definite subjects render nongeneric readings.)

31 Note that a proposition formed on an individual-level predicate may also *form* such a stage (in this case, a situation in which a farmer owns a donkey). What is excluded is only for a sentence with an individual-level predicate to be predicated of an indexed stage topic.

32 Donkey sentences with relative clauses differ from the *if*-clauses in certain details involving the subordinate f-structure in the antecedent: the topic of the antecedent is confined to the *head* of the relative clause. See also section 2.4.3.2.

33 The generic stage defined here belongs to the class of "imaginary" stages discussed in section 2.1.3.

34 One might think of the process of positioning an individual on stage as type shifting if individual topics and stage topics are considered to be different topic types. As we shall see in a minute, the reverse type shifting, making a stage into an individual, is not possible.

35 Note that the sentence passes muster if it is taken to mean that the man *falls in love with her*. But if we give it this interpretation we have in effect assigned a stage-level interpretation to the predicate in the consequent and we are no longer dealing with the f-structure (94).

36 Chierchia (1992) points out that only the universal reading is available in cases such as (i). Lappin (1992) adds that the universal reading is also required for cases such as (ii). Finally a reviewer notes that the negative version of (87) renders an existential reading as in (iii).

(i)   No person who had a hat wore it to the concert.
(ii)   Every person who had a hat did not wear it to the concert.
(iii) No man who owned a slave owned its offspring.

An f-structure theoretical analysis of negation (as outlined in chapter 3), together with the analysis of donkey sentences presented here, turns out to predict these facts. The story for (i) and (ii) has to do among other things with the impossibility of putting "no one" on stage. In the case of (iii) the set of slave-owners is partitioned into two, the empty set and the rest. The empty set is the topic of which the consequent is predicated, rendering the correct reading.

37 A specific slave would be pragmatically unfeasible here. The interpretation would be that it is a property of men in general that they own a specific slave, i.e., this specific slave is owned by all men.

In addition to the generic slave reading, we also have a cardinal reading in which the indefinite "slave" is treated as a cardinal, i.e., a single member of the genus slave is derived. This reading is available only if contextual clues indicate that each man has exactly one slave.

3 Negation, questions, and contrast

1 The discussion of negation is much inspired by Horn (1989), in particular pp. 68–9, where he presents the views of Ryle, and pp. 509–15 in which he shows that the scope of negation is determined pragmatically.

2 Predicates which are negated by term negation, by affixal negation, or which are lexically negative must be focused. This has repercussions for the f-structure in which they occur. I touch on this briefly in chapter 6 in the context of *wh*-movement.

Note that negation with *not* can either be taken as term negation, or as predicate denial (see immediately below) with different repercussions for f-structure.

3 The cases of negation in which a predicate-internal constituent is focused are often referred to as "narrow" focus negation.

4 Zucchi (1990) offers a totally different explanation. He argues that it is the distinction between *do* and *be* which is at stake here. Zucchi uses the following contrast to argue his case:

(i)   ??While John didn't own a house, Mary bought a car.

Informants find (ii) as bad as (i), however.

(ii)   While John was not a homeowner, Mary bought a car.

5 Katalin É. Kiss (pers. com.) notes that *a man* in these sentences can be located in topic position in Hungarian. This would, however, render the interpretation that *a man* is selected from a set of contextually specified men. Such an interpretation is consistent with my view that the subject here must function as the main topic. I leave for future research the issue of how overt topic and focus marking (as in

Hungarian) explains why an indefinite in topic position can be interpreted restrict-ively, whereas the equivalent case in English cannot.

6 The effect of a question on a context differs from that of an assertion in that the speaker's (rather than the hearer's) information state is examined.

7 This basic idea will be developed in chapter 6 where I discuss the Subject Constraint, an f-structure constraint on *wh*-traces which are argued to form I-dependencies.

8 Note that restrictive sets may be infinite: the set of numbers, for example, is infinite, but it is still possible to define it as a partionable restrictive set. We can thus partition the set of numbers into the subsets "even" and "odd" numbers, i.e., we are implementing a partitioning into *kinds* of numbers. See also section 3.3.

9 See Erteschik-Shir (1992) for an initial version of this discussion.

10 For the connection between downward entailment and the approach to negative polarity taken here, see Kadmon and Landman (1993) and Krifka (1990a). Krifka offers a semantic approach to negative polarity which incorporates a theory of focus which uses the device of alternative sets. His approach thus bears some similarities to the one proposed here.

11 The literature on association with focus is vast. See Horn (1969), Jackendoff (1972), Rooth (1985) and Vallduví (1992) for important contributions. Discussion of focus is often limited to this topic. My main concern is to show that the view of f-structure developed here, which is intended to account for a much wider array of areas, can also account in a natural way for association with focus.

12 I do not take a stand here as to whether *only* is inside or outside the focus constituent.

13 *everything else* can be defined as (U-[Mary]) where U= the universe of discourse or more simply, the complement set of MARY.

14 Note that *Mary* is annotated as a focus as well as a topic. The topic set includes Mary and the rest of the members of the set of alternatives. This set is partitioned by the operator *only* into the focused member *(Mary*, in this case) and the set containing the remainder of the set of alternatives.

15 Note that contrary to custom I assume that *only* partitions the set of alternatives into two subsets: one which is defined by the focus with which *only* associates, the other the complement set. For convenience I use "everyone else" as the name of this complement set.

16 Note that negation also fixes the focus structure. Neither of the following is ambiguous:

(i)   We are not required to study only SYNTAX.
(ii) We are required not to study only SYNTAX.

17 For another analysis of *only* in terms of topic and focus, see Atlas (1991).

18 In Danish, the interjection "ja" (=yes) has the same function as does *even* ("endda"). Hansen (1967: 3,333) describes this function as adding an extension, rise or climax.

19 *Even* is distinguished from negation and *only* in that the latter two partition restric-tive sets and *even* does not. It may be possible to extend the f-structure account of stressed *any* to an explanation for the fact that *only*, but not *even*, can be stressed as noted in Krifka (1992).

20 I have left many issues concerning *even* undiscussed. An important one is the interaction between *even* and negation. In order to account for the whole array of data, Rooth (1985) argues for the existence of two different *evens*. See Wilkinson (1992) for arguments that only one *even* is necessary, if a more detailed analysis of old and new is taken into account. Her approach does not preclude a language such as German in which the two *evens* assumed by Rooth are disambiguated.

21 Actually the whole VP is stressed and an initial pitch rise can be detected in the beginning of the constituent. This is the intonation which indicates VP focus elaborated in chapter 4.

22 Notice that (68) entails that there is a set of fish that Bill did catch (although its size is not entailed).

23 In the metalinguistic *John didn't catch TWO fish*, the proposition is not denied and it may be true that John actually caught two fish. What is denied is therefore the assertability of the sentence, i.e., that it is wrong to assert that John caught two fish, when, in fact, he caught three.

4 The phonological interpretation of f-structure

1 See Pierrehumbert (1980), Pierrehumbert and Hirschberg (1990) for analysis. I use Pierrehumbert's * to indicate nuclear stress. (H indicates high tone, H* indicates high tone alignment with a stressed syllable. L, in Pierrehumbert's system, indicates low tone. % is used to indicate boundary tone.) By stress I mean what Bolinger and others call *accent* or *pitch accent* and I use all three terms interchangeably.

2 In section 4.4.1 I discuss stress assignment to subordinate f-structures and show how stress is assigned to topics in those cases in which a subordinate f-structure is involved.

3 For a more elaborate discussion of the rhythm rule involved in the lowering of initial and intermediate accents assigned to a focus constituent, see Erteschik-Shir and Lappin (1983) and references cited therein.

4 I relate to the fact that different verbs can be more or less "focusable" in section 4.4.4.

5 See section 4.3 for an account of stress assignment in questions.

6 For such an approach to coordination see Goodall (1987).

7 J. Taglicht has pointed out to me that British English differs from American English in starting with H* in (26)a.,c., and d.

8 This set is generated by examining possible alternate topics for the predicate, which for the purposes of the metalinguistic process provides a topic. The noncontrastive part of contrastive sentences thus has a dual function. It may provide the predicate for the purpose of the main assertion and at the same time perform the function of topic of the metalinguistic contrast.

9 The latter belongs to the same class as "except" in the following:

   (i)   Everyone went to the beach, except Peter.

   In which I assign a parallel structure factoring "everyone" and "Peter" as one vertical constituent.

10 J. Taglicht (pers. com.) notes that subordinate f-structures are also assigned to indefinite topics that consist of just an article and a noun:

(i)   This is a tricky problem. *A colleague* has suggested the following solution.

This explains the accent on the subject topic in such cases.

11 I will use the term "focusability" of a lexical item X to mean that the X^{max} can be predicated of a topic.

12 For the view that colorless expressions cannot be focused see also Rochemont (1986).

13 According to Berman and Szamosi (1972) this idea was originally Perlmutter's, but Berman and Szamosi consider destressing redundant items a "tendency."

14 See the discussion of "Discourse," chapter 2 Section 2.2.

15 This is a rather superficial report of the work reported in P&H. See P&H for details.

16 Clearly, I am making gross generalizations here. Attitudinal factors can interact with these generalizations to achieve different results as pointed out to me by J. Taglicht.

17 In British English, according to J. Taglicht, a typical polar interrogative question would have H* on the first accented word.

18 I wouldn't be surprised if it were found in future research that the pitch accent on the restrictive topic is one of the complex ones rather than H* as indicated. I believe that P&H's claims with respect to what these pitch accents convey can be fruitfully examined in the context of the theory of f-structure developed here.

19 See also Ladd's (1980) discussion of "paralanguage", in particular chapters 5 and 6 and Gussenhoven's (1983) [+counterassertive] feature.

20 Oehrle (1991) gives an analysis of L% vs. H% boundary tones occurring both intrasententially and in sentence-final position. The analysis employs categorial grammar together with a dynamic approach to interpretation similar to the one argued for here. The flexibility of categorial grammar allows very flexible constituent bracketing allowing for the definition of a variety of intonational phrases. I leave it for further research whether the flexibility afforded by f-structure can also achieve these results.

21 Selkirk (following Bolinger and Ladd) associates contrast with "narrow" focus. In this we differ. Contrast (metalinguistic focus), in the current view, occurs on sub-constituents, "narrow" constituents, complete VPs and even whole sentences.

22 See also my discussion of Selkirk's embedded foci in chapter 3, Section 3.4.1. On these issues see also Fretheim (1988 a,b).

23 In chapter 1, I suggested that the rule of predication can be applied to subordinate topics by accommodation. This is, however, contingent on the nature of the subordinate topic. Here it is unlikely that the sentence be taken to be *about* books as well as about John.

24 In order to get the verb destressed Jacobs assumes that integration in VPs goes from left to right in German while in NPs it goes from right to left. No explanation is offered for this hypothesis.

25 In Jacobs' framework this data follows from the fact that the verbal heads must be autonomous because the modifiers are nonfunctional. I take the opposite tack in arguing that the modifier is integrated into the verb.

26 In chapter 1, section 1.6.3.2 I argued that this scrambling rule is not necessary at LF.

5 Scope and R-dependencies

1 Landman's definition of "sum" differs from Massey's. For Landman, the distributive reading is associated with the "sum" interpretation of the plural.

An immediate problem would seem to be posed by my view that distributivity is a feature of NPs since distributivity may be marked elsewhere:

(i)   The children got an apple each.
(ii) The children each got an apple.

I assume reconstruction to trace position in a derivation in which the quantifier and NP start out as a constituent (in spec,VP), enabling the view that it is the NP which distributes.

2 Massey (1976) replaces the *fusion* operator introduced by Leonard and Goodman with a *sum operator* with the same effect. See Massey for the details.

3 See chapter 1, section 1.6.2.3, for an initial analysis of partitives.

4 Landman argues that plural NPs can shift from *sums* to *groups*. His sum reading is parallel to Massey's set reading. His group reading is parallel to Massey's sum reading. In both systems one reading results in a distributive or "interior" perspective of the plural, the other in a collective or "exterior" reading. In the latter reading access to the individuals within the set is blocked. The terms distributive vs. collective will be used here to avoid terminological confusion.

5 With too pronounced stress contrastive readings are derived. Contrastive stresses and tunes should therefore be avoided.

6 LF movement has been motivated by other linguistic phenomena such as crossover and superiority. In chapter 6 I offer an f-structure theoretical account for these phenomena as well.

7 Stressing *someone* (rendering the partitive reading in which "someone" is selected out of a context-defined set) allows for a reading in which *someone* is the topic.

8 For more details on the differences between *each, every, any*, and *all* see Vendler (1967).

9 As Katalin É. Kiss (pers. com.) noted, these quantifiers *can* be used with individual-level predicates as follows:

(i)   Swedes always/sometimes/often/ have blue eyes.

Here, the quantifiers do not provide stage topics, however, but operate on the subject topic generating the set of all/some/most Swedes, respectively.

10 For a study which relates to dialectical differences see Labov (1972).

11 See Labov (1972) for discussion.

12 For a preliminary discussion of some of these points and a wider range of examples see Erteschik-Shir (1986a). Also relevant here is Pesetsky (1987).

6 I-dependencies in focus structure

1 The idea that I-dependencies are involved in this array of phenomena was indirectly inspired by the discussion of dependencies in Higginbotham (1983).

An account of the interaction between bound anaphora and ellipsis will be given in Erteschik-Shir (in prep. b) in which I discuss the f-structure of parallel formatted structures.

2 The constraint is revised in section 6.4.1 to include f-structures with stage topics.
3 Reflexives are further constrained to occur only in the domain of lexical structure. See Reinhart and Reuland (1993) and below.

There are potentially cases where c-command holds, but in which the Subject Constraint is violated. This issue will be examined below.
4 This is also the case when the pronoun uniquely identifies the antecedent:

> Q: Who recognized who?
> A: John recognized Mary and Peter recognized Jim.
>   *She has blue eyes.

5 See also Comorovski (1989) for this point and further relevant discussion.
6 Experiencer predicates may be exceptional here:

> (i)   What frightens who?

Here the question can be asked in the context of a set of *who*s only. In Erteschik-Shir (in prep. a) I argue for an analysis of such predicates in which the surface object functions as a stage topic. The Subject Constraint, as it is revised below, licenses this interpretation with the proposed f-structure.
7 In this sense strong quantifiers and strong readings of weak quantifiers are all d-linked.
8 Pesetsky (1987: 104 (his (20b)) gives the following examples:

> (i)   ??What did you persuade *who(m)* to read t?
> (ii)   ??What did you promise *who(m)* to read t?

Here *who(m)* is not a subject, hence the Subject Constraint correctly rules these out. Note further that overt d-linking improves (i) but not (ii):

> (iii) ?Which book did you persuade which student to read t?
> (iv)   *Which book did you promise which teacher to read t?

This effect follows if the Subject Constraint applies to the infinitive in (iii) and the PRO subject controlled by *who(m)* functions as the subject topic. This option is not available for (iv) since here PRO is not controlled by the *wh*-phrase.
9 Manzini (1995) distinguishes two representations for *wh*-phrases: reconstructed (operator, variable) and nonreconstructed (bound pronoun construal). This is essentially the same distinction made here. Manzini also derives island effects from this distinction, however, without direct recourse to f-structure. I leave a detailed comparison of the two approaches for further research.
10 "e" (as opposed to "t") is used to distinguish cases in which reconstruction is not required. As shown in chapter 3, fronted topic *wh*-phrases are interpreted via update.
11 See Kim and Larson (1989) for a discussion of psych verbs in these construction types. Kim and Larson claim that psych verbs allow a family-of-questions reading in examples parallel to (34b). In note 6, I suggested that surface objects of such predicates function as stage topics, thus rendering a canonical f-structure. This would explain the fact that psych verbs allow family-of-questions readings in both of the following:

(i)   Who did everyone frighten?
(ii)   Who/what frightened everyone?

12 In Reinhart and Reuland (1993) the c-command constraint is derived from a general condition on A-chains. Here it suffices to show that the Subject Constraint makes the same predictions as the c-command constraint with respect to bound anaphora.

For relevant discussion of the relationship between *syntactic* predication and bound anaphora, see Williams (1980) and Rothstein (1991) as well as references cited below.

13 Reinhart (1983) accounts for this distribution by claiming that fronted sentential PPs are c-commanded by the subject but not by the object.

14 *Nobody* is analyzed as a (negative) proform along the lines of the pronouns *someone* and *something* discussed in chapter 4, section 4.4.3.

15 Note that a preposed stage topic takes precedence over an object as main topic as predicted by the Topic Constraint. This is apparent in view of the fact that the following is unproblematic:

(i)   Peter placed nobody near his child's crib.

16 In this example inversion has occured allowing the subject to be dependent. Similar examples without inversion are degraded:

(i)   ??In every chair its owner was sitting.

Inversion blocks the interpretation of the subject as a (subordinate) topic. In the uninverted case in (i), the subject is most naturally interpreted as a topic in violation of the Subject Constraint which requires that the dependent be in focus.

17 Reinhart and Reuland (1993) view Binding Theory as constraining the reflexivizing function which must be matched with predicate reflexivity. (See also Riad 1988 for the same basic idea.) The structural (c-command) constraint on local anaphora follows from A-chain theory. I am in general sympathy with this type of division of labor. Here, the hierarchical constraint follows from the Subject Constraint on I-dependencies, which in turn also constrains movement (A-bar movement in this case). Other constraints on reflexives are accounted for in terms of properties of lexical structure and its interaction with f-structure. An overall comparison between RR's theory and the one proposed here must await a more detailed analysis of anaphora within the current view.

18 Riad (1988) presents a theory of reflexivity which anticipates a number of the basic ideas presented in Reinhart and Reuland (1993). I will only relate to those aspects of the two theories which are relevant to the discussion of I-dependencies in the framework of f-structure.

19 "Sig," however, has two separate functions. In addition to its function as a marker of an I-dependency, it can also be cliticized onto a predicate, forming a reflexive predicate as in the following intransitive examples (from Vikner 1985, his (13)–(15)):

(i)   a. være doven af sig, "be lazy of___" = be naturally lazy
       b. skynde sig,   "hurry___"   = hurry

Transitive examples are also possible:

(ii)   a. Peter$_i$ barberede sig$_i$
       b.   sig selv$_i$
          Peter shaved

In the transitive cases the object can be realized as in (iib) or cliticized as in (iia). I assume that cliticization generates a reflexive predicate. In English no overt marking of the cliticization need appear. Other languages mark reflexive predicates of this sort in a variety of ways. I ignore this use of "sig" below.

20 RR account for the fact that the antecedent of anaphors such as "sig" (their se-anaphors) must be a subject by assuming that these anaphors adjoin to I(nfl) where they inherit the subject's features. This would account for the distribution of "sig," but not of "sig selv" which takes subjects of small clauses as its antecedent. A further locality constraint on "sig," however, is that the antecedent must be within the smallest tensed clause containing the anaphor. It is doubtful that f-structure theoretical considerations could contribute to this locality effect. I therefore leave this issue aside here.

21 I here adopt the general view of Hellan (1986) presented in Riad (1988: 35) that "self" is "a sort of 'closeness' element."

22 I adopt RR's proposal for the projection of pronouns as determiners of full NP constructions.

23 I show immediately below that any pronoun which can be interpreted via an I-dependency must be. It follows that locality constraint (ii) applies to nonself-marked pronominals as well as anaphors (i.e., *sig*).

24 Note that imposing a c-command condition is not sufficient:

(i)   Susanne$_i$ fortalte Tine$_j$ om   sigselv$_{i/*j}$.
       Susanne told   Tine   about herself.

In Danish the reflexive can only refer to the subject although the object stands in a c-command relation with it and it doesn't help if this object is the topic in f-structure.

25 Jane Grimshaw (pers. com.) has suggested that these principles of interpretation could fruitfully be rephrased in terms of Optimality. I leave this for future research.

26 The parallel data in Danish follows:

(i)   Læreren   talte   med hver eneste pige om   hendes karakterer.
                                                   *sine
       the teacher talked to   every single girl about her   grades

With the relevant interpretation only the pronominal form "hendes" and not "sine" is possible in view of the fact that "sine" requires a subject antecedent. Still, an I-dependency is licensed with the nonsubject antecedent.

27 RR note that the same data is to be found in Norwegian in Hellan (1988). Danish is no different. Dutch "zich" and "zichzelf" equal Danish "sig" and "sig selv," respectively. RR refer to "zich" as SE = simplex expression.

28 When *believe* selects a propositional *that*-clause, no stage is involved blocking the f-structure (72c).

29 It is not totally impossible to assign a subordinate f-structure to the small clause in this context, since "Susan" is also introduced in the question and hence qualifies as a topic in the answer. This is why the data is not totally clear-cut.

30 A small clause cannot be assumed here correctly ruling out

   (i)   Max examined the carpet$_2$ underneath itself$_2$.

31 Anaphoric pronouns that are not c-commanded by their antecedents are necessarily logophoric according to this view. However, no claim is made to the effect that a logophoric pronoun cannot be c-commanded by its antecedent. For a detailed analysis of logophoric pronouns and their properties in a variety of languages see Huang (1994).

32 According to Ben Shalom and Weiler, quoted in RR, speakers vary in their intuitions of such examples. The contrastive use of reflexives may make it difficult to isolate purely logophoric uses. Speakers may also vary as to the ease with which they allow logophoric entries.

33 See Kuno (1987), Zribi-Hertz (1987) and the sources quoted therein for detailed discussions of both kinds of logophors.

34 For RR "myself" is not an argument of the verb in this f-structure, the relevant argument is the complex constituent indicated. This f-structure therefore affords a way for RR to maintain their theory of reflexivity without recourse to LF Focus Movement.

35 In notes 6 and 11 I mentioned that the surface object of psych predicates may function as a stage topic. This accounts for the fact that "reverse" *wh*-quantifier I-dependencies can occur in such constructions. The explanation for the distribution of reflexives in these constructions is more complex:

   (i)   *Himself worried John.
   (ii)   Rumors about himself worried John.

   (i) will not be licensed by the Subject Constraint if the antecedent functions as a stage. This follows from the fact that the reflexive pronoun cannot be identified by a stage. I leave for future research the question as to whether the reflexive in (ii) is logophoric. For pertinent discussion see Pesetsky (1990).

36 Lasnik and Stowell (1991) disagree with Chomsky (1982) that WCO effects are totally absent in restrictive relative clauses. Chomsky (1982) pursues an explanation in terms of predication for the lack of the effect in relative clauses.

37 In Appendix A, Lasnik and Stowell mention that WCO effects are absent in clefts as well. Although the clefted item is focused, the focus here is metalinguistic. The relation between the clefted NP and its clause is still one of predication in which the NP functions as the topic. Note that a topicalized NP can also be constrastive:

   (i)   JOHN$_1$, I believe his$_1$ mother loves t$_1$, not PETER.

   The extra metalinguistic subordinate f-structure does not interfere with the function of the fronted NP as the main topic of the sentence.

38 This sentence is actually not so terrible. See discussion of (103) above.

39 A more detailed discussion is called for here involving an analysis of the f-structure of NPs as well as the relation between this data and parasitic gap constructions. See also the discussion in section 6.4 in which I argued that a subordinate topic contained in the main subject topic can be the antecedent in an I-dependency.

40 I exclude from discussion the locality constraints on negative polarity items. Progovac (1991) distinguishes two kinds of polarity items in Serbo-Croatian with different locality constraints. She argues that the locality constraints on these polarity items parallel those of two kinds of anaphors (more or less parallel to the distinction between "sig" and "sig selv" in Danish). Progovac thus views negative polarity items as dependent items parallel to bound anaphors. This provides support for my position that both exemplify I-dependencies.

41 Kuno (1976) and Grosu (1982) propose that extraction is conditioned by the accessibility of the extracted NP to interpretation as the topic of the domain of extraction. This constraint follows from the interpretation of the *wh*-phrase as topic and will not explain all the cases excluded by the Subject Constraint on I-dependencies. For discussion see also Erteschik-Shir and Lappin (1983).

42 The following examples show that stage topics do not interfere with *wh*-movement:

(i)   In Jerusalem, what did you buy?
(ii) At 5 o'clock, who left?
(iii) When you left the house, who arrived?

43 See Rizzi (1990), who argues this general point, for much relevant discussion of this issue as well as the idea that negation and *wh*-questions, both being affective operators, cause ECP violations in the same way.

44 The reason why the reflexive is not so bad here is given above in the section on logophoric reflexives (section 6.4.2).

45 This question is improved if the *wh*-phrase is taken to range over a context-specified set. In that case, however, reconstruction does not occur and no I-dependency is invoked.

46 See Fiengo (1987) for an account of extraction out of picture NPs in the general spirit of the current proposal. There quantifier scope is also taken to belong to the same class of phenomena:

(i)   He picked out the picture of everyone.
(ii) He picked out a picture of everyone.

In (ii), but not in (i), *everyone* is confined to NP-internal scope. This would follow in the current framework from the fact that *everyone* cannot function as the main topic when it is embedded in a definite NP. The whole NP takes precedence as a potential topic.

47 See Erteschik-Shir (1981) and Diesing (1992) for discussion of the lexical properties of the predicates which license extraction. These predicates are either creation verbs or other "light" verbs such as *see* which select stages. Creation verbs, for example, make a stage come into existence.

48 Subordinate foci including metalinguistic ones and their associated stress, can, of course, occur within islands. The Subject Constraint is, however, sensitive to main foci.

49 For arguments that no other f-structure is assignable to such sentences see Erteschik-Shir (1973) and Erteschik-Shir and Lappin (1979).

50 I assume that the head of the relative clause and the relative pronoun are coindexed via an I-dependency governed by the Subject Constraint. It follows that the head of the clause must be a specifier of a constituent dominating the clause.

51 An issue addressed in Erteschik-Shir (1982) is the relative ease with which these and other constructions license extraction in Danish compared to English, for example. I related this to the prevalence of topicalization in Danish. This connects well with the claim that it is not the Subject Constraint which is violated in these cases in Danish.

52 See among others Cinque (1990), Kroch (1989), Rizzi (1990) and the references they cite. An initial version of the account given here also appeared in Erteschik-Shir (1992).

53 See Erteschik-Shir (1992) for further discussion of adjunct extraction.

54 It is not clear whether *wh*-reasons can form an I-dependency with another *wh*-phrase at all:

(i)   *Who went why? (vs. Who went and why?)
(ii) *What did John do why? (vs. What did John do and why?)
(iii) *Why did John do what?

55 The issues discussed in S&Z only partially overlap those covered here. It will be a challenge for anyone to address the interesting and extensive coverage of data to be found in S&Z from an f-structure perspective. See also the discussion of Hungarian in the Conclusion.

56 The term "bridge verbs" is derived from Erteschik-Shir (1973). There I argue that verbs that must be inherently focused block the interpretation of the complement as a focus in violation of the constraint on extraction (here rephrased as the Subject Constraint). In Erteschik-Shir (in prep. a) I show that lexical structure identifies this class of predicates.

57 In the discussion of picture NPs above, I argued that a subordinate f-structure with a subject topic blocked an I-dependency triggered by an antecedent or operator outside it. This is only the case for subordinate f-structures which themselves are predicated of a stage topic which is not the case for the examples discussed here. The exact details of this phenomenon needs further investigation.

58 This is the class of predicates which licenses negative polarity items in their complements such as *regret* and *doubt*. Note that many predicates which are classified as factives have nonfactive uses and occur in an f-structure which licenses extraction.

59 I discuss how the complement clause is interpreted by the file change semantics in Erteschik-Shir (in prep. a). Essentially the clause is processed as a separate predication retaining from the matrix that the source of the assertion is Peter.

60 I discuss Fiengo and May's proposals in the context of ellipsis in Erteschik-Shir (in prep. b).

Conclusion

1. For these distinctions see Fodor (1983).
2. One might consider certain creative or artistic domains to have topics. A story may be "about" something and a picture may be "of" something.
3. For different views concerning the organization of the grammatical components with attention paid to the role of focus in this discussion see Kidwai (1996), Reinhart (1995) and Simpson (1995).
4. Chomsky (1995: 220) ignores "surface effects" on interpretation such as topic focus, theme–rheme structures and figure–ground properties, but notes that incorporating these effects into the analysis may require qualification of the theory.
5. In chapter 6 English clefts were viewed as contrastive. É. Kiss views them broadly as restrictive. This issue is not relevant to the discussion here.

References

Akatsuka, N. (1986) "Conditionals are discourse-bound," in E. C. Traugott, A. ter Meulen, J. S. Reilly, and C. A. Ferguson (eds.), *On Conditionals*. Cambridge University Press, 333–51.

Anderson, T. (1991) "Subject and topic in Dinka," *Studies in Language* 15.2, 265–94.

Ariel, M. (1990) *Accessing Noun-Phrase Antecedents*. London: Croom Helm.

Atlas, J. D. (1991) "Topic/comment, presupposition, logical form and focus stress implicatures: the case of focal particles *only* and *also*," *Journal of Semantics* 8, 127–48.

Bayer, J. (1996) *Directionality and Logical Form: On the Scope of Focusing Particles and Wh-in-Situ*. Dordrecht: Kluwer.

Berman, A. and M. Szamosi (1972) "Observations on sentential stress," *Language* 48, 304–25.

Bolinger, D. (1972) "Accent is predictable (if you're a mindreader)," *Language* 48, 633–44.

    (1980) "Syntactic diffusion and the indefinite article," reproduced by the Indiana University Linguistics Club.

    (1983) "Affirmation and default," *Folia Linguistica* 17.1–2, 99–116.

Bresnan, J. (1971) "Sentence stress and syntactic transformations," *Language* 47, 257–80.

Bresnan, J. and J. Kanerva (1989) "Locative inversion in Chichewa: a case study of factorization in grammar," *Linguistic Inquiry* 20, 1–50.

Bresnan, J. and S. A. Mchombo (1995) "The lexical integrity principle: evidence from Bantu," *Natural Language & Linguistic Theory* 13, 181–254.

Brody, M. (1995) *Lexico-Logical Form: A Radically Minimalist Theory*. Cambridge, MA: MIT Press.

Büring, D. (1994) "Topic," in P. Bosch and R. van der Sandt (eds.), *Focus and Natural Language Processing*, vol. 2: *Semantics, Working Papers of the Institute for Logic and Linguistics*. Heidelberg: IBM Deutschland Informationssysteme GMBH, Scientific Centre.

Carlson, G. N. (1977) "Reference to kinds in English," Ph. D dissertation, University of Massachusetts.

Carlson, G. N. and F. J. Pelletier (1995) *The Generics Book*. University of Chicago Press.

Chafe, W. L. (1974) "Language and consciousness," *Language* 50,1.

(1975) "Givenness, contrastiveness, definiteness, Topics and Points of View," in C. Li (ed.), *Subject and Topic*, New York: Academic Press.

Chastain, C. (1975) "Reference and context," in Keith Gunderson (ed.), *Language, Mind, and Knowledge*, Minnesota Studies in the Philosophy of Science. University of Minnesota Press.

Chierchia, G. (1991) "Functional WH and weak crossover," *Proceedings of the West Coast Conference on Formal Linguistics (WCCFL)* 10, 75–90.

(1992a) "Anaphora and dynamic binding," *Linguistics and Philosophy* 15, 111–83.

(1992b) "Individual level predicates as inherent generics," MS, Cornell University.

Chierchia, G. and S. McConnel-Ginet (1990) *Meaning and Grammar: An Introduction to Semantics*. Cambridge, MA: MIT Press.

Chomsky, N. (1971) "Deep structure, surface structure and semantic interpretation," in D. Steinberg and L. Jakobovits (eds.), *Semantics: An interdisciplinary reader in philosophy, linguistics and psychology*. Cambridge University Press.

(1976) "Conditions on rules of grammar," *Linguistic Analysis* 2, 303–51.

(1982) *Some Concepts and Consequences of the Theory of Government and Binding*. Cambridge, MA: MIT Press.

(1992) "A minimalist program for linguistic theory," *MIT Occasional Papers on Linguistics I*, Department of Linguistics and Philosophy, MIT.

(1995) *The Minimalist Program*. Cambridge, MA: MIT Press.

Cinque, G. (1989) "Long wh-movement and referentiality," paper presented at the II Princeton Workshop on Comparative Grammar.

(1990) *Types of A'-Dependencies*. Cambridge, MA: MIT Press.

(1993) "A null theory of phrase and compound stress," *Linguistic Inquiry* 24, 239–98.

Comorovski, I. (1989) "Discourse and the syntax of multiple constituent questions," Ph.D dissertation, Cornell University.

Condoravdi, C. (1992) "Individual level predicates in conditional clauses," paper presented at the LSA meeting, Philadelphia, PA.

Culicover, P. W. (1993) "Evidence against ECP account of the *that-T* effect," *Linguistic Inquiry* 24, 557–61.

Culicover, P. W. and M. S. Rochemont (1983) "Stress and focus in English," *Language* 59, 123–65.

Daneš, F. (1974) "Functional sentence perspective and the organization of the text," in F. Daneš (ed.), *Papers on Functional Sentence Perspective*. Prague: Academia. 106–28.

(ed.) (1974) *Papers on Functional Sentence Perspective*. Prague: Academia.

DeCarrico, J. S. (1985) "Scope islands and indefinite NPs," *Proceedings of the Chicago Linguistics Society (CLS)* 21, 65–74.

De Hoop, H. (1992) "Case configuration and noun phrase interpretation," Ph.D dissertation, University of Groningen.

De Swart, H. (1991) "Adverbs of Quantification: a generalized quantifier approach," Ph.D dissertation, University of Groningen.

Diesing, M. (1989) "Bare plural subjects, inflection, and the mapping to LF", in *Papers on Quantification*. Department of Linguistics, University of Massachusetts, Amherst.

(1992) *Indefinites*. Cambridge, MA: MIT Press.

Donnellan, K. S. (1966) "Reference and definite descriptions," *Philosophical Review* 75, 281–304.

(1978) "Speaker reference, descriptions and anaphora," in P. Cole (ed.), *Pragmatics, Syntax and Semantics* 9. New York: Academic Press.

(1981) "Intuitions and presuppositions," in P. Cole (ed.), *Radical Pragmatics*. New York: Academic Press.

Dowty, D. R. (1979) *Word Meaning and Montague Grammar*. Dordrecht: Reidel.

(1991) "Thematic proto-roles and argument selection," *Language* 67, 547–619.

Eckardt, R. (1994) "Focus with nominal quantifiers," in P. Bosch and R. van der Sandt (eds.), *Working Papers of the Institute for Logic and Linguistics*. Heidelberg: IBM Deutschland Informationssysteme GMBH Scientific Centre.

Enç, M. (1990) "The semantics of specificity," *Linguistic Inquiry* 22.1, 1–27.

Engdahl, E. (1986) *Constituent Questions*. Dordrecht: Kluwer.

Erteschik-Shir, N. (1973) "On the nature of island constraints." MIT Ph.D dissertation. Reproduced by the Indiana University Linguistics Club, Bloomington, IN.

(1979) "Discourse constraints on dative movement," in T. Givon (ed.), *Syntax and Semantics* 12 *(Discourse and Syntax)*. New York: Academic Press.

(1981) "On extraction from noun phrases (picture noun phrases)," in A. Belletti, L. Brandi, and L. Rizzi (eds.), *Theory of Markedness in Generative Grammar: Proceedings of the 1979 GLOW Conference*. Pisa: Scuola Normale Superiore di Pisa. 147–69.

(1982) "Extractability in Danish and the pragmatic principle of dominance," in E. Engdahl and E. Ejerhed (eds.), *Readings on Unbounded Dependencies in Scandinavian Languages*. Sweden: Umeaa.

(1986a) "Wh-questions and focus," *Linguistics and Philosophy* 9, 117–49.

(1986b) "Der," *Nordic Journal of Linguistics* 8.1, 131–48.

(1987) "Right node raising," in M. A. Browning, E. Czaykowski-Higgins and E. Ritter (eds.), *MIT Working Papers in Linguistics* 9.

(1988) "Topic-chaining and dominance-chaining," in Y. Tobin (ed.), *The Prague School and its Legacy*. Amsterdam: John Benjamins.

(1992) "Focus structure and predication: the case of negative wh-questions," *Belgian Journal of Linguistics*, volume on Predication, 35–51.

(1994a) "Donkeys on stage," *Proceedings of IATL*.

(1994b) "Dependencies in focus-structure," in P. Bosch and R. van der Sandt (eds.), *Working Papers of the Institute for Logic and Linguistics* 7, vol. 2: *Semantics*. Heidelberg: IBM Deutschland Informationssysteme GMBH Scientific Centre. 291–300.

(in prep. a) *Focus in the Lexicon*.

(in prep. b) "Coordinate focus structures."

Erteschik-Shir, N. and S. Lappin (1979) "Dominance and the functional explanation of island phenomena," *Theoretical Linguistics* 6, 41–85.

(1983a) "Dominance and extraction: a reply to A. Grosu," *Theoretical Linguistics* 10, 81–96.

(1983b) "Under stress: a functional explanation of sentence stress," *Journal of Linguistics* 19, 419–53.

(1987) "Dominance and modularity," *Linguistics* 25, 671–85.

Erteschik-Shir, N. and T. R. Rapoport (to appear) "Verbal projection," in Gabriela Matos and Matilde Miguel (eds.), *On Interfaces in Linguistic Theory*, selected papers from the International Conference on Interfaces in Linguistics, Oporto, November 1995. Lisbon: APL/Ediç es Colibri.

(in progress) "Verbal projections."

Evans, G. (1980) "Pronouns," *Linguistic Inquiry* 11, 337–62.

(1977) "Pronouns, quantifiers, and relative clauses (I)," *The Canadian Journal of Philosophy* 7, 467–536.

Faber, D. (1987) "The accentuation of intransitive sentences in English," *Journal of Linguistics* 23, 341–58.

Fiengo, R. (1987) "Definiteness, specificity, and familiarity," *Linguistic Inquiry* 18.1, 163–6.

Fiengo, R. and R. May (1994) *Indices and Identity*. Cambridge, MA: MIT Press.

Fillmore, C. (1971) *Santa Cruz lectures on Deixis*. IULC.

Fodor, J. A. (1983) *The Modularity of Mind*. Cambridge, MA: MIT Press.

Fodor, J. D. and I. Sag (1982) "Referential and quantificational indefinites," *Linguistics and Philosophy* 5, 355–98.

Frampton, J. (1991) "Relativized minimality: a review", *The Linguistic Review* 8.1, 1–41.

(1992) "The fine structure of wh-movement and the proper formulation of the ECP," in W. Chao and G. Horrocks (eds.), *Levels, Principles and Processes: The Structure of Grammatical Representations*. Berlin: de Gruyter.

Fretheim, T. (1988a) "'Broad focus' and 'narrow focus' in Norwegian intonation," MS, University of Oslo.

(1988b) "Intonational phrases and syntactic focus domains," MS, University of Oslo.

Goodall, G. (1987) *Parallel Structures in Syntax: Coordination, Causatives and Restructuring*. Cambridge University Press.

Gordon, P. C., B. Grosz and L. Gilliom (to appear) "Pronouns, names, and the centering of attention in discourse," *Cognitive Science*.

Grimshaw, J. (1991) "Extended projection," MS, Brandeis University.

Grimshaw, J. and A. Mester (1988) "Light verbs and o-marking," *Linguistic Inquiry* 19, 205–32.

Grosu, A. (1982) "Extragrammatical motivation for certain island phenomena," *Theoretical Linguistics* 9, 17–67.

Grosz, B. (1986) "The representation and use of focus in a system for understanding dialogs," in B. K. Grosz Spark Jones and B. L. Webber (eds.), *Readings in Natural Language Processing*. Los Altos, CA: Morgan Kaufmann Publishers.

Grosz, B. and C. L. Sidner (1986) "Attentions, intentions, and the structure of discourse," *Computational Linguistics* 12.3, 175–204.

Guéron, J. (1980) "On the syntax and semantics of PP extraposition," *Linguistic Inquiry* 11, 637–78.

Gundel, J. K. (1974) "The role of topic and comment in linguistic theory," Ph.D dissertation, University of Texas at Austin. Reproduced by Indiana University Linguistics Club, 1977.

(1994) "On different kinds of focus," in P. Bosch and R. van der Sandt (eds.), *Working Papers of the Institute for Logic and Linguistics* 7, vol. 3: *Discourse*. Heidelberg: IBM Deutschland Informationssysteme GMBH Scientific Centre. 457–66.

Gussenhoven, C. (1983) "Focus, mode, and the nucleus," *Journal of Linguistics* 19, 377–417.

Haiman, J. (1978) "Conditionals are topics," *Language* 54, 564–89.

Hale, K. L. and S. J. Keyser (1993) "On argument structure and the lexical expression of syntactic relations," in K. L. Hale, and S. J. Keyser (eds.), *The View from Building 20: Essays in Honor of Sylvain Bromberger*. Cambridge, MA: MIT Press.

Halliday, M. A. K. (1967) "Notes on transitivity and theme in English," Part 2, *Journal of Linguistics* 3, 199–244.

Hansen, A. (1967) *Moderne Dansk*. Copenhagen: Grafisk Forlag.

Heim, I. (1982) "The semantics of definite and indefinite noun phrases," Ph.D dissertation, University of Massachusetts.

(1987) "Where does the Definiteness Restriction Apply?" in E. Reuland and A. G. B. ter Meulen (eds.), *The Representation of (In)definiteness*. Cambridge, MA: MIT Press.

(1989) "E-type pronouns and donkey anaphora," *Linguistics and Philosophy* 13.

Hellan, L. (1986) "On anaphora and predication in Norwegian," in L. Hellan and K. K. Christensen (eds.), *Topics in Scandinavian Syntax*. Dordrecht: Reidel.

(1988) *Anaphora in Norwegian and the Theory of Grammar*. Dordrecht: Foris.

Higginbotham, J. (1980) "Pronouns and bound variables," *Linguistic Inquiry* 11.4.

(1983) "Logical form, binding, and nominals," *Linguistic Inquiry* 14, 395–420.

(1987) "Indefiniteness and predication," in E. Reuland and A. G. B. ter Meulen (eds.), *The Representation of (In)definiteness*. Cambridge, MA: MIT Press.

Horn, L. R. (1969) "A presuppositional analysis of *only* and *even*," *Proceedings of the Chicago Linguistics Society (CLS)* 5, 97–108.

(1985) "Metalinguistic negation and pragmatic ambiguity," *Language* 61, 121–74.

(1989) *A Natural History of Negation*. University of Chicago Press.

Huang, C.-T. James (1984) "On the distribution and reference of empty pronouns," *Linguistic Inquiry* 15.4, 531–74.

Huang, Y. (1994) *The Syntax and Pragmatics of Anaphora, A study with special reference to Chinese*. Cambridge University Press.

Ioup, G. (1975) "Some universals for quantifier scope," in J. P. Kimball (ed.), *Syntax and Semantics* 4. New York: Academic Press.

Jackendoff, R. (1972) *Semantic Interpretation in generative Grammar*. Cambridge, MA: MIT Press.

Jacobs, J. (1991) "Focus ambiguities," *Journal of Semantics* 8, 1–36.

(1994) "Informational autonomy," in P. Bosch and R. van der Sandt (eds.), *Focus and Natural Language Processing*, vol. 1: *Intonation and Syntax. Working Papers of the Institute for Logic and Linguistics*. Heidelberg: IBM Deutschland Informationssysteme GMBH, Scientific Centre.

Jespersen, O. (1933) *Essentials of English Grammar*. London: George Allen & Unwin.

(1954) *A Modern English Grammar on Historical Principles*. London: George Allen & Unwin, and Copenhagen: Ejner Munksgaard.

Kadmon, N. (1987) "On unique and non-unique reference and asymmetric quantification," Ph.D dissertation, University of Massachusetts, Amherst.

　(1990) "Uniqueness," *Linguistics and Philosophy* 13, 273–324.

Kadmon, N. and F. Landman (1993) "ANY," *Linguistics and Philosophy* 16.

Kamp, H. (1981) "Evènements, représentations discursives et référence temporelle," *Language* 64, 39–64.

Kamp, H. and U. Reyle (1993) *From Discourse to Logic.* Dordrecht: Kluwer.

Karttunen, L. (1974) "Discourse Referents," in J. McCawley (ed.), *Notes from the Linguistic Underground, Syntax and Semantics* 7. New York: Academic Press.

Kayne, R. (1984) *Connectedness and Binary Branching.* Dordrecht: Foris.

Kennedy, B. (1990) "Performative operators and context theory," MS, Harvard University.

Kidwai, A. (1996) "Word order and focus positions in Universal Grammar," MS presented at Focus Workshop, Paris.

Kim, Y. and R. Larson (1989) "Scope interpretation and the syntax of psych-verbs," *Linguistic Inquiry* 20.4, 681–87.

É. Kiss, K. (1991) "Logical structure in syntactic structure: the case of Hungarian," in J. Huang and R. May (eds.), *Logical Structure and Linguistic Structure.* Dordrecht: Kluwer, 111–48.

　(1996) "The focus operator and information focus," *Working Papers in the Theory of Grammar,* 3,2, Research Institute for Linguistics, Hungarian Academy of Sciences.

Klima, E. S. (1964) "Negation in English," in J. Fodor and J. Katz (eds.), *The Structure of Language, Readings in the Philosophy of Language.* New Jersey: Prentice-Hall, 246–323.

Kratzer, A. (1989a) "Stage-level and individual-level predicates," in *Papers on Quantification.* Department of Linguistics, University of Massachusetts, Amherst.

　(1989b) "An investigation of the lumps of thought," *Linguistics and Philosophy* 12,5.

Krifka, M. (1990a) "Polarity phenomena and alternative semantics," in M. Stokhof and L. Torenvliet (eds.), *Proceedings of the Seventh Amsterdam Colloquium, Part I,* ITLI publication, University of Amsterdam. 277–301.

　(1990b) "4000 ships passed through the lock: object induced measure functions on events," *Linguistics and Philosophy* 13.

　(1992) "A compositional semantics for multiple focus constructions," in J. Jacobs (ed.), *Informationsstruktur und Grammatik.* Opladen: Westdeutscher Verlag, 17–53.

　(1994) "Focus and operator scope in German," in P. Bosch and R. van der Sandt (eds.), *Working Papers of the Institute for Logic and Linguistics* 7, vol. 1: *Intonation and Syntax.* Heidelberg: IBM Deutschland Informationssysteme, GMBH Scientific Centre. 133–52.

　(1995) "Generics and focus," in G. N. Carlson and F. J. Pelletier, *The Generics Book.* University of Chicago Press.

Kroch, T. (1989) "Amount quantification, referentiality, and long wh-movement," MS, University of Pennsylvania.

Kuno, S. (1976) "Subject, theme, and the speaker's empathy – a reexamination of relativization phenomena," in C. Li (ed.), *Subject and Topic*. New York: Academic Press.

(1982) "The focus of the question and the focus of the answer," in *Papers from the Parasession on Nondeclarative Sentences from the Regional Meeting of the Chicago Linguistics Society*.

(1987) *Functional Syntax, Anaphora, Discourse and Empathy*. University of Chicago Press.

Kuroda, S.-Y. (1972) "The categorical and the thetic judgment (evidence from Japanese)," *Foundations of Language* 2, 153–85.

Labov, W. (1972) "Negative attraction and negative concord in English grammar," *Language* 48.4, 773–818.

Ladd, D. Robert (1980) *The Structure of Intonational Meaning*. Bloomington: Indiana University Press.

Lambrecht, K. (1994) *Information Structure and Sentence form. A theory of topic, focus, and the mental representations of discourse referents. Cambridge Studies in Linguistics*. Cambridge University Press.

Landman, F. (1989a) "Groups, I," *Linguistics and Philosophy* 12, 559–605.

(1989b) "Groups, II," *Linguistics and Philosophy* 12, 723–44.

(in prog.) "Events and plurality. The Jerusalem Lectures," MS, Linguistics Department, Tel Aviv University.

Lappin, S. (1982) "Quantified noun phrases and pronouns in logical form," *Linguistic Analysis* 10.2, 131–59.

(1985) "Pronominal binding and coreference," *Theoretical Linguistics* 12, 241–63.

(1988–9) "Donkey pronouns unbound," *Theoretical Linguistics* 15, 263–86.

(1992) "The syntactic basis of ellipsis resolution," in *Proceedings of the University of Stuttgart Workshop on Ellipsis*, Stuttgart.

Larson, R. J. (1988) "On the double object construction," *Linguistic Inquiry* 19.3, 335–91.

Lasersohn, P. (1993) "Existence presuppositions and background knowledge," *Journal of Semantics* 10, 113–22.

Lasnik, H. and T. Stowell (1991) "Weakest crossover," *Linguistic Inquiry* 22.4, 687–720.

Leonard, H. and N. Goodman (1940) "The calculus of individuals and its lies," *Journal of Symbolic Logic* 5, 45–56.

Li, C. and S. Thompson (1976) "Subject and topic: a new typology," in C. Li (ed.), *Subject and Topic*. New York: Academic Press.

Lumsden, M. (1988) *Existential Sentences, Their Structure and Meaning*. London: Croom Helm.

Manzini, R. (1995) "Form dependency and the theory of locality," MS presented at The Limits of Syntax Workshop, Ohio.

Massey, G. J. (1976) "Tom, Dick, and Harry, and All the King's Men," *American Philosophical Quarterly* 13.2, 89–107.

May, R. (1977) "The grammar of quantification," Ph.D dissertation, MIT.

(1985) *Logical Form. Its Structure and Derivation*. Cambridge, MA: MIT Press.

(1989) "Interpreting logical form," in R. May (ed.), *Studies on Logical Form and Semantic Interpretation, Linguistics and Philosophy* 12.4, 387–435.

McCawley, J. D. (1981) *Everything that Linguists Have Always Wanted to Know about Logic (but were ashamed to ask)*. University of Chicago Press.

McNally, L. (1993) "Adjunct predicates and the individual/stage distinction," MS, Indiana University.

Milsark, G. L. (1974) "Existential sentences in English," Ph.D dissertation, MIT.

(1977) "Toward an explanation of certain peculiarities of the Existential Construction in English," *Linguistic Analysis* 3.1, 1–31.

Mittwoch, A. (1983) "Backward anaphora and discourse structure," *Journal of Pragmatics* 7, 129–39.

Newman, S. (1946) "On the stress system of English," *Word* 2, 171–87.

Oehrle, R. T. (1991) "Grammatical structure and intonational phrasing: a logical perspective," AAAI Fall Symposium on Discourse Structure in Natural Language Understanding and Generation, Asilomar, November 1991.

Partee, B. H. (1975) "Deletion and variable binding," in Edward L. Keenan (ed.), *Formal Semantics of Natural Language*, Cambridge University Press.

(1992) "Topic, focus and quantification," in *Proceedings of the 1991 SALT Conference*, Department of Modern Languages and Literatures, Cornell University.

(1994) "Focus, quantification, and semantics-pragmatics issues, preliminary version," in P. Bosch and R. van der Sandt (eds.), *Working Papers of the Institute for Logic and Linguistics*. Heidelberg: IBM Deutschland Informationssysteme, GMBH Scientific Centre.

Pesetsky, D. (1987) "Wh-in situ: movement and unselective binding," in E. Reuland and A. ter Meulen (eds.), *The Representation of (In)definiteness*. Cambridge, MA: MIT Press, 98–129.

(1990) "Experiencer predicates and universal alignment principles," MS, MIT.

Pierrehumbert, J. (1980) "The phonology and phonetics of English intonation," Ph.D dissertation, MIT.

Pierrehumbert, J. and J. Hirschberg (1990) "The meaning of intonational contours in the interpretation of discourse," in J. R. Cohen, J. Morgan, and M. L. Pollack (eds.), *Intention and Communication*. Cambridge, MA: MIT Press.

Polanyi, L. and R. Scha (1989) "A syntactic approach to discourse semantics," *Text*. Tilburg.

Postal, Paul M. (1993) "Remarks on weak crossover effects," *Linguistic Inquiry* 24, 539–56.

Prince, E. (1981) "Toward a taxonomy of given-new information," in P. Cole (ed.), *Radical Pragmatics*. New York: Academic Press, 223–56.

(1988) "Information-status," in W. Bright (ed.), *The Oxford Dictionary of Linguistics*. Oxford University Press.

Progovac, L. (1991) "Polarity in Serbo-Croatian: anaphoric NPIs and pronominal PPIs," *Linguistic Inquiry* 22:3, 567–72.

Quine, W. V. O. (1960) *Word and Object*. Cambridge, MA: MIT Press.

Rapoport, T. R. (1991) "Definitely arguments," presented at the Canadian Linguistics Association.

Reinhart, T. (1976) "The syntactic domain of anaphora," Ph.D dissertation, MIT.

(1979) "Syntactic domains for semantic rules," in F. Guenthner and S. J. Schmidt (eds.), *Formal Semantics and Pragmatics for Natural Language*. Dordrecht: Reidel.

(1981) "Pragmatics and linguistics: an analysis of sentence topics," *Philosophica* 27, 53–94.

(1983) *Anaphora and Semantic Interpretation*. London: Croom Helm.

(1986) "Center and periphery in the grammar of anaphora," in B. Lust (ed.), *Studies in the Acquisition of Anaphora*, vol. I, 123–50.

(1995) "Interface strategies," *OTS Working Papers*, Utrecht University.

Reinhart, T. and E. Reuland (1993) "Reflexivity," *Linguistic Inquiry* 24.4.

Riad, T. (1988) *Reflexivity and Predication, Working Papers in Scandinavian Syntax* 36.

Rizzi, L. (1990) *Relativized Minimality*. Cambridge, MA: MIT Press.

Roberts, C. (1987) "Modal subordination, anaphora and distributivity," Ph.D dissertation, University of Massachusetts.

Rochemont, M. S. (1986) *Focus in Generative Grammar*. Amsterdam: J. Benjamins.

Rochemont, M. S. and P. W. Culicover (1990) *English Focus Constructions and the Theory of Grammar*. Cambridge University Press.

Rooth, M. (1985) "Association with focus," Ph.D dissertation, University of Massachusetts, reproduced by GLSA.

(1987) "Noun phrase interpretation in Montague Grammar, file change semantics, and situation semantics," in Peter Gärdenfors (ed.), *Generalized Quantifiers*. Dordrecht: Reidel. 237–68.

(1992) "A theory of focus interpretation," *Natural Language Interpretation* 1, 75–116.

Ross, J. R. (1971) "Variable strength," MS, MIT.

(1982) "Pronoun deleting processes in German," paper presented at the annual meeting of the Linguistic Society of America, San Diego, California.

Rothstein, S. (1991) "Binding, C-command, and predication," *Linguistic Inquiry* 22:3, 572–78.

Schmerling, S. F. (1973) "Aspects of English sentence stress," Ph.D dissertation, University of Illinois.

Schwartz, A. (1976) "On the universality of subjects: the Ilocano case," in Charles N. Li (ed.), *Subject and Topic*. New York: Academic Press.

Sgall, P., E. Hajicová, and J. Panevová (1986) *The Meaning of the Sentence in Its Semantic and Pragmatic Aspects*. Dordrecht: Reidel.

Selkirk, E. (1984) *Phonology and Syntax*. Cambridge, MA: MIT Press.

Sidner, C. L. (1986) "Focusing in the comprehension of definite anaphora," in B. K. Grosz, Spark Jones and B. L. Webber (eds.), *Readings in Natural Language Processing*. Los Altos, CA: Morgan Kaufmann.

Simpson, A. (1995) "Wh-movement, licensing and the locality of feature checking," Ph.D dissertation, SOAS, University of London.

Stalnaker, R. (1978) "Assertion," in P. Cole (ed.), *Pragmatics: Syntax and Semantics* 9. New York: Academic Press.

Steedman, M. (1991) "Structure and intonation," *Language* 67.2, 260–96.

(1994) "Remarks on intonation and focus," in P. Bosch and R. van der Sandt (eds.), *Focus and Natural Language Processing*, vol. 1: *Intonation and Syntax. Working Papers of the Institute for Logic and Linguistics*. Heidelberg: IBM Deutschland Informationssysteme GMBH, Scientific Centre.

Strawson, P. F. (1964) "Identifying reference and truth-values," *Theoria*, vol. 30. Reprinted in D. Steinberg and L. Jakobovits (eds.) (1971) *Semantics*. Cambridge University Press.

Szabolcsi, A. (1995) "Strategies for scope taking," *Working Papers in the Theory of Grammar* 2,1. Research Institute for Linguistics, Hungarian Academy of Sciences, Budapest.

Szabolcsi, A. and F. Zwarts (1993) "Weak islands and an algebraic semantics for scope-taking," *Natural Language Semantics* 1.

Taglicht, J. (1984) *Message and Emphasis, On Focus and Scope in English*, English Language Series. London: Longman.

Uechi, Akihiko (to appear) "Toward syntax-information mapping," *Japanese/Korean Linguistics* 5. CSLI, Cambridge University Press.

Vallduví, E. (1992) *The Informational Component*. New York: Garland.

(1994) "The dynamics of information packaging," MS, University of Edinburgh.

Vallduví, E. and R. Zacharsky (1994) "Accenting phenomenon, association with focus, and the recursiveness of focus-ground," in Paul Dekker and Martin Stokhof (eds.), *Proceedings of the Ninth Amsterdam Colloquium*, ILLC, Amsterdam. 683–702.

Vendler, Z. (1967) *Linguistics in Philosophy*. Ithaca, NY: Cornell University Press.

Vikner, S. (1985) "Parameters of binder and of binding category in Danish," *Working Papers in Scandinavian Syntax*, 23, Dragvoll, Norway.

von Fintel, K. (1989) "Theticity in Generative Grammar," in *Papers on Quantification*. Department of Linguistics, University of Massachusetts, Amherst.

von Stechow, A. (1989a) "Topic, focus and local relevance," in W. Klein and W. Levelt (eds.), *Crossing the Boundaries in Linguistics*. Dordrecht: Reidel.

(1989b) *Focusing and Backgrounding Operators*, Technical Report 6, Fachgruppe Sprachwissenschaft, University of Konstanz.

(1991) "Current issues in the theory of focus," in A. von Stechow and D. Wunderlich (eds.), *Semantik/Semantics: An International Handbook of Contemporary Research*. Berlin: de Gruyter.

Ward, G. and J. Hirschberg (1985) "Implicating uncertainty: the pragmatics of fall-rise intonation," *Language* 61.4, 747–76.

(1986) "Reconciling uncertainty with incredulity: a unified account of the L*+H L H% intonational contour," Linguistics Society of America (December).

Webber, B. L. (1986) "So what can we talk about now," in B. K. Grosz, Spark Jones, and B. L. Webber (eds.), *Readings in Natural Language Processing*. Los Altos, CA: Morgan Kaufmann Publishers.

(1988) "Tense as discourse anaphor," *Computational Linguistics* 14:2, 61–73.

Wasow, T. (1979) *Anaphora in Generative Grammar*. Ghent: E. Story-Scienta.

Wilkinson, K. (1986) "Genericity and indefinite noun phrases," MS, University of Massachusetts, Amherst.

(1991) "Studies in the semantics of generic noun phrases," Ph.D dissertation, University of Massachusetts, Amherst.

(1993) "Bare plurals, plural pronouns and the partitive constraint," MS, Ben Gurion University of the Negev.

(to appear) "Towards a unified semantics of *even*: a reply to Rooth," *Proceedings of SALT Conference*, March 1993, Irvine, CA.

Williams, E. (1980) "Predication," *Linguistic Inquiry* 11, 203–38.

(1988) "Is LF distinct from S-structure? A reply to May," *Linguistic Inquiry* 19.1, 135–46.

Zribi-Hertz, A. (1989) "A-type binding and narrative point of view," *Language* 65, 695–727.

Zucchi, A. (1990) "The aspect of negation," MS (submitted to *Selected Papers from the Third Symposium on Logic and Language*).

Index of names

Index of subjects

A-accent *see* accent
"about" 10, 236
all 176, 178–80, 251 n. 8
any 109–10, 118, 119, 176, 220, 222, 251
　　n. 8
　Free Choice 109–10
absolute uniqueness *see* uniqueness
accent (= pitch-accent, pitch) *see also* tunes
　　125, 126, 129, 131, 132, 133, 152, 154,
　　249 n. 1
　A-accent (fall) 178
　B-accent (fall–rise L+H*) 149, 150–2, 178
　derived from focus assignment 130
　high (H*) 125, 126, 132, 133, 149
　high boundary tone 147, 149
　intermediate 249 n. 3
　L+H* *see* tunes
　L*+H *see* tunes
　low (L*) 126, 133, 137, 146, 147, 242 n. 39
　metalinguistic 136
　phrase 146, 147
　and rhythm rule 132
　rise–fall 182
　and semantics of lexical items 139, 144
　on subject topic 250 n. 10
　and subordinate focus 134, 137
　stress rule assignment of 127
　and theme/rheme 161
　and tunes (*see also* tunes) 146–52
accentability 154
accommodation 46, 72–3, 74, 154
affective operator *see* operator
alternative question 102
amplitude 124
anaphora (anaphoric) 3, 5, 11, 59, 60, 72,
　　89, 92, 138, 184
　backward 60, 78–9
　bound 184, 185, 196–200, 205
　and c-command 253 n. 17
　in Danish 200–3, 205
　donkey 96–7
　and double-object constructions 208–9,
　　211

and ECM 208
and ellipsis 251 n. 1
locality constraint on 200–4, 206–11,
　212, 214, 215
and locational predications 209–11
logophoric, *see also* logophors 241 n. 24
negative polarity items (as anaphors) 256
　n. 40
plural 72
pragmatic 60
and prepositional phrases 209–11
reflexivity 11, 200–15, 224, 227
amplitude 124
arbitrary representative (instance) 77, 86, 91
argument structure 35, 153–6, 200, 207
articulatory-perceptual system 236
assertability 119
assertion 2, 10, 13, 61, 64, 120, 133, 134,
　135
　main 14, 39, 55, 78, 249 n. 8
　and negation 100
　possible pragmatic assertion (PPA) 10
　and presupposition 56, 112
　and question 248 n. 6
　speaker 61
　true 105
assessment (for truth value) *see also*
　　evaluate 5, 8, 10, 25–8, 33, 37, 39, 42,
　　46, 72, 78–9, 90, 91, 98, 124, 135,
　　138, 153, 163, 167, 168, 169, 175, 178,
　　180
　collective and distributive 166–8, 178–80
　and contrast 121, 123
　of negative 100–2, 104
　with *only* 116
　and partitioning 168–70
　of restricted set 31, 42, 72, 86, 246 n. 29
　and scope 170–2
　with stage topic 27–8, 52, 79, 86–7, 104,
　　177, 180
　topic, pivot of 8, 9, 10, 15, 32, 45, 51,
　　242 n. 45
　of *wh*-questions 105

273

single task-specific mechanism 236
spatio-temporal argument 8, 26, 36, 51
spatio-temporal heading 26
spatio-temporal location 35, 51
spatio-temporal parameters 10, 32, 63, 172
specific 60, 61, 62, 64, 65, 66, 73, 87
  indefinite 39–42, 43, 62, 63, 65, 67
  reading 44, 60, 65, 67, 68, 110, 168, 173
  to speaker 44, 164
  topics 60, 61
  and R-dependency 166
specifier 224, 257 n. 50
spell-out 3, 7
stage level 8, 26–9, 35–7, 51–2, 59, 60, 63, 82, 177
  interpretations 51–2
stage topic 8, 26–9, 32, 33, 36–7, 49–50, 51–2, 53, 54, 55, 56, 57, 58, 59
  and conditionals 86–95, 97
  and negation 103–5
  extraction of 228
  and I-dependent pronouns 198, 199
  and intonation 128, 136, 159, 162
  introduced by existential 227
  locative and directional PPs as 209–11
  and minimal predication 206–8
  multiple *wh*-questions with 193–5
  negative stage topics and canonical f-structure 223–7
  predicates with select 207, 224, 227
  and psych predicates 255 n. 35
  and scope 163, 165, 171, 172, 173, 175, 176–8, 180, 181, 183
  sentential adverbials as 232
  as specifiers 224
  subordinate 227
  and *wh*-movement 256 n. 42
stative 103
stress 1, 12, 24, 25, 26, 37, 38, 43, 45, 56, 65, 81, 84, 109, 111, 113, 115, 120, 122, 124–62, 218, 230
  and scope 168, 173, 176, 178, 181, 182, 183, 251 n. 5, n. 7
stress rule 124–7, 130, 131, 132, 134, 135, 136, 137, 138, 145, 146, 152, 154, 158, 161, 162
  syntactic 158, 159
strong crossover *see* crossover
strong determiners 168
structural account 114
structural constraint *see* constraints
Structural Description (SD) 3, 7
subject constraint *see* constraints
subordinate f-structure 39–44, 52–5
  and scope 168, 169, 173, 175, 177, 178, 181, 183

and I-dependencies 188, 194, 199, 204, 207, 209, 211, 212, 213, 214, 218, 219, 224, 225, 257 n. 57
and intonation 136–8
and Topic Constraint 164
subordinate update 39, 40, 41, 43, 44, 46, 53, 54, 65, 67, 68, 71–4, 77, 78, 80, 84, 85, 90, 91, 107, 110, 115, 122, 123, 140, 179, 199
subset 3, 8, 10, 26, 43, 52, 59, 72, 74, 91, 108, 151, 169, 185, 238
sum (individual) reading 166, 171
superimposing f-structures 208
superiority 189–90, 192, 194, 216, 217, 251 n. 6
symmetric interpretation 45, 47, 95–6, 173
syntactic modules (*see also* modules of grammar) 185, 233–5

temporal adverb 63
term negation *see* negation and scope 178
tests for focus 14–15
tests for topic 14–15
test question 108
that-clause 230–2, 255 n. 28
that-complement 230, 232
that-t effect 233, 234
thematic progression 69, 73, 75
theme 31, 161, 239 n. 4, 241 n. 31
thetic-categorical 241 n. 27
time and place 26, 29, 36, 52, 87, 221, 228
Topic Chaining 69–71, 77
Topic Constraint *see* constraints
topic drop 129, 237
topic rule 4, 5, 18, 20, 21, 43, 52, 54, 101
topic-marked 54
topic-prominent language 6, 237
topic-set *see* restrictive (topic) set
topicalization 34, 55, 127, 211, 217, 218, 224, 225, 232
tough-movement 217
trace position 183, 190, 191, 223, 226, 237, 228, 229, 251 n. 1
transitive f-structures 44–51
transparent 170, 181
tripartite (discourse representation) 4, 8, 32, 57, 85, 241 n. 24
truth conditions 4, 8, 29, 31, 101
truth value 8, 10, 15–16, 17, 23–4, 26, 29, 32, 33, 37, 42, 46, 55, 56, 59, 64, 65, 72, 73, 85, 96, 97, 105, 123, 137, 154
gap 9, 29
and scope 167, 170, 178, 183
of quantifier 169

Printed in the United Kingdom
by Lightning Source UK Ltd.
119736UK00001B/195